CONTENTS

Damodar Mauzo is one of Goa's best-known Konkani fiction writers. He is a novelist, short story writer, critic and scriptwriter. His works include *Ganthan*, *Zagrannam*, *Rumadful Bhurghim Mhugelim Tim*, *Karmelin*, *Sood*, *Tsunami Simon* and more. He wrote the screenplay for the National Award-winning film, *Aleesha*. He was awarded the Jnanpith Award, India's highest literary honour, in 2023. He has won the Sahitya Akademi Award in 1983 for his novel *Karmelin*; other awards include the Konkani Bhasha Mandal Award (twice), Goa Kala Academy (twice), the Janaganga Award, Goa State Cultural Award and several more.

Jerry Pinto is the author of *The Education of Yuri* (2022), *Murder in Mahim* (2017) and *Em and the Big Hoom* (2012; winner of the Hindu Prize and the Crossword Book Award), and the non-fiction book *Helen: The Life and Times of an H-Bomb* (2006; winner of the National Award for the Best Book on Cinema). His other books include *Asylum and Other Poems*, *Surviving Women*, *A Bear for Felicia*, *Monster Garden*, *When Crows Are White* and, as editor, *A Book of Light: When a Loved One Has a Different Mind*, *Reflected in Water: Writings on Goa*, *The Greatest Show on Earth: Writings on Bollywood*, *Bombay, Meri Jaan: Writings on Mumbai* (with Naresh Fernandes) and *Confronting Love: Poems* (with Arundhathi Subramaniam). He has also translated (from Marathi) Daya Pawar's classic autobiography *Baluta*, and the memoirs *I Want to Destroy Myself* (*Mala Udhvasta Vhachay*) by Malika Amar Shaikh and *I, the Salt Doll* (*Mee Mithaachi Baahuli*) by Vandana Mishra.

Boy, *Unloved*

DAMODAR MAUZO

***Translated by* Jerry Pinto**

SPEAKING
TIGER

SPEAKING TIGER BOOKS LLP
125A, Ground Floor, Shahpur Jat, near Asiad Village,
New Delhi 110049

First published by Speaking Tiger Books in 2024

ISBN: 978-93-5447-889-5
eISBN: 978-93-5447-866-6

10 9 8 7 6 5 4 3 2 1

Typeset in Sabon LT Std by SŪRYA, New Delhi
Printed at Impressions Printing & Packaging Ltd., Noida

1

The Marriage of the Banyan and the Mango

Once again, the urge for a cup of tea.

I light the gas and put the water to heat.

The water begins to boil.

Eureka!

Archimedes came to mind, but something else brought me up short.

At that age, just out of school, the arts and the sciences had always seemed like separate silos to me. But when I learned how to make tea, I understood how deep the relationship between the two is, a matter of chemistry and gastronomy. I could have learned a lot about how tea leaves become tea but I was far more concerned with how the brew tasted.

I go through the motions quickly, barely containing my impatience. And then raising the cup to my lips, the first sips, the joy.

'Arre, I can smell tea. If you've made some, bring me a cup,' my mother calls from within.

I add some water, let the brew bubble for a while, splash some milk in and take it to her. She sips, makes a face.

'The tea you were drinking smelled different. This isn't that tea. And there's not enough sugar.'

I set my jaw, go to the kitchen, bring a spoonful of sugar and put it in her cup.

I want to say, 'Now stir it, or must I do that too?' but stop myself.

She had always been lazy, Daddy would say. That was why he had never hired a servant, he would add, so that she might move her body around a bit. But her desire to be served hand and foot had not abated. She cooked for us, making the basic rice and curry, but it was tasteless. Even when she was in the kitchen, she had one eye on the television. To avoid her cooking, Daddy would eat out.

*

Until the time I got to the tenth standard board examinations, I had never had tea. Somehow, I had got it into my head that children don't drink tea. And I was never tempted to try. But then something happened to arouse my curiosity about it.

I must have been about seven or eight at the time. It was late in the night when I was awakened from my sleep. At first, I thought it was the tomcat next door. Then I realized it was Ma's voice, coming from the next room. I could hear, 'Aah!—No...Please, enough.' Daddy was growling, 'Hunh, Hunh...' Were they fighting? Should I do something? I tried closing my eyes and then I heard: 'Get up and get me a cup of tea.'

'It's two in the morning...'

'I didn't ask you the time. I asked you for tea.'

Then the sound of the stove being lit.

What could it be, this tea, that Daddy might want some so late in the night? Was it that good?

*

As soon as Daddy's scooter took him off to work, I asked Ma: 'Ma, does tea taste good?'

'If it's made well, it tastes good.'

'Daddy told you to make some in the night, no?'

Ma's eyes widened.

'You were awake?'

'I got up for a moment and fell asleep again.'

I think she forgot about the whole thing. But I was still intrigued.

*

Like scars, these memories will stay with me for a lifetime. What age was I when the windows and doors of the house last stood open? When Daddy and Ma sat and actually talked to each other, discussed things? When someone said a word of praise to me?

When I had grown up a little, she would say, 'You turned up in my tummy and took my happiness with you.' Or, 'You came along and your father drifted away from me.'

Ma seemed to have the notion that it was my duty to help her with her work. She blamed Daddy for the fact that we had no help at home. Daddy blamed Ma. I have a vague memory of Durgamma, who was our household help in some distant past. One day, something happened at home and Ma dismissed her. When Daddy came home, Ma began to complain about Durgamma and he slapped her, used his fists.

Then he roared, 'A cup of tea, right now!'

I went and sat in the dark, alone.

I fell asleep there.

Our house in Merces was not one of those antique beauties but it could not be called new either. Although my grandfather had built it, Daddy told me that his parents had never had the good fortune of living in it. There was no balcao in front but the house was not small. The main door opened into the living room. To the right was Daddy's den. To the left was the room Ma had taken over when she was delivering and which she had continued to use. Passing through, one came to the kitchen on one side and on the other the storeroom which had now fallen to my lot. Behind these, the bathroom and the toilet. When my grandparents died suddenly, the doors and windows had not even been put in. It was the dowry Ma brought with her that made it possible for these to be put in and which gave Daddy his scooter—or so Ma said.

The front door had a latch on either side. If by some remote chance we were all to go out, the front door would be locked. But one day something happened that lead to both the latches breaking at the same time and one latch being installed which could be opened from the outside with a key.

In front of our neighbour Pascoal's house, Dr Someshwar had opened a clinic. 'An ayurvedic doctor?' my father scoffed. 'Which Goan is going to go to him?'

My mother must have felt sorry for him. One day she told me, 'I have a pain in my chest. Go and fetch Dr Someshwar. No one else.'

Dr Someshwar came eagerly. That was the first of many visits. When he came, Ma would send me out to play or sit me down in the hall to study. When I asked why she would say, 'When doctors give injections, children should not see what's going on.'

Anyway, Ma's health seemed to improve under his treatment.

One day, when Daddy was feeling under the weather, and he was setting out to meet Dr Costabir, I asked, 'Shall

I get Dr Someshwar? Ma always calls him when she's not well.'

Daddy forgot whatever was troubling him and beat Ma mercilessly.

The next day the carpenter arrived. He took out both the latches and put in one latch on the outside which opened with a key. From then on, Daddy took the key with him when he left.

*

Most people had some kind of garden in front of their homes. We had land in front of our house but it was left untended, bare except for a stand for a tulsi plant. There was a nondescript mango tree and further down a banyan. Daddy said that the mango tree belonged to us but the banyan was not ours. In the summer, the banyan would put out bunches of red fruit. I would go outside and stand under the tree, hoping one of those fruits would fall on me. But the banyan would have nothing to do with me. When the mango flowered in the cold weather, it looked beautiful. In the summer, the dull green bulbs of raw mangoes would appear. When these ripened, the breeze would make them fall. I would hear the dull thumps and run to get the sour-sweet treats before the other children did.

Ma would make saasav, a ripe mango curry with them. Daddy didn't like saasav so she didn't make it on Sundays or holidays. When she made it, I would eat it. When the children threw stones to knock the mangoes down, she would shout at them. She would tell me to drive them off. I never had to. The children ran away as soon as they saw me, never turning back, even if I called them.

But one late evening, they did not run away. My sharp

ears had picked up the sound of two mangoes falling, one after the other. There was a settlement of migrant labourers from Karnataka not far from where we lived. I thought a couple of children would come running to collect them. I wanted to let them have this treat so I sat still and did nothing. But I heard no sound of footsteps.

'Arre, Babu, I heard some mangoes falling. Go and get them quickly,' Ma said. I was frightened of going out into the darkness to look for fallen mangoes but I obeyed. I found the mangoes quickly and when I had picked them up and was about to return, I saw someone there. I went forward quietly. There were two of them. One was a girl in a ghaghra and blouse and the other was a much older boy. I thought they had come to find mangoes. I walked forward and put out my hands with the two mangoes.

'Do you want some mangoes?' I asked.

'I already have two mangoes here,' the boy said with a mean laugh, as if he had made a joke of which I was the butt.

I got angry. I could see that both his hands were inside the girl's blouse. How could he have any mangoes?

'Show them to me, then!' I said and went forward. The girl covered her face with her hands and I could see that she might even be crying.

'Get away from here,' he said.

That annoyed me even more. Why should I leave just because he said so? But then I heard Ma calling me and I ran home. I gave Ma both the mangoes and said, 'There are two people there, near the mango tree. A boy and a girl. He's so stupid, no, I asked him if he wanted mangoes and he said he had two already. But his hands were in her blouse so where could he have any mangoes, na, Ma? Why did he lie?' Ma stuck her head out of the door and screwed up her eyes to get a better view. 'Can't see anything in this darkness. Who knows whether he's squeezing those mangoes or sucking them? Come on inside.' Ma closed the door, ending any chance of seeing the mangoes the boy said he had found.

*

The banyan and the mango seemed to have some kind of relationship going on. When the mangoes fell from the tree, the children came running to get them but the banyan fruit lay on the ground, ignored. I felt the two trees were communing with each other. The banyan was growing well, and it was swathed in dark green leaves. It looked tall and handsome, and reminded me of my mother's brother, my Uncle Junior, dressed up for his wedding.

One day, the banyan must have wanted to tell me something. One of its fruits fell with a 'tonk' on my head. The mango tree was also laden with fruit that year and looked like the banyan's bride. I thought of getting the banyan tree married. An idea sprang up in my mind—call the children together and get the banyan married to the mango. On that day, saasav could be cooked and served to the children in cones made from the leaves of the banyan.

One evening, a wild wind began to blow. The mangoes began to fall with those familiar dull thuds. Ma sent me out with a bag to collect them. The other children had gathered with the same idea.

It was great fun collecting mangoes with them. When I got home with a bag full of mangoes, Ma began to complain that the 'ghati' children had taken the pick of the windfall. Even before Daddy's scooter stopped at the gate Ma began to whine, 'All those kids from the village come and steal our mangoes. Bring someone to pluck them.'

'Why? So you can make some dreadful saasav?' Daddy said, to bait her.

'We could sell them.'

'You want me to sit on the street and sell fruit now?'

Daddy dealt it with in his own way. He brought someone and showed him the tree. For the next week or so, we scrabbled about, hunting for mangoes. And then the tree was cut down. The banyan was alone. It broke my heart.

2

Losing My Marbles

I had no idea who Devu was. I saw him only much later. But Daddy spoke of him as if he were God; he called him Baba. He took no step without consulting Baba first. Daddy spent many a Saturday evening at his place. Ma referred to Devu as that *ghaadi*—how was I to know what a ghaadi was? Only years later would I learn of its pejorative meaning: a man who thought himself an exorcist, who dealt with demons.

When Daddy was in an expansive mood, he would talk about Baba: 'Today, Baba was channelling the divine,' he'd say or 'He asked for a cockerel today,' or he reminded us that an offering was needed for the guardian spirit and 'Maybe I forgot to offer the roti and liquor once and so a malignant spirit is waiting for revenge.'

I understood nothing of all this. But I thought it might be a good idea to imitate Daddy's way of speaking.

When I entered my fourth year, Ma reminded Daddy, 'Babu should be sent to kindergarten now.' It took me some time to understand what this kindergarten business was. But one Saturday night, after he had come home, Daddy told Ma, in my hearing: 'Baba says that education is not in Babu's fate.'

'What does that mean?' Ma asked. 'All children go to school.'

'You think I don't want an educated son? He has to look after us in our old age. How is he going to do that if he hasn't studied? But what can we do if that is his fate?'

'So are we supposed to keep him sitting at home?'

'Baba says dont send him to school until he's six. Let's see if he shows some signs of being able to manage by then.'

Daddy closed his eyes and folded his hands in a salutation to his absent guru.

'If we don't send him to school now, it will be the ruin of him,' Ma insisted.

I was happy to see that Ma was concerned about me.

'I know what you're thinking. Once he's out of the way, the field will be clear for you. And I'm supposed to stand by and watch?'

Daddy's eyes grew red and Ma changed the subject. And one thing became clear: kindergarten would remain a mystery for me.

*

In the afternoon when I heard the voices of children playing far away, I would stand by the window and listen. Sometimes I would see two or three children of my age playing tip cat or seven stones. When they threw the ball or sent the stick close to the window, they would see me. One or the other might wave; my hand would rise but before I had completed the action, it would fall back again. Often, I would play with them in my imagination. As soon as Daddy left, we would pick up pebbles and throw them at each other. I enjoyed these imaginary games.

One day, I saw them playing marbles. One of the marbles

landed near the window. 'Hit it, go on,' the boy who had followed the marble challenged the other.

The other boy threw it and it landed close by me. As he picked up his marble, he asked me, 'Coming to play?'

'I don't have any marbles,' I said.

'Come and watch then,' he said and ran off. I went in and asked Ma, 'Can I go out?' Ma was dozing, her eyes about to close. When she nodded sleepily, I was out of the door in a flash. Then I stood by watching the game.

'Twenty,' shouted a boy. He had obviously won because he pocketed both the marbles. They turned and came towards me, marbles rattling in their pockets.

'I'm Ravi. He's Pitoo. You?'

'Babu,' I said. I knew there was another name, Vipin, but it had never seemed to belong to me.

'I have no marbles,' I repeated and one of them said, 'Then you play cricket, right?'

'No.'

'Football?' the other asked.

When I said I played no games, they wouldn't believe it. 'Not even in school?'

'I don't go to school,' I answered which surprised them. They looked at me with pity which I didn't like, not one bit.

Ravi said to Pitoo, 'You lost twice. Now play with him. He doesn't know how to play at all. You might even win this time.'

I said, 'I have never played. I don't have any marbles.'

Ravi said: 'I'll lend you one. Not for keeps, okay? When you're finished, give it back.'

Pitoo laughed at this. 'If he loses, I get the marble. How will he return it?'

'That's between us. Don't butt in,' Ravi said, and pushed a marble into my hand.

Then he began to explain the rules of the game to me. There was a small circular depression called the *meel.* If you threw a marble and it hit another marble that was a 'shot'. To start the game, you had to get the marble into the meel. You had twenty shots to do this. The eighteenth shot had to get the marble in the meel. Nineteenth too. And then at twenty, you were the winner.

I began to play. When I got to seventeen, Pitoo was on eight. He was somewhat startled by my aim. He tried to extend the game by throwing the marbles a distance away. But I won when he was still struggling at eight.

So I popped Pitoo's marbles into my pocket and returned Ravi's to him. Ravi began to tease Pitoo who got cross and challenged him: 'You play against him and show.'

Ravi was waiting for that. We started a new game and by the time Ravi got to fifteen, I had won again. This time, Pitoo clapped for me.

I suggested that we should all play but just for fun. Not to win or lose marbles. Not to count shots. Just to play. This went down well and we played for a long time. Then I said, 'I have to get home before Daddy gets back.'

Ravi asked: 'You're scared of your Daddy?'

That puzzled me. What did that mean: to be scared? Was I scared? I told the truth, 'I don't know.'

After that I began to play with them every day. Pitoo liked that because we played my style and he got to keep his marbles. He would say, 'After you came, we have so much fun. Now we don't win or lose, we just play!'

One day Pitoo didn't show up, so Ravi and I played. Suddenly he said, 'Aai told me to get a kilo of rice. But I forgot to take the money. I have to go home and get it. Coming?'

Their home was a hut erected between two fields owned by the Church. Ravi's mum was at home. 'Is this your friend Babu?'

Ravi must have told her about me. She stroked my hair and said, 'Poor fellow. He's had his childhood taken away from him. Run along and play.'

I knew all about marbles being taken away but how was one's childhood taken away?

Ravi and I walked towards my house, chatting away. It was getting close to my deadline. Ravi said, 'I'll walk you home.'

We went on talking and when Ma opened the door, we just walked in, chatting and laughing. And then Daddy arrived: 'Who is this? Why is he here? How dare you bring him here?'

Ravi took off, running.

After that I never saw Ravi near our house. For the next eight days I waited for him but he didn't come. Nor did Pitoo. They must have just gone somewhere else to play.

But I had two marbles in my pocket. Marbles I had earned. In the afternoon when Ma went for a snooze, I would go out and played on my own. And I found it was fun. The marbles began to play with me.

As I remember it, one of the marbles rolled near a bush. I was going to throw the other marble at it when I saw a snake uncoil its hood and hiss. It was as long as a man's arm extended. I was mesmerised by its glittering skin and its sinuous shape. Its small beautiful eyes were fixed on my hand. If I had thrown the marble, I would have certainly hit the snake. Without knowing it, I lowered my hand and the snake furled its hood and slithered into another hole.

Perhaps Ma was watching from a window. 'Babu, come

in right now,' she shouted. I took my shot, hit the other marble foursquare and then delighted, picked them both up and went inside. The moment Daddy returned home, Ma told him all about this snake.

'A rat snake or a cobra?' Daddy asked.

'The second and let's not talk about it in the evening.'

It was later that I learned that one does not mention snakes in the evening for fear that they will take it as an invitation. 'It was an aristocratic snake, what a hood it had. I had never seen one like him before,' Ma said.

'Show me where it was.'

Ma took Daddy to the window and showed him. He turned and shouted at me, 'Idiot, why did you go out to play? Who gave you marbles? Bring them here.'

The two marbles I had earned were taken from me.

'Don't you dare step out of the house now,' Daddy snapped and banged the window shut.

I lost interest in windows.

*

Marbles gone. Doors and windows closed. But I never understood why Daddy was always in such a bad mood. That 'aristocrat' (we didn't call it a snake) had done me no harm and simply gone its way. All these questions were too large for my limited understanding.

But Daddy seemed quite frightened.

'This is his territory, it seems. I hope Babu did not hurt him. We have to tell Baba about this. He'll have to work his magic.'

Then he ordered Ma: 'Remind me on Wednesday. We'll have to make the offerings.'

3

The Race Is Not to the Swift

When I was young, I thought all children were alike. When I joined school, I realized all fathers are not alike. Nor are all mothers. But one thing became clear then: one had to accept one's parents as they were. When I entered the class the first day, someone said mockingly, 'Look, the master has come.'

Giggles all around.

I knew they meant it for me but it didn't matter. All the other children were five years old. I was six. And big built. It wasn't as if I was angry but when I did stand up to see who had said it, all the other kids put on their not-me faces. The one who did say it hid his face. Maybe he was just scared of my size. After that no more comments.

Another thing I didn't know was that there were books besides the ones we used in school. I enjoyed reading the lessons in the textbooks. And then one day, books made their way to me.

And to my surprise, Daddy did not tear them up. It happened when I was in primary school, in the third standard.

The year had just begun. There was an annual gathering in the churchyard. At the same time the finals of the sporting events took place. I was in the finals of the 100-metre dash. The chief guest arrived and my event was announced

'Don't bother running too hard,' a classmate, Gary, said to me. 'Roy will come first.'

'Then Roy wins,' I said and shrugged.

We got on our marks, we got set, the whistle blew and we ran. I didn't bother to look around but just focused on running. I could hear the kids chanting, 'Roy, Roy, Roy!'

Then a whistle blew and we were told to stop. I looked behind and saw that Roy had fallen over a rope left on the ground and the referee had decided that we should run the race again.

On your marks, get set, go and we ran. No one was ahead of me and I breasted the tape first. But the referee came up to me and said: 'You're disqualified. You started before I blew the whistle.' And it was announced that Roy had won. The crowd was silent. Some kids clapped. Gary came up to me and whispered: 'I told you, na? Roy is the MLA's son. He had to win. His Dad is the chief guest.' I was a little surprised. How could this happen? I was certain I had not started before the whistle blew. This wasn't right.

When Roy received his prize, the chief guest announced, 'The boy who came first had to be disqualified because of an early start. But he ran so well I would like to gift him a special prize: two hundred rupees.'

My name was announced. But my feet would not move. Gary jabbed me in the shoulder. 'Go! They're calling you.' But I simply walked away. I turned my back on everyone and left the ground. I wanted to run. My hands were balled into fists, my nails digging into my palms. My eyes felt like they wanted to jump out of their sockets.

I sensed that someone was following me but I refused to

turn back. That someone put his hand on my shoulder and stopped me. 'That was brave of you. I am proud of you. Come with me,' he said. He took my hand and led me away. When he had put his hand on my shoulder, I wanted to jerk it off. But his calm, deep voice had its effect on me. He led me into the Parish House, next to the church. He went to his room and when I saw the crucifix pinned to his shirt, I realized he was the curate.

'Today you showed great spirit in front of that crowd. I'm proud of you...' Father said. He continued to talk but only half of what he said got through to me. I didn't know what I had done to be proud of. The referee had cheated. I was angry that I had not been able to express my feelings and here this priest, sitting in front of me, was telling me that he was proud of me.

'In the name of Jesus Christ, I have to say that I'm ashamed of myself. I was on the grounds when this happened and I did nothing about it. I have sinned against God and you. Please forgive me.'

He knelt and began to pray. His eyes were wet! I was rather surprised by all this.

After a while he rose again, went to a cupboard and took out a couple of biscuits and gave them to me. 'Will you have a cup of tea?'

I said no. I had not started my life-long affair with tea then.

'Today people have no value for the truth. Lies have value instead. We all seem to have abandoned our self-respect. It has become a commodity. And we are all helpless in front of the power of money. But you have courage. You spat in their faces.'

'Father, may I leave?'

But he was not listening to me.

'Tell me something: do you read?'

'Yes.'

'What do you read?'

'My textbooks.'

'Other than those?'

He got up and took out two small books from a shelf. 'Read these. There are stories about Christ from the Bible.'

I just wanted to get out of there. I grabbed the books and ran home. Daddy had arrived. Someone must have told him that I had insulted the MLA by refusing to take the two hundred rupees he had offered me. As soon as I entered the house, my father took me by the collar and shook me: 'Where did you go to eat shit?'

'Father took me...'

But he had seen the books in my hand and grabbed them.

'Did that priest give them to you? What does he want? To convert you? And this priest is more important to you than an MLA?'

He slapped me across the face.

*

The other children in the school seemed odd to me.

Accustomed to closed doors and windows and to my father's rule, I had become a creature of habit.

I knew that I should not look at the kind of bags other children had. I must simply carry the bag Daddy gave me. When there were rusks at home, Ma gave me rusks in my tiffin; occasionally she boiled an egg for me. I must eat what I was given and not dream of cakes and laddoos, or sheera or sandwiches. One Sunday, I hesitantly asked, 'Daddy, can we go to Miramar or Dona Paula today? Raju's father takes them to Calangute or Bondla.'

Daddy said: 'Sunday is my only day of rest. After six days of work, this is the only time I have to myself. You also should just stay home and rest.'

Then he thought of something else: 'Tell you what. Every morning, get up and do some exercise. Ten surya namaskaras and twenty squats.'

He showed me what a squat was. Although he could not manage a surya namaskar himself but he put me through the paces of one. I found the whole thing quite exciting and it became a part of my routine.

*

When I was in the fifth standard, Cajetan asked me: 'When is your birthday?' Up to that time I had thought that only other children had birthdays. I knew about birthdays because one of the children would wear party clothes and would bring toffees for everyone. I didn't think I had a birthday. Sometimes Ma would say, 'When you were born, I was born again.' I had never asked what this meant. But when Cajetan asked, I thought to ask my father. Daddy pointed at Ma and said, 'The day she almost died is your birthday. Get it?'

I did not get it, so I asked again, 'Daddy, Cajetan is asking when we'll celebrate my birthday. What should I tell him?'

Daddy didn't like this kind of question. 'Tell him that your birthday brings back memories of the time your mother was at death's door. So we don't celebrate.'

I still didn't understand what he meant and when I told Caji what my father had said, he didn't understand it either. When I was in the sixth standard Nilesh invited me over for his birthday party. By then I knew enough to check Daddy's mood before asking.

That day Daddy came home whistling. Ma had an explanation for this: 'He's only in this mood when he's had a good feed of mutton at Sher-e-Punjab in Panjim. Or if he's met some flirt.'

I quietly asked Daddy, 'There's a birthday party. Nilesh invited me. May I go?'

His mood changed instantly. That mutton must have been some ornery goat for he bared his teeth and snarled. 'No coming and going from people's houses.' Then he got hold of my ear and twisted it and issued an order: 'You're not to go anyone's house and you're not to invite anyone over. You understand?'

This wasn't only a law meant for me. No one came to our house except for a rare visit from Ma's brothers and Dr Costabir.

4

Tea, Filter Coffee and Me

I knew there were things called festivals like Ganesh Chaturthi, Diwali and Christmas and that these seemed to be occasions for holidays. But then one day it seemed as if Christmas crossed our threshold. It was Daddy who opened the door when Christmas knocked.

'Merry Christmas!' said the woman at the door and proceeded to come right in.

'We are Hindu,' Daddy said and I thought he was going to get angry.

The woman proffered a bag full of cake and cookies and replied cheerfully, 'What of that? We are Nasraani, Tamil Christians.'

I was standing right behind Daddy. 'Take,' she said to me and offered me the bag while she shook hands with Daddy and added: 'I'm Elsie.' Quite contrary to what I had expected, Daddy ordered me to take the parcel: 'Why are you standing there like an idiot? Take that packet.' Hesitantly I came forward.

'Hello little fellow. What a cutie!' she said and pinched my cheek. 'Which class are you in?'

'Sixth.'

'Aiyaiyo. Only sixth?' Then she turned to Daddy: 'He's big for his age.'

She looked like my aunt but she was dressed differently, in a sleeveless white blouse and a white sari with a red border. Around her neck there was a delicate gold chain from which hung a locket. Her hair was loose around her shoulders. I liked her smile. She seemed South Indian from the way she spoke and dressed. Daddy pulled up a chair for her to sit down but she said, 'No, no, I must be going.' But then she didn't move. Ma must have heard a voice and came out.

'Madrasi?' Daddy asked.

She must not have liked that but she smiled anyway. 'I'm Sri Lankan. But my husband is Tamilian.'

She told us that her husband had just been transferred and they had come to live in the house behind Pascoal's. She said, 'One day you must come over for coffee.' As she left, she turned and said to Daddy, 'I'm all alone when my husband goes to work. I get bored. Send Babu to keep me company. I'll even take care of his homework.' Then she stroked my cheek again and said, 'Come tomorrow, haan? I'll give you some lovely coffee.'

When Ma saw Daddy following our visitor with his eyes, she said loudly, 'She invited Babu, not you.' And then she scuttled off inside to avoid an outbreak of Daddy's anger.

Nothing like this had happened before. No one came over and no one invited us over. This was the first time I had heard the words, 'Merry Christmas' in our house. That day we all gorged on cake. The next day I waited eagerly for her hoping that she would come to take me home. Of course, I could have gone myself but I didn't have the guts. Finally, I asked Ma, 'That woman who came over yesterday? Her house is not so far away. Can I go?'

Ma sniffed at that and said, 'All she has to do is crook her finger and off you go, hopping and skipping. She seems like a proper coquette to me.'

I didn't ask Ma what a coquette was. When I asked Daddy, he said: 'She thinks every woman is like herself.' So I didn't get an answer to my question but Daddy did say, 'If she calls again, you can go.'

Two days later, she came by again, around four o'clock.

This time she was wearing a long skirt and a white blouse. Her hair was loose, lying against her neck as if she had just stepped out of her bath. 'Where's Amma?' she asked just as Ma came out. She gave Ma a packet and said, 'Special South Indian sweet for you.'

Ma took the packet and though Elsie smiled sweetly at her, her face remained frozen. Elsie took my hand and said, 'Come, I'll give you sweets.' Then she looked at Ma for approval. Ma did not say no and so I went off with her, hopping and skipping.

Elsie kept up a steady flow of prattle. When we got to her place, she put on water for coffee. As it was heating up, she gave me a laddoo. It was made with ghee and very sweet. She brought the coffee to the table and sat down and pulled me into her lap. This had never happened to me before. I don't remember having sat on Ma's lap. Nor did I remember ever inhaling the scent of another woman before this. When I finished my laddoo and reached for the coffee, she pulled my hand back and said, 'No, no, the coffee is hot. Wait.'

And she pulled me into her arms and gave me a smacking kiss on my cheek. Another new experience. I felt I should say something to her. But I didn't know what to call her. Teacher? Miss? Then I thought 'Aunty' would be the best. But when I said it, she protested, 'No, no, call me Elsie, just

Elsie.' I could not call an adult by her first name. I pointed at a photograph lying on the table and asked who that was.

'My husband.' I wanted to ask if she had children but did not know how. So I pointed at her and asked, 'Baby?'

For a moment her face clouded over. But then she smiled again and said, 'No baby. But you play with me, okay?' Then she blew on the coffee and brought it to my lips. 'Like it? It's filter coffee. Our speciality.'

We only ever had watery instant coffee at home. Daddy and Ma drank tea. As a child I wasn't allowed either. This was the first time I had coffee like this.

'Did you like the coffee?' she asked again.

I thought it was okay but I said yes. She gave me another tight hug and kissed me again. Then she took out some toys: playing cards and a Snakes and Ladders board.

'Do you play?' she asked, pointing at the cards. I shook my head so we settled on Snakes and Ladders.

'Come on, let us sit on the bed,' she said.

I sat cross legged and she tucked her legs beneath her. And we settled down to play. We rolled the dice and she would respond excitedly with cries of 'Oh no!', 'Ayyaiyo!', 'Very good!'.

I enjoyed that. Though I was not in the habit of talking much, I grew quite animated and found myself clapping. I won the first game and she was happier than I was. She pulled me to herself and hugged me so hard, the breath was squeezed out of my body. We started another game. We rolled the dice and I got two sixes. I moved my token and looked for the dice to roll again but one of them was missing. We looked for it everywhere but couldn't find it. Nothing had fallen on the ground. It had to be on the bed. She made me raise my legs and rooted about under my buttocks. Then she raised her legs and told me to look around. Finally, I saw the dice tucked into the folds of her skirt, under her thighs. I slipped my hand underneath and retrieved it, much to her delight. She kissed my hand and said, 'Enough now.' I was a little disappointed but then she added, 'Come tomorrow. We will play more. Okay?'

I was about to leave—home wasn't far off—but she stopped me. She said she would accompany me and changed her clothes, right there, in front of me.

*

That day, as we enjoyed her delicious South Indian sweets, Daddy asked me more questions than he had ever asked before. What was her house like, how many children did she have, what did her husband do, did she have servants. Up to now, Daddy had not cared for me to talk at all. But now he found my answers too short for his liking. The same man who did not like me asking questions was now asking so many himself. I told him what I could.

'She's called me tomorrow again. Should I go?' I asked.

Daddy grunted. The next day I didn't wait and left for her house.

'Oh, good, you've come,' she said, stroking my hair. She looked a little different today in a filmy nighty, her hair lying on her shoulders as if she had just bathed. 'Sit down. I will make us some coffee.'

I said I didn't want any but she paid no attention.

'No, no, you must have some coffee.'

She went on to tell me how good coffee was: how it gave you energy, how you felt alert afterwards and other things like that. After we drank our coffee, she gave me some biscuits. And then she asked me to sit on her lap.

'I like you, Babu,' she said and pulled me closer to her. Then she presented her cheek to me and said, 'Your turn to give me a *mutta*.'

I didn't know what she meant, but I figured out that I was supposed to give her a kiss. I still had some biscuit in my mouth but I kissed her anyway and some crumbs ended up on her face. 'Oh, you naughty man...' she said dusting her cheek. Then she patted my thigh and said, 'Eat first' and then kept on patting my thigh. No one had ever been so affectionate before. And so all this seemed quite strange but it was not unwelcome. Until I finished my coffee she didn't let me get down from her lap nor did she drink her coffee herself.

'Would you care for some more?' she asked, presenting her cup to me. I refused and tried to get up but she would not let me go. She moved up a little and pulled me down to sit next to her.

'Do you like me?' she asked.

I was quite surprised. I couldn't think of a reason for disliking her except for all this kissing and hugging which had got a bit too much.

'Come, you like me, no? Hold me tight!' she said and took both my arms and pulled them around her. I pulled back. I wanted to run away. But she said, 'Wait. I will give you chocolate. Come.' She could not see my nervous face as she hugged me again and stroked my body. Her hands ran over my chest, my stomach and then further down. Before she could put her hands into my shorts, I shouted, 'You're old, you're old.' As she started fondling me, I felt terribly disgusted. With all my strength I pushed her away. Somewhere I heard the sound of a coffee mug falling and breaking. I had no idea whether she fell over too because I threw myself out of the door and ran all the way home.

I was filled with shame and rage that I had not seen this coming. The coffee she had offered me came back into my throat, I felt as if I were about to vomit. But somehow, I didn't want to vomit it out and empty myself. When Daddy returned home, I would tell him and all would be well again. Then I thought: 'He'll give her good. He screams at Ma even for a small mistake and this? He won't spare that Elsie.'

But this time his scooter did not return from the usual direction. Instead, it came from the direction of Elsie's house. When I saw him, I got up and before I could say anything, he let fly and slapped me.

'So you broke a coffee cup at that Madrasi's house and ran away.'

At this all the coffee made its way out and I vomited.

Daddy went inside. He told Ma, 'No tea for me. I had a great cup of coffee.'

*

After that I kept my distance from Elsie. Nor did she come over to our house. Daddy would visit them from time to time. I knew when because he would say, 'I don't want any tea, I've had some coffee.'

And from then onwards I developed a great dislike of coffee.

The next Christmas Ma was hoping for some cake.

Daddy told her, 'Forget about the cake now. He's transferred and they're gone.'

5

Another Kind of Father

I enjoyed school. It was not that I had any friends. But at least I was out of the cage of the house in which I had begun to feel suffocated. When Ma felt ill, she would stay in bed. At such times, Daddy would say, 'Stay at home and help her, got it?' I don't know why Daddy thought to say that. For him, missing a day at school was no big deal but he also felt that I was big enough to help my mother.

At these times, I didn't understand why we had no servants. There was a washing machine for the clothes but we needed someone to clean the house. Ma would wash only those vessels which were needed again and she would sweep only every alternate day.

When the house began to look a bit messy, Daddy would shout at her. And then he would say to both of us, 'Do you feel ashamed to take a broom and do a bit of sweeping?' I didn't ask for Daddy's help with my homework. One day we were studying simplification in Algebra and I asked him, 'Daddy, minus 8a upon 2b. How would I simplify that?' Daddy took the textbook from my hand and looked at it carefully. After thinking about it for a while, he said, 'Why? What do you learn in school?'

'Daddy, it's minus...'

'Now look here, minus means subtract. Minus 2a means...Why don't you go to school tomorrow and tell your teacher to explain things properly? Tell her I'll complain otherwise.'

When the teacher did explain, I was surprised at how easy it was. So why didn't Daddy solve it for me? Maybe he had wanted me to learn it myself.

*

One day our English teacher set us an essay on 'My Home'. I wrote the essay telling the truth. I described our home, how we had space for a garden but nothing was planted and tended. How the mango tree had been cut down because the children threw stones at it. How with the mango tree gone, the sparrows and crows had abandoned us...How the front door was kept closed for fear of robbers and the back door was kept closed because animals might get in. How the windows were closed because mosquitoes might get in. How I swept and cleaned because Ma couldn't manage and how I got ample time to study because no one came to our house.

The next day the teacher returned all the books but not mine. I was a little startled. Martin Sir, the English teacher, never got angry with us and after the period was over, he called me to him. He gave me my book and said, 'I want to talk to you. Can you come in the evening to my house? I don't live very far. It's just after the Horse Dam.'

I went and what a surprise I got! A woman who must be Sir's wife was outside watering the garden and Martin Sir himself was sweeping the verandah. Could that be true? A man, a teacher that too, doing housework?

He saw me and said, 'Come on up.' But he did not stop

sweeping. When I mounted the steps, he set down the broom and said, 'Will you have some tea?'

I said, 'I don't drink tea, sir.'

He gave me a glass of water. If I had said I wanted tea, would he have made it himself and served me?

He sat down next to me and asked about me how were my studies going. What did Daddy do? He asked after my mother as well. Then he asked, 'Why don't you play any sports?' I had no answer to this. I just didn't play. All the other boys played something or the other. So why didn't I? But after Ravi and Pitoo went away, I had played nothing.

'What books do you read?'

I liked reading. From time to time the Konkani teacher would give me books from the library.

'Have you read any English books?'

When I said I hadn't, he went inside and brought out two books and gave them to me. One was *Oliver Twist* and the other was *Tom Sawyer*.

'Read and return. And then tell me whether you like them. And if you like them what you liked about them.'

At that moment a girl came in, carrying a basketball. I assumed this was Martin Sir's daughter. A hairband held her hair back and her white shirt and skirt were so dirty that I thought Martin Sir was going to scold her. But lo and behold!

'Hey Stella! How did the tennis go? Better go in and clean up. Mumma has some soup ready. Give me a moment and I'll come and heat it up for you. Call me when you're ready.'

This seemed to be my cue. As I was leaving, he asked, 'Do your parents read?' I said they didn't. He must have read these lines in my essay: 'Ma watches TV. Daddy brings files home and reads them. The doors and windows are closed. But when the door opens, I enjoy the way the breeze rushes in. I am in awe of closed windows...'

That day, I saw another kind of father, Stella's father.

6

Setting Down the Burdens of the Heart

The first death I witnessed.

Early in the morning, the news came. My grandfather had died.

Ma hurriedly stuffed some clothes into a bag. Mine went in, too. Daddy had called for a taxi. Ma made tea, took out some biscuits. She told me, 'Fill up. You won't get anything to eat in a house where death has visited. Lunch will also be late.' Ma also ate her fill. I didn't need to be told that Daddy would eat out. The seventh standard examinations were in a couple of days but I was ready so that didn't bother me much.

The taxi arrived. In my memory, this was the first time I had ever sat in one. We reached Mapusa by ten in the morning.

This was also the first time I had ever seen a corpse. My grandfather was lying on the floor, on a satrangi. His hands had been tied. Or did I feel that way? And that he was staring at me through his half-opened eyes? Ma had often said to me, 'How your uncle and aunt harass that poor man.' But now they had placed a garland over his body. Ma often said that my aunt would not give my grandfather enough food. But now she was sobbing her heart out. And through her tears, my aunt was saying, 'He was fine yesterday. Got up as usual, drank his tea, ate his chapattis. Good fish there was yesterday, fried fish. He ate well, two pieces more than his usual.

'He praised my cooking and had a nice nap in the afternoon. In the night, rotis were made specially for him to eat with some of the fish curry from the afternoon. He slept well too and then go to see in the morning...'

To which someone said, 'An easy death. What a beautiful way to go. Only God knows what Fate has written for us.'

Powered by the biscuits and tea, Ma too burst into an energetic bout of tears. I was rather surprised and went out to have a look around. Daddy was chatting to the neighbours. My uncles were wandering about, with forlorn faces. They were telling all and sundry about their father. I heard praise of him that I had never heard before. Then I heard Daddy mutter to someone, 'That's as much hypocrisy as a man can take in a day.'

Kalpesh, my cousin, came looking for me and dragged me off outside. With his hair combed into a quiff and his red t-shirt, he looked like a guest in his own home. The bier was being constructed and Kalpesh gave me a guided tour: how they would load Grandfather on the bier, how he would be carried off to the cremation grounds, how the wood would be arranged and how the body would be laid on it...I wasn't very keen on seeing all this.

I said: 'I'll come with you. Let's stick together.'

'Tscha. We don't get to go. If your dad's around, you don't go to the cremation grounds,' he said. Then he pointed to a teenager who was also standing there. 'You see that Ulhas? He gets to go. His dad's dead, see?'

The day was well advanced by the time the body was placed on the bier. Daddy went with the rest to the cremation. Ma sent me off for a bath. Daddy returned and went up to Ma.

'I'll wait out the mourning period here,' she told him. 'You go and take Babu with you.'

'And dance after him for the next twelve or thirteen days?'

'He has exams from day after tomorrow.'

'He will stay where you are. These are only the seventh standard exams. They can't fail anyone until the eighth standard. That's the rule now. I'll see who fails him.'

'Oh and you get to play the field for the next fortnight...' Ma mumbled.

*

The next three days were spent in much the same way. Trapped at home for three days, Uncle Senior wandered about, mumbling and muttering. His younger brother, Uncle Junior, a lawyer by profession, occupied himself with his files. Aunt Senior was concerned about how she would manage the three days of vegetarianism inflicted upon her by this death. She sought to assuage her hungry tongue by thinking up various options to pull through. Uncle Junior's wife had taken to peering at herself in the mirror each time she happened to pass it. When the corpse was taken away, she happened to notice that she looked a little more fetching when she let her hair loose over her shoulders. The dilemma she now faced was whether to let her hair hang down her back or whether she should bring her locks to lie over her breast. She polled the house and even asked me for my opinion three or four times. Meanwhile Ma enjoyed a holiday. 'Does a daughter who has returned to her mother's home ever have to work?' she asked rhetorically, and settled down delightedly to doing nothing. Kalpesh was kept busy with the small chores that can be entrusted to a boy. He would drag me along when he was doing them. I did not like trailing about after him at all. But I went along anyway. In those three days, Kalpesh kept up a steady stream of information about his rather advanced ways.

When the two uncles left the house on the fourth day, Kalpesh heaved a sigh of relief. 'There. The eclipse is over at last,' he said. 'Only nine days left for the sutak to end.'

When Uncle Senior returned after his sojourn in the outside word, he had his lunch and then went off for a nap, a good one by his snores. The lawyer had left in the morning; he would not return until nightfall. But after lunch Kalpesh was restless. Finally, he powdered his face, tucked his shirt into his trousers and put on socks and shoes. It was obvious that his feet were itching to go out. He called me to one side and said, 'I have some work to do. I'll be home by evening. Right now, they're all sleeping but if anyone asks where I am, you're to say: "He's gone to Babush's to fetch the bananas from Moira for the halwa for the thirteenth day ceremony." And whenever they ask, you're to say, "He just left", okay?'

He didn't wait for a reply. I had no desire to lie for him. I didn't want to be asked so I kept away from everyone. But no one made any inquiries until he returned at dusk so I was spared the need to lie. And to give him his due, he did bring the bananas when he came home.

When both the uncles had left the house the next day, Kalpesh told me his secret.

'Do you know where I went yesterday?' he asked.

'To Babush's...'

'Tscha. What Babush-Babush? There's no one called Babush. That's a story I invented for them. That some MLA has a personal assistant called Babush who likes me. When I say that I'm going to see Babush, no one asks any questions. And then I come back I bring bananas sometimes or cake. And everyone's happy.'

'But what if your father asks about the MLA?'

'They won't ask. But let me tell you where I went. You have to promise to keep it a secret.'

Taking my silence for assent, he began, 'Today, I went to Calangute. Where? Not to the beach. Did you know this?' And so saying he put a finger to his nose. When he saw that I did not understand he said, 'You only look big. I keep forgetting that you're four years younger than me. Wait, I'll show you.'

He went inside and brought out a shabby pamphlet. He checked that no one was around and then opened it and showed it to me. A woman was lying down, her legs spread wide open and a man was lying on top of her. Both of them were naked.

Then we heard the sound of footsteps. Kalpesh quickly slipped the book under his shirt and into his shorts. One of our aunts had come down to check whether the lamps had been lit in Grandfather's room to keep vigil. Kalpesh took my hand and dragged me out into the verandah and then in the manner of someone telling a ripe tale, he told me that some months ago he had met an American woman who had come to live in Calangute. She was the mother of two but did not look it. She had lots of money and threw it around happily. She was plump and out for a good time. It seems she had seen Kalpesh when she had come to the market in Mapusa.

When their eyes met, she smiled. She had had four bags in her hands. They weren't heavy since they had fruit, biscuits, cakes, stuff like that. She asked Kalpesh to help her carry them back to the place where she was staying in Calangute. From then on, twice a week, she would call him and he'd go over. Then they would do things together like the couple in the book. She would even give him some money.

I had a flashback and asked, 'Does she give you coffee as well?'

'How did you know? Great coffee! Like the stuff you get in America. They call it Starbucks or something.'

I felt a little sick. From that day on, until we went back, I stayed away from Kalpesh.

*

During those holidays I must have read at least fifty books. Out of them, twenty to twenty-five were given to me by Martin Sir. At the beginning when I returned a book after two days, he was suspicious. He started asking me questions. When I returned *The Fault in Our Stars* in two days, he asked, 'You finished it?'

'Yes sir.'

'All of it?'

I had. He asked me about Hazel's diagnosis and the city the young couple visits. When I answered he gave me *The Book Thief*. When I returned that one, he asked me questions about the Jews in Germany under Hitler, about the Final Solution and about the young German girl in the book. And then he asked: 'Would you write such stories?'

I shook my head.

'Why not try?' he asked.

I shook my head even more firmly.

Martin Sir looked steadily at me. 'Vipin, I know you have stories in you but I think you are afraid to bring them out. Telling a story is an art. And from your essays, it seems that you have some talent for writing. So do write. Write it down, whatever it is, as it comes...'

*

That day I did write. I put everything down. Daddy and me, home and school, the banyan and the mango, Sir and Stella. When I read it back, I felt very strange. I did not like the comparisons I had made. It was as if I had stripped myself bare and was looking at my naked body in a mirror. What if Sir were to ask to read it tomorrow? I tore up the pages. But two days later I was at it again. This time: Kalpesh, Elsie. Once again when I was finished, I tore it all up. But I discovered one thing: that you could set down the burdens of the heart onto paper and after that paper became the place where I could clear my head. It was as if I had been carrying a headload and came to a place where I could set it down and stretch my body, rest my back and legs. When my head grew heavy, I could write it all down, write it out of my system. When I was done, I could tear up the paper. And my mind would be light...calm...quiet.

*

'The eighth standard is very tough,' all the kids would say and I grew apprehensive.

In June we got our textbooks. I was eager to read them but was soon done. The language textbooks were disappointing. They seemed to be kid stuff. I turned to the history textbook, looking for stories. Science fascinated me and the idea of going to the laboratory seemed exciting. But here too disappointment. We were not allowed to construct our own experiments. But it was still interesting to watch experiments being demonstrated. Inspired by that I went home and opened up whatever came to hand: a torch, a remote, a light switch. I would put them back together again.

Sometimes I would not understand the meaning of a word. Martin Sir said, 'When you don't understand a word, stop and check a dictionary before you go any further.'

We had only a small pocket dictionary at home. I preferred to use the big *Oxford Dictionary* in the library. One day I chanced upon *Webster's Dictionary and Thesaurus* which aroused my curiosity. I issued the book and brought it home. I enjoyed the lists of synonyms and antonyms. I rationed myself to twenty pages a day to prolong my enjoyment. I began to see patterns in words and looked up derivations and etymology. There were only ten or twenty pages left on the day Gaonkar Sir was teaching history. I knew all about the period he was describing in our freedom struggle since I had read the history textbook.

So, I stopped listening and read my thesaurus under the desk. Gaonkar Sir asked the class a question and then he noticed that I was reading something. He made me stand up and asked for the answer. I asked him to repeat the question. This angered him but he repeated the question which I promptly answered. Seeing the open book on my desk, Gaonkar Sir thought I had read the answer out of it.

'Bring that book here!' he commanded. He was quite surprised to see what I was reading. 'Here I'm killing myself to teach you history and you're looking up a dictionary? What are you looking in the dictionary for?'

'The meaning of words, Sir.'

'What were you looking for?'

'I wasn't looking for anything, Sir.'

'So why read a dictionary then?'

'I was learning it up, Sir.'

'Learning up the dictionary?' He laughed aloud and my classmates took their cue and laughed with him. He asked, 'Have you finished?'

'Almost.'

'So what does history mean?'

'The study of the past, sir.'

That annoyed him. He opened the dictionary and asked, 'What does historiography mean?'

'The study of history and written histories.'

'Proletariat?'

'Working class people.'

He saw all this as a challenge to his authority.

'And the antonym is?'

'Aristocrats.'

He didn't like this at all.

'Now tell me what palimpsest means?'

I was about to say 'over-written manuscript' but I knew this would upset him further so I said nothing. And then Gaonkar Sir's angry face lit up with signs of victory.

'Says he's reading the dictionary! Try to get past this class first!'

And for the rest of the period he lectured us on how if we didn't pay enough attention to our eighth standard syllabus, we were certainly not going to be able to do well in the tenth standard.

At the end of the class, he took the dictionary with him.

I met Martin Sir after school. When he saw me, he said, 'Come and see me at home this evening, if you can.'

I was puzzled. I did not have any of his books and so I

had nothing to return to him. Perhaps he had a new book for me?

*

'Where are you going? When will you be back?' Ma's usual questions but I did not feel like answering them.

'Take your time. It's Saturday today. *He* will be going to that ghaadi.'

Baba obviously would be meeting Daddy at dusk, at *kaatorvel*, the time of dusk, when it was neither day nor night.

None of this made any difference to me.

I got to Martin Sir's a little early. As I entered, Stella told me that Martin Sir was waiting for me in the hall. His wife was sitting at her sewing machine. Martin Sir asked me to sit down. The sound of the wheel and the click-click-click of the needle stopped when Sir said, 'Agnes, if that work is not urgent, could you join us for a minute? I want to talk to this young man. And I'd like you to join us.'

She turned her chair around to face us. 'So, Agnes, first a little background,' and Sir told her what had happened in the school that day. Apparently, Gaonkar Sir had told the story of the boy who was reading the dictionary in the class to the staff room, no doubt adding his own flourishes. 'Does one have to *read* a dictionary? One *consults* a dictionary,' Gaonkar Sir had said. 'I asked him the meanings of some simple words which he got but then I chose a tough word and the boy fumbled.'

Turning to me, Martin Sir asked, 'What was that word?'

'Palimpsest,' I said.

'Didn't you know the meaning?'

'A manuscript with many layers of use, Sir.'

'Then why didn't you answer?'

'Gaonkar Sir would have got even more angry, Sir,' I said.

Martin Sir smiled. 'Agnes, the *Webster's Dictionary and Thesaurus* was bought for staff use but the staff doesn't refer to it. Now this boy seems to have it off by heart. Right?'

I did seem to remember a lot of it but I said nothing.

'I shouldn't say it in his hearing, Agnes, but he is brilliant. I've seen his reading speed and his grasping power. And now this ability to remember things, this memory. These are God's gifts.'

I was walking on air. I felt as if someone were showering me with parijat flowers. When Stella brought me a slice of cake and a soft drink I refused because I didn't want anything to interfere with my feeling of bliss but when Sir insisted, I couldn't refuse. I walked home and though it was not raining, my mind was in a green, wet space.

*

I had hardly set foot on the threshold when a growl greeted me: 'Stop right there!'

I froze.

Framed in the door was my father.

Behind him his godman. He had a greasy towel around his waist. Across his shoulders, a dirty red scarf. His head was swathed in black cloth.

In the background, I could see my mother sitting on a rug with her back to the wall. In the middle of the room, a *ghamela w*ith embers crackling and smoking in it. The atmosphere was tense, serious. It reminded me of the time of my grandfather's death.

Waving a broom made of four palm fronds tied together, Baba approached me.

'Quiet. Not a word. Not a move,' he ordered and I was not sure whether he was talking to me or to someone unknown.

'Who are you? Where are you from? Will you not talk? Don't baulk!' he snarled as he advanced to the door. I was still standing on the threshold. With his red eyes whirling and his strange clothes, he looked a little mad to me.

Seeing my father with his hands respectfully folded behind this man was even more weird. This was the man who was always in a bad temper, who lashed out at my mother for every small offence, who kept me on a short leash and here he was, tail between legs.

'The day is done. The dusk has come...'

Whirling his broom, Baba approached me. 'Raise your spell. Go back to Hell,' he said and was about to hit me with a broom when I raised my hand and stopped it by grabbing his wrist firmly.

'You dare to touch my body? You dare to mess with a ghaadi! Will you pay no heed? Must I make you bleed?' he began to shout. 'Let go of my arm or I will burn your palm!'

Daddy ran forward and freed his arm from my grasp. He whispered in my ear. 'Listen to what Baba says. Let him finish his ritual. He wants to free you from the spirit that possesses you.'

I remained quiet. Baba looked at Daddy and asked, 'You want your son back, right?'

Daddy said, 'Yes, Saiba.'

Did he use 'saiba', a word for master but also for God, by mistake? Why didn't he just say, 'Yes, Baba?'

Then the Baba hit me on the head three times with the broom but he took care not to hurt me too much.

'He's gone. It's done. Now let him come in,' said the

Baba and walked away from the door and sat down by the smoking ghamela. He threw some crystals of rock salt on the coals which crackled angrily.

'The threat has passed, right, Baba?' Daddy asked.

Baba took out a pinch of vermillion and put it in Daddy's hand and said, 'Smear his forehead with this. Then take him inside and lock him up. No one is to go near him tonight. Do not put on the light. No food, no water. Tomorrow is Sunday, right? When the first crow caws, you can open the doors.'

This was obviously my punishment for having grabbed his hand.

'Yes, Saaiba,' Daddy said, as he made his promise, with the fire throwing shadows on the walls as witness.

Before extinguishing the contents of the ghamela with water, this Baba asked my father, 'Any other issues?'

'This spell of bad luck, this *saade-saathi* will ease, won't it?'

'You're only half-way through seven-and-a-half years of a difficult period but you have no cause for worry. I have everything under control.'

And then I heard him pouring water into the ghamela. Smoke filled the room. I could hear my parents coughing. Locked into my own room, I was spared the thick smoke that filled the other room.

*

Restrained by invisible shackles, I was filled with anger and shame to be locked up in this manner. I wanted to hide myself away from the world but at least I was alone. Even my shadow that went everywhere with me was missing. I opened my eyes and looked towards the door. The shadows that danced on the wall would now have gone. I was glad that there was no one to witness this disgrace. I began to enjoy my solitude. I had always enjoyed the darkness and now whether I opened my eyes or closed my lids, darkness was my companion. I made darkness into a friend.

That night, that closed room showed me my place in the world. Yes, there must be some relationship between this unrelieved darkness and the cycle of birth and death through which I was passing. This darkness allowed me space to sharpen my sensibilities, to evoke joie de vivre inside me. Ever since my father had driven Ravi away, I had adopted darkness as one of my own. And now I had a positive enjoyment of the dark. Now the realization came that I could be myself in the dark. On the night that Daddy's Baba had pronounced that the saade-saathi was half done, my ears taught me a new mantra.

I had no watch on my wrist; nor was there a clock on the wall but I could hear a ticking in the room, a ticking that did not stop. I realized that it was my heart beating in my chest. I focused on that sound, losing myself in it. All my senses were now denied me. Whether I closed my eyes or opened them made no difference. My ears had become my eyes. And so sounds that would not normally reach me, became clear. Pascoal's dogs barking, the owls hooting, the bats swooping down on their prey, all these came to me with the clarity that horns hooting and breaks being slammed would in daylight. From far off, along the edge of the fields, the sounds of the trees, the rustling of the leaves, as I listened to all this, I remembered what I had read once: that nocturnal birds navigate in the night and hunt their prey by the use of the echoes, by the use of sound. The world of sound came to life for me. Sound was no longer just sound.

Sound became tangible. Sound had consciousness. Sound took human form. Sound began to make contact. Sound began to challenge me. I became conscious for the first time of the fractional difference between the beat of my heart and the throb of my pulse. I felt the slow rush of my blood as I began to grow conscious of how each of the nodes of my body was ticking simultaneously.

By drawing into the sense of hearing alone, the world expanded and that was how I got through that night: with an epiphany as sound made itself present and absolute in that darkness.

7

Tea for Two

When I entered the tenth standard, the other students said that they had to spend a huge amount of time studying and when they studied late into the night and began to feel drowsy, tea would refresh them. I said, 'Wouldn't your mother get angry?'

They looked at me as if I were mad.

'My mum makes tea for me herself,' one of them said.

But when I asked my mother, she baulked. 'Where do you sit up late to study?'

She was right. I never had to pull an all-nighter. But my new relationship with the dark helped me decide that I would sit up in the night and study too. I told my mother, 'This is the tenth standard and that means I have to study a huge amount. And I don't even take tuitions like all the others do. So, I'm going to have to sit up at night.'

That night I asked her to make me some tea. She called me into the kitchen and said, 'If you're going to sit up in the night, I won't be able to sit up late and make it for you. So, you'd better learn how to make tea.'

'I've never...'

'Learn. You're not a little boy anymore. I'll show you today.'

And she demonstrated how to make tea. I didn't care much for this. But one day I went to Martin Sir's house to pick up a book. From time to time, he would lend me English novels to read.

That day his wife brought us a cup of tea. I enjoyed that very much and told her so. She said, 'I make tea with milk.'

That night I made tea, boiling the tea leaves in the milk. It was very satisfying.

*

When I brought home the book Martin Sir lent me, I thought of the priest who had once given me a book to read. I had read those Bible stories and a question had risen in my mind: 'Jesus Christ had fought for the rights of the poor and the downtrodden. And yet he died on the cross. The perpetrators went scot-free. Still, you say that we should fight for the rights of the downtrodden?'

But I never did meet that curate again. Someone must have objected to his ways and he was transferred.

*

From outside, the cry of a vendor, a man trundling along with pots, saplings on a wheelbarrow and calling, 'Plants, cuttings...' When I had seen him some days ago, I had told him what I wanted. Now he was waiting by the gate for me.

'Ma, give me fifty rupees. He's brought the tulsi plants.'

Seeing Martin Sir's garden, the desire to have one around our house had been fired up in me. I had been working on this for the past two years. In the summer, people would prune their plants and I would take some cuttings home. I made a start with hibiscus, jasmine and periwinkle. A few days ago, when the vendor of plants were passing by, I asked him the price of a rose. He told me that an ordinary local rose cutting would cost fifty rupees. I went in and asked Ma and she snapped, 'Flowers! What do you want with flowers? I have no love of flowers. Ask him if he has tulsi.'

When I asked, he laughed and said, 'Babu, you can get tulsi anywhere. If you want, I'll get you some next time. Only ten rupees. But buy these rose cuttings. They're local so they're cheap. Hybrids cost two hundred.'

I agreed and asked him for two rose cuttings for fifty.

Which was why he was here.

'Fifty rupees for tulsi? Tell him we don't want.'

'But Ma he was asking for thirty rupees for one. I told him we will take two for twenty-five each.'

'What do we want with two? One will do.'

'What if one withers? So, I asked for two.'

And so I got a rose cutting, knowing that Ma would never come and check. The man said that it was a creeper. I would have to give it some support. I walked around looking for a suitable place.

We had about eight or ten square metres of land around the house. That was where I built my garden. I dug up the soil and planted the rose, firming its base up with soil that had been washed away by the last rains. I chose a good spot where the roses would get some sun. Then I looked around me for a while. The hibiscus Jose has given me last year had taken firm root. The bougainvillaea was growing wild. The white hibiscus had a fine showing of buds; there would be flowers in the next couple of days. The crotons were doing well. They were good healthy bushes. I planned to plant frangipani. As long as Daddy didn't notice, I was going to have a fine garden here. The thought made me happy and I went in to celebrate with a cup of tea.

*

The prelims were close.

Everyone was now studying hard in order to score high marks. I had finished my revision and whenever I seemed to have some free time, Daddy would try and quiz me. 'What's heavier: ten kilos of iron or ten kilos of cotton?'

I said, 'Both weigh ten kilos, right?'

That annoyed him. He said, 'I asked: which is heavier, cotton or iron?'

'Of course, iron is *denser*,' I said. He didn't like that either.

One day he asked how atom bombs were made. I said I didn't know. He got angry and said, 'You're going to sit for your Matric. What do they teach you?'

Then another question: 'What's more important for Goa: agriculture or mining?' I didn't remember if this question had ever been addressed in class. But I took a guess and said agriculture. Daddy was angry enough to raise his hand but not enough to hit me. 'What an idiot you are. I hope you'll pass the exams!'

When he saw me with a book in my hand, Daddy would say, 'Study, study. Is anything going into your head?'

If he knew that I was holding a novel, who knows what he would have said.

*

Martin Sir had sown the seed of a love of reading deep inside me. I had scarce finished a book when I wanted to start another. Sometimes he would give me two books at a time or suggest other titles I might like to read. He would refer me to books I could get from the library. I would consume the books, reading greedily, and return them only to get more.

I worked my way through the Hardy Boys all the way up to *Pride and Prejudice*.

After we had once visited my mother's birth home when my grandfather died, we never went anywhere again. Not even to the neighbour's house. I'd go to Martin Sir's house to get books. Now that the prelims were close, he handed over the books but he said, 'You will keep up with your studies, won't you? First make sure you have done what you need to and then sit down to read, okay?'

*

On the day before the prelims, Ma began to run a fever. Ma told Daddy, 'I can't do anything. You better take a holiday tomorrow.'

'I have taken a holiday already. The manager has a Satyanarayana Pooja at home. He's called me to help. I have to go; it will help my career. If I don't go, it will cause problems. And I have to keep on his good side, do you understand?'

'And how am I supposed to manage? Do you want to see me dead?' Ma moaned.

'Don't talk rot. No one dies of a little fever. Babu will stay at home. Show him how to cook. He'll make some rice and curry. And you, run off to Vasudev's and get some vegetables. You can put something together for the curry. I'll be home by three or four o'clock.'

'Daddy, I have prelims. If I don't pass, they won't let me sit for the finals.'

'So? Will the world come to an end? You can always sit next year.'

Daddy left in the morning. Ma's fever began to come down. But never once did she say, 'Go to school.' I picked up *To Kill a Mockingbird* and jumped right in.

At around 4 p.m. the doorbell rang. It was Uncle Senior.

Had he come because Ma had told him she was not feeling well?

I brought him to Ma's room.

'Arre, Babu, go to Vasudev's and get four or five batata vadas. You can't have had a very good lunch.'

I was hungry. We hadn't had much. I ran off to get the vadas. When I got back, Daddy had returned. He looked at Uncle Senior and said, 'What are you doing here?' I knew that Daddy did not like my uncle. Still, it didn't seem right for him to say this right at the door. Daddy turned to me: 'You must have called and whined that your mother was ill.'

'Nothing of the kind,' said Ma, 'Anyway, when has he ever come running when I called?'

'Whatever. Have you asked him if he'll have a cup of tea?' Daddy asked. Ma understood what he actually meant. Daddy wanted a cup of tea.

'How could I? I can hardly get up. Has that boy brought the batata vadas?'

'Babu, take the thermos and run over to Vasudev's and get a couple of teas.'

'Never mind, never mind. Water will do for me,' Uncle Senior said.

'Daddy, should I make tea?'

Daddy frowned at me: 'You know how?'

'I taught him,' Ma piped up.

'Okay then. Let's try you out.'

I made the tea. I poured three cups for them and set some aside for me. By that time, they had made quick work of the batata vadas. I barely managed to save one for myself. They slurped the tea but no one said whether it was good or bad. I cleared away their empty cups.

'Put them to soak,' Ma said, 'And if there's a vada left, keep it for me. I'll eat it later when I feel better.'

Meanwhile Daddy was asking our guest: 'So what brings you here? We never see you unless you have some work.'

'I did indeed have something to ask. You know, Kalpesh is quite grown up now.'

'Are you thinking of getting him married?

'No, no, not so soon. He's hardly twenty. I'm talking about a job for him.'

'How far has he studied?'

'You know his situation. He failed the SSC twice.'

'He won't even get a peon's job then.'

'That's as may be. But he doesn't want a job. He wants to be an independent businessman.'

'So my nephew is going to be an entrepreneur?'

'He wants to have his own tourist taxi,' Uncle did his best to ignore my father's sarcasm.

'Oh, he'll be a driver then?'

'He says in one year he'll be able to pay off the loan on a car. Then he'll get another car and have a driver for this one. And then a third car of his own. He says he'll have a travel company at the end of it.'

'A fine plan! He will soon be the owner of a company. And you will be an industrialist's father!'

'But only if we have your support,' my uncle kept his voice even.

'What support can I give you? I won't even be able to push the car if it stalls.'

'We need a loan to buy the car. If you could stand guarantor…'

'Ah so! If tomorrow your son crashes the car, I will be responsible. What a great idea! Push my brother-in-law into a mess,' Daddy's voice began to rise.

Ma was worried that he would lose his temper and insult her brother. She intervened. 'Will you listen to me?'

And just then she farted. I don't remember when I started laughing. My uncle coughed a bit but Daddy was vastly amused. In between chuckles he said, 'Now everyone has heard what you wanted to say. Anything left? If so, we all will step out.'

My mother's face fell and I felt sorry for her.

'I have to leave soon but now that I'm here I might as well talk about another matter I have in mind,' said Uncle Senior, clearing his throat.

'I knew there was going to be something else. You're not the kind to turn up without an agenda.'

'Now look here, what I'm going to say will benefit everyone.'

'By everyone, you mean you and your brother will benefit, right?'

'Please first listen to me. I'm under a lot of stress right now. We are dividing the property.'

'Amongst whom?'

'Us brothers. You know my younger brother, he's a lawyer, right? He is out to cheat me. And so…'

'And she's to be cut out?' Daddy pointed at Ma.

'We did well by her at the time of her wedding, right? Didn't we?'

'You did?'

'Means our father did.'

'I remember some baubles. Nothing much there.'

The edge in Daddy's voice began to worry me.

'My father said we gave everything: necklace, earrings, bangles, armbands, pendants, anklets, everything. And so Baba said…' Uncle Senior's voice trailed off.

'So, you have it all worked out. You'll do as you please. So why have you come?' Daddy said and got to his feet.

'Please sit down and listen to me. Let me explain. We want this division of property to be painless. For that we need her power of attorney. It's just one signature. I'll see to the rest.'

'No such luck. She won't sign anything. And now you can get up and get out of here. I'll see how you divide the property and keep your sister out of it.'

And Daddy grabbed my uncle by the arm and almost shoved him out of the house.

*

Greatly disturbed, I went into my room and began to read *To Kill a Mockingbird* again. The character of Scout seemed deeply familiar. Even though she was a girl she seemed to be telling my story. But now I began to envy her.

There were many people around her who kept trying to tell her what she should and should not do. She had a companion in Finch, her tomboy friend. She had someone to understand her. And this made it clear that I was no Scout.

In the bright light of day, I felt blinded.

When I heard someone outside, I felt no interest in finding out who it was. Then I recognized the voice and I was frozen in position.

'Who are you?' Daddy was asking.

'My name is Martin TK. I teach in Vipin's school.'

'So what brings you to my house?'

'How is Vipin?'

'What's wrong with him?'

'Today, the prelims started.'

'I know.'

'He didn't appear for today's paper.'

'He'll be there tomorrow.'

'Don't take this lightly. These irregularities could cost him dearly.'

'So they're not the finals, no? And if he fails this time, he can sit next year.'

'Please don't take it casually, Mr Parob. You know he's the brightest student in our school. He might even feature in the merit list...'

But Daddy was in no mood to hear anymore.

'Right, right. I said I'll send him tomorrow.'

And I heard the door banging.

For a moment I thought of Martin Sir as Finch and Daddy as Radley Boo. There was a lump in my throat, as if I were suffocating.

While I had served my uncle tea, Daddy had kept poor Martin Sir on the threshold, not even inviting him in. I would have made him tea. He could have had that last vada. I felt like having a cup of tea but when I went into the kitchen Ma was eating the last batata vada. I just drank some water and came out again. Ma had the TV on and a song was playing, '*Tvameva maata cha pita tvameva*'. This was a familiar prayer; I had never paid much attention to it. But this time I stopped and really listened to the words. What I understood was: 'You are my mother and you are my father'. And this was addressed to God. My hair stood on end. So, were parents supposed to be my God or was God supposed to be my parents? Was my father supposed to be like God? Or was God supposed to be like my father? I switched off the television.

*

The next day I sat for the second paper. Martin Sir was invigilating but I did not meet his eyes. He came up to me and as if nothing had happened the day before, said, 'Now do your best with the rest of your papers. No one will hold you back for missing just one paper at the prelims.'

I felt I could breathe again.

*

The final exams ended. Under Martin Sir's instructions I read at least ten or twelve novels in Marathi and Konkani through those vacations. None of them seemed to have much to say. I read Saratchandra in translation. There was something there. But the *Tale of Genji* swallowed me whole. I had read nothing like it. I had no idea what Japan was like in the thirteenth century but I got lost in those thousand plus pages. And then I bumped into Kafka's *Metamorphosis*. That was life changing. I thought one day I too might become an insect and encounter a variety of reactions from all the people I met. In those two months I wandered through different worlds. Such experiences! I found out more about Goa. *The Discovery of India* introduced me to my own country. The Partition of India, the American Civil War, apartheid in South Africa, the lives of Dalits, the attacks on M.F. Husain...There was so much to discover and so much to read. As I read about all this, I felt I were lost to myself. *War and Peace* with its extraordinary combination of celebration and violence, of reality and imagination seemed like an entire alternative universe into which I could step at will.

8

My Future Decided

I passed the SSC with good marks. All my classmates congratulated me. I didn't see what the big deal was. I had studied and I wrote what I had learnt. Someone said, 'Martin Sir's waiting for you.'

When I went to his house he said, 'I thought you'd make it to the merit list.'

But he didn't seem very disappointed that I had not scored as high as he had expected.

'You must keep your quest alive. You should try to understand other people. They're human like you. What seems different may simply be a product of a different reality and you must find out what that reality is. But before that, you must know yourself. I don't think you're the kind to be interested in the pleasures of the world. They say the way to a person's heart is through the stomach. I don't think you're built like that either. If anything, the books you read will show you the way. Keep company with books; they never let you down.'

He might have said more but then Maggie from my class turned up. 'Sir, these pedas are for you.'

And Martin Sir's wife also came out.

'Congratulations Maggie. I heard you did well.'

'Yes, Ma'am. I got a distinction.' Then looking at me she said, 'But not as well as he did.'

'Don't talk like that, Maggie. Comparisons are odious. You worked hard and got the marks you deserved. Congratulations again,' said Martin Sir. Maggie gave me a peda too.

And I had gone there empty handed.

*

I don't think anyone expected me to do well. My mother had signed my report cards blindly, simply making sure that there were no red lines to indicate failing marks. That I had stood first consistently seemed to be of no interest to her. When I told my father I passed he said, 'Good. At least you didn't waste a year. How much did you get?'

When I told him I scored ninety-one per cent he looked suspicious. 'You're not joking? Well then, not bad but nine less than a hundred!'

This was a line he had used a day before to describe Ma's increasing weight.

The headmaster wrote to Daddy saying that the school would like to felicitate him and Ma because I had stood first in the school and the village. The next day Daddy took the letter and showed it to everyone in his office. The manager could not believe it. When he praised Daddy in front of everyone, Daddy was delighted. The manager told Daddy that he should educate me well. He told him that I had the potential to be a doctor or an engineer. Daddy took that to heart. The office demanded a celebration. He bought a cake for three hundred rupees and distributed it among his colleagues. He brought four slices home: one for me, one for Ma and two for him.

*

Ma was happy because Daddy was happy. The reason why I got to study further was the manager's response. Since he was a disciplinarian, Daddy didn't like him much.

'He won't eat and he won't let others eat either. The idiot!'

But the manager had been very impressed by my results. 'Where did he go for his tuitions?' he had asked. When he was told that I had taken no tuitions at all, he was even more impressed. He made some back-of-the-envelope calculations and told Daddy that I had saved him at least twenty-five thousand rupees. And so, he said Daddy owed me a nice gift. Perhaps a scooter, he suggested but then realized that I would not be able to get my license until I was eighteen. Get him a computer, he suggested. Daddy couldn't afford that either but one of the clerks said: 'When he goes to the eleventh standard, the Goa government will give him a laptop.' Finally, the manager settled on a smart phone and Daddy fell in line.

And so that day I got my first mobile, that too a smart phone.

My future was decided in that office. The consensus was that I was smart and so I should become an engineer. But Daddy wanted a doctor son. In either case, I would have to do science because they all agreed that this had 'scope'. Even where I was to study was decided there. I couldn't go to a higher secondary school because Daddy wanted me to go to a junior college. I found it odd: my father who had never wasted a word enquiring about my studies was now deeply involved in every decision.

'I'm going to make you a doctor. And then I shall strut about happily. What do I need that rubbish job for? And if that manager falls ill, let him just come and ask for free treatment and see!'

Ma had no interest in whether I was going to study science or join a technical course, the last resort of the not very bright students. It made no difference to her. No one asked my opinion but then I didn't feel I had the right to have one.

*

Dr Costabir's dispensary was right next to Vasudev's restaurant. The doctor was always busy. But that day I saw him outside his clinic. He must have heard about the results for he congratulated me. I thought he would be a good person to ask the question that had been bothering me. 'Doctor, what is the difference between arts and science?'

He put a hand on my shoulder and tried to make things simple. 'Science teaches you how you came to be born. Arts teaches you how to live after you've been born,' he said.

That made me think I should rather like to study arts. But since Daddy had put me down for science, so I simply went with the flow. Later when we were studying microscopic anatomy and procreation, Dr Costabir's words came back to me. Science teaches you how you came to be born.

In my mind's eye, I saw my father and mother coming together physically, making love. Their meeting, their mating, pregnancy, childbirth...and then there I was. From that day on, my way of looking at my parents changed.

*

On Sunday Daddy said, 'Today we must go and see God.'

'Which one?' I asked.

'All of them.' Daddy said, rather grandly. 'I've ordered a taxi. We leave at nine.'

I was rather surprised. I had not seen the temples of Goa but I knew there must be at least a hundred. 'How are we going to see all the temples on a single day?'

Daddy got angry. 'You think I'm a tour guide? We will go and see our family deity and your mother's. Then to Shanta Durga and the gramadeva of our region, Jambavlicha Damodar. Got it? Now stop asking stupid questions and get ready.'

Since my father's Godman had told him that the seven-and-a-half years of his trial were not over yet, my father had gone to an astrologer to figure out how this miracle of good marks could have happened. The astrologer said, 'This saade-saathi is not always a bad time. Good things can also happen. Since you have Saturn in a good aspect in your astrological charts, good things can also happen. In the next six months, this period will end. But Saturn will not be in opposition during that time...'

The same astrologer must have advised my father to go to the temple and pray for the intercession of the gods. When we made our offerings in the temple, I discovered why we were doing this. Daddy was praying that I should get good marks in the twelfth standard. I wanted to ask him whether God would increase my marks? But I thought it wise to shut my mouth rather than listen to another tirade.

'Since we have come to Marcel remind us. We'll swing by Old Goa and light a candle to Saint Francis Xavier,' he said. I rather suspected that this was advice from the manager. After we had visited the Bom Jesu Cathedral, my father made one-rupee offerings at every temple we passed. My mother uttered a small prayer each time we passed a shrine, a cross, or a village goddess smeared with vermillion. At Damodar's temple in Zambaulim my father sought a verdict from the petals with which the deity was propitiated. He wanted a word from the gods. But since we were getting late Daddy snapped at the officiating priest and told him to hurry up. The priest snapped at the God. And then he divined the God's answer for us: 'You will get your heart's desire if you pay careful attention to the child's education.'

All the way home, Daddy kept turning the oracle's pronouncement over for hidden meanings.

It was 8 p.m. by the time we got back from Cuncolim. Daddy dropped us home and said, 'How will you get any cooking done now? I'll go out and get us all something to eat.' He got onto his scooter and left. He returned only at nine with one packet of pulav. 'You two share it,' he said. 'I'm not hungry.'

*

One Sunday, after the eleventh standard academic year had begun, I went to meet Martin Sir. I told him that I had taken admission in science. I thought he would be happy to hear that, but he seemed disappointed.

'Science! Why?' he asked. 'What do you know about science?'

I thought about what Dr Costabir had told me about the difference between science and the arts but I didn't have the courage to say it in front of Martin Sir.

'Daddy said I got good marks and there was a good future in science,' I mumbled.

'So, you did this because Daddy…' he seemed to want to say more but stopped. I was silent too.

'What did he say about science?' Sir asked.

'A bright future.'

'Whose?'

That surprised me.

'So what will you do afterwards?'

'Daddy said I should study medicine.'

'So you will become a doctor.'

'Daddy says...'

But I didn't know what I wanted to say.

'Got it. Your father is keen that you should be a doctor, right?'

I nodded.

'Have you ever thought what you want to do?'

Martin Sir seemed a little sad. I wanted to answer him but I had to think. I realized that I have never asked myself what I wanted to do.

'I thought you were different from the others. You've read so many books. You write such good essays. I thought you were capable of independent thought...but never mind. Study hard, study well. But also try to learn to think for yourself.'

That day Martin Sir didn't ask me what I was reading. He didn't suggest a book that I should read. But when I was leaving, he said simply, 'There's no freedom like the freedom of the mind.' All the way home I pondered the meaning of that sentence.

*

To think independently, I would have to step out of the daily round of habit. I found I could not.

I went as usual to class.

I made tea as usual for Ma.

I bought what Daddy wanted me to buy from the market.

I did my homework.

I made no attempt to open the door to independent thought. Part of the reason was my personality: I was bound by routine. I held aloof from other people. This meant that both the students and the teachers behaved well with me. Except for the biology teacher, Namshikar Sir. There were two reasons for this. The first was that I had not joined his tuition classes. The second was that his son who studied in the same class as me, scored less than I did in every subject, except biology.

After the Diwali vacation that year the government gave every student a laptop. Some of the students already had laptops at home but since they were being handed out free, they took them as well.

For me it was a complete revolution, something that erupted into my everyday world. It was a whole new landscape that unfolded in front of me, as the internet flung the doors of my world wide open.

I had no idea about how I should navigate this world but a student called Amrut Patel came to my rescue. He helped me get an internet connection and taught me everything I needed to know about surfing, chatrooms and downloading. In return I helped him with Konkani and English, subjects in which he was weak. When I finally set my own password for the first time, I realized what joy Ali Baba must have felt when he uttered, 'Open sesame' and the stone rolled way from the cave of treasures. It was as if the treasures of knowledge, of information, were suddenly laid out in front of me. I took to this new world with delight.

*

Around this time, I began to sprout hair above my lips and in my armpits. But it didn't occur me to shave. One day a boy called Ninad appeared in class with freshly shaved cheeks which caused a storm of teasing comment.

'Did you go to the barber or the laundry?'

'Tell us the name of your saloon.'

Then they began to ask for a 'first time' party. Ninad said proudly, 'I shaved myself with a foreign razor.' And then he added, 'Daddy taught me how to shave.'

When I got home, I told Daddy and he said, 'Why do you need teaching? As your beard grows your brain grows and you will learn how to do these things yourself.'

'May I use your razor?'

'Certainly not. What do I give you pocket money for? Get your own.'

The next day I bought one and the day after I shaved.

No one in class so much as noticed.

*

One Sunday during the holidays, our neighbour Pascoal's daughter Flavia, was getting married. Pascoal himself came over with the invitation. Daddy did not care much for Pascoal. He told me to go. I was not very keen. I thought I would go to the library and read the whole day and come back and say I had gone.

But then that was to risk Pascoal coming the next day to ask why none of us had come. And that would cause an explosion. The only saving grace was that one of my classmates, Ignatius, was also going. At least I would have company. The wedding was in Mapusa. Pascoal had organized a bus to take his guests there and back. I got dressed in freshly ironed clothes and found that the bus was full but everyone urged me to get in. I saw Ignatius sitting on the front seat and he called me over, shifting up to let me sit down. I squeezed in somehow.

First there were the nuptials at the church and then the reception. They said it would start at eight but it didn't begin till nine. I hung around with Ignatius. We annexed a table at which there were three girls, Ignatius, another friend and me. They kept the conversation going with a stream of jokes and laughter. Ignatius tried to include me in the conversation from time to time. Beer and snacks were served. I didn't want to drink but Ignatius said that his friends would think it odd if I refused and so I accepted a glass. I raised it in a toast and touched it to my lips. Yuck. Yuck. How do people drink this stuff and enjoy it? It was really bitter. I set my glass down and ignored it for the rest of the evening. When the music started to play, Ignatius and his friend got up to dance. I remained seated. The third girl at our table also remained seated. And then suddenly Martin Sir came up to me. I didn't see him until he was right up close. What must he have thought seeing a glass of beer in my hand? He asked a little about my studies. Then, 'Have you kept up with your reading? Or don't you get time?'

I told him that I was reading P. Sainath's *Everybody Loves a Good Drought*. He was happy to hear that. I got up only when the line for the buffet began. By the time we had eaten, it was eleven p.m. I got into the bus quickly and sat down on the front seat. The bus began to fill up. At the end two ladies hoisted themselves in and I had to give up my seat and stand. If it had been full when we came, it was now packed to bursting. I found myself standing in the middle of a bunch of girls. They were all around me, chattering to each other in a carefree manner and ignoring me completely. I tried to take up as little space as possible so as not to touch any of them by mistake. But each time the bus took a turn or the driver hit the brakes, we bumped into each other. Someone's buttocks made contact with my genitals. Someone's breasts were rubbing against my arm. I began to wonder if this was deliberate. By the time we crossed the Mandovi Bridge my breath was keeping pace with the bus. I was awash with all kinds of emotions.

At home, I threw myself onto the bed in my clothes. I fell asleep and was troubled by a series of dreams. These did not feature Martin Sir. Nor Ignatius. Instead those girls in the bus showed up. I woke up abruptly in the middle of the night.

My first wet dream.

I went to the bathroom and cleaned up.

9

Stay-at-home Dad

When Daddy had gone to make an offering to our village god, he had asked as a special favour that the God should personally pay attention and get me good marks in my examinations. And then whether it was something to do with the pact he made with the deity or whether he wanted to get the money together for medical college, Daddy took voluntary retirement.

'Now, Babu, there are going to be no more monthly salaries. But I will pay for your education. All you have to do is become a doctor.' That was a lot of pressure for someone my age to deal with. But I did as I normally did. I decided that I would become a doctor as my father wanted me to.

*

On the day Daddy took voluntary retirement, my mother's elder brother turned up, bearing jackfruit which he knew his sister liked. He asked Daddy, 'Why take retirement so young?'

'Young? How old do you think I am?'

'I have a vague notion. Couple of years older than me.'

'Must be. But I want to take it easy for the rest of my life.'

'And you think VRS is a way to do that?'

'Simple maths. In the next few years Babu becomes a doctor. Then we'll have a doctor at home to look after both of us. And we can live long, happy lives.'

'From your lips to God's ears. But who can say that you won't die tomorrow? You should give some thought to that too.'

I don't know whether these words had any effect on Daddy but they left me thinking. If one were to die tomorrow, what would be the point of living today? That night I suddenly wanted a cup of tea. Now I had begun to need tea whether I was studying or not. And I decided that from then on, I would drink tea as if there were no tomorrow.

Daddy had taken VRS to make sure I studied for my twelfth standard. This was an easy calculation for him: if Babu had managed good marks in the tenth standard without much effort then with effort he would score even better.

He would remind me every day. 'Bear this in mind. I've put you in a good college. I expect good marks.' He didn't care to call it the higher secondary.

I would get home around five o'clock. As soon as I arrived, he would ask: 'So what did you study today? You made notes, no? You must study hard. If you want guides or anything, just let me know.'

One day he met Professor Namshikar. He said, 'The boy is doing well. But if he has to get into a medical college, I would advise you to put him into twelfth standard biology tuition now itself and see if he doesn't get a full hundred out of hundred with my help.'

This persuaded Daddy. I kept telling him that there was no need. This went on until he met another of my professors who said that if I were studying hard there was no need for tuition. And that was the end of that. That helped me get out of that.

And then a tragedy occurred. Madan, a boy one year my senior at school, killed himself. The news appeared in the papers. The whole state was talking about it. I knew Madan from school. He was a fine sportsman who gave his all to every game he played. At school, he played cricket; outside with the kids, football. He was actually crazy about football. Since he was so good at it, everyone wanted him on their team. But his family made it clear: if he wanted to take part in sports, it would have to be cricket. There were prospects in cricket. Football was a poor second. And so Madan played for two years in the school cricket team. He was an excellent batsman and a good fielder. He did well at the SSC. Since he got ninety-six per cent in mathematics, he was packed off to engineering. Despite all their efforts, Madan signed up for the football team in junior college. He was managing his studies quite well but quite well was not enough to get him into engineering. His parents forced him to quit the football team. Then began the grind of tuitions, college, practicals, classes, homework…eventually he could take it no longer and killed himself. This terrified Daddy. He did not want his careful calculations upset by something like this and so he laid off me.

The news of Madan's death depressed me deeply. It was only after I had a cup of tea that I felt a little better.

*

I had always felt that the people I read about in stories and novels bore very little resemblance to the people I encountered in real life. In the books I read about love and lust, struggles and sentiments, but it all remained literary. I didn't believe that these things happened in real life but when I got my laptop, I discovered that there were many people who lived their lives according to their own beliefs. Not unlike the literary characters I read about.

After the eleventh standard, I had a long break and much free time. But Ma took advantage of this. She began to assign all kinds of little tasks to me. When she felt too lazy to get up, she would say, 'Babu, get me a glass of water.' If she felt peckish it would be, 'Get us a couple of batata vadas from Vasudev's.'

She hated cleaning fish so she stopped the fish seller coming to the house and sent me to the market with orders to get a couple of slices of kingfish. Daddy was not at home most of the time. When he was, he would suddenly say, 'I feel like a good xacuti today,' or 'I'd like a nice mackerel kismur'. Sundays were particularly bad for Ma. There was always something amiss: one or more of her various aches and pains would surface. Then Daddy would say, 'Babu, go get some mutton from Ankush's. Tell him we want lots of gravy and get some sliced bread from Rocky's.'

Perhaps it was all the reading but my sensitivity was getting sharper. I began to realize that my retiring personality was getting in the way of Martin Sir's attempts to liberate me from myself. I wanted now to break these invisible fetters. I was under no illusion: they were of my own making. I did not think that I would be praised for being an obedient child who never opposed his parent's wishes. Would such praise have mattered? Absolutely not and yet everything went on the way it had always gone on—the way they wanted it. I had developed some pursuits of my own which I enjoyed during the vacation: going to the library to change my books, reading about technology on my laptop, the usual round of exercises, a little gardening in and around the house and punctuating all of this with cups of tea.

*

One day I met my classmate Ignatius on the road. He said, 'There is a mango sapling coming up right next to the wall of our house. If we let it grow, it will break the wall. Papa says we should uproot it and throw it away. Would you like to take it?'

This brought back memories of the mango tree near the house that Daddy had cut down. Maybe he would...but that was so long ago.

There was such a lot of space, I told myself, and went to fetch the sapling. It was almost as tall as I was. I thought Daddy would say something slighting about me being in the twelfth standard and should I be mucking around in the garden. So, I chose a corner he was unlikely to notice. I dug a pit nearly two feet deep and filled it with cowdung, ash and coir. Then Ignatius brought me some alluvial soil and I planted the sapling. When I was done, I poured a mug of water over its roots.

But the very next day Pascoal came with a complaint. 'What were you thinking planting that mango tree so close to the border? Didn't you see the boundary stone right there?'

I had never had any reason to exchange words with a neighbour so I immediately apologised, 'Sorry Uncle. I'll replant it somewhere else right away.'

'You will do nothing of the sort,' Daddy snapped, giving me a start. I had not seen him arrive.

'It is within our plot. And how did that boundary stone get so close. I know you shifted it. Let's get the survey people to come and check.'

'Bring all the survey people you want. As if I care,' Pascoal said and marched off.

The next day the mango sapling went missing.

I was angry with Daddy. I would have replanted it somewhere else. Now it was completely gone. And we had a fight with the neighbour for no real reason.

10

Vipin Parob, Hero?

I was working at my laptop when Ma said that she wanted tea right now. I told her to wait a little. She began to mutter angrily under her breath. I got up annoyed. I made the tea and gave it to her.

'*You* drink this. And give me what you have kept for yourself,' she said.

'I haven't made myself any,' I said peaceably.

'Why not?'

'I don't want tea now. I'll have some later.'

'Then give me some when you're making it for yourself.'

'So, you don't want this tea?' I asked even as she raised the cup to her mouth. I turned to go to my room when she said in a voice designed to reach my ears: 'I never get tea the way I want.' I thought of something Oscar Wilde had said, 'There are only two tragedies in life—one is not getting what one wants; the other is getting everything one wants.' If Ma had not got anything she wanted, how did she live? What kept her going? I could not remember seeing her happy ever. Had she been happy at least when I was born? Or had she wanted a girl, someone to make tea for her, to look after her?

Perhaps even as a child she had not been given what she wanted. Had her parents not tried to make her happy? Her elder brother would come over occasionally to meet her, pretending it was to find out how she was doing but he only came if he had an agenda. Their family did not keep up with traditions like Bhau Beej and Raksha Bandhan. She said they never had. It must have been twenty-five years since she had married and come into this house. What hopes and dreams had she brought with her? Daddy was the earning member, the master of this house. Had she missed out on the love of a father-in-law and a mother-in-law? What did it mean when she said that she had never got what she wanted when she wanted it? What had she wanted? Marital bliss, jewellery, sex? She was not very old yet. Forty-seven meant old age was a way off. Madhuri Dixit had turned fifty and looked like she was in her thirties. But if you told someone Ma was sixty, they might believe it. When had Daddy last hugged her or kissed her?

A memory from childhood: Uncle Senior had come to ask after his sister and Daddy had said to him in my hearing: 'From the time we got married she's never given me a moment's happiness. Just this gibble-gabble, gibble-gabble...' It was true that Ma liked talking. Daddy could not stand that. And so, when he was at home, she put on the TV and sat down in front of it. Of late, she had developed the habit of mumbling to herself even as she watched.

Daddy was the earning member. Had he got everything he wanted? Probably. For instance, he would eat out and come home. Did he eat out because Ma didn't cook anything at home or was it because he ate out that Ma never cooked anything at home? I had no idea. But it was true for a long time she had cooked only the bare necessities. Daddy had complained to my uncle that Ma had never given him any happiness in life. Today I understood what he meant. So, was it true that Daddy satisfied all his needs outside?

Perhaps Oscar Wilde was right. Getting everything you wanted could be a tragedy. But surely one might be entitled to some amount of what one desired?

And me? I had never even given thought to what I wanted. Was it because I got everything I needed and so had no cause for complaint? I was given a laptop. I was given a mobile. Was there something that I didn't get? I thought I should read *The Picture of Dorian Grey* again. Yes. They say Oscar Wilde's life ended in tragedy. What happened to him? Did he get all that he wanted? Did he get nothing? He had married, had two children but he was gay. He was thrown into jail for his homosexual encounters and there too he wrote poetry. My head began to spin with my thoughts. Inside, Ma was still muttering to herself, probably cursing her fate. I felt sorry for her. I got up and went into the kitchen and made two identical cups of tea. And I took them both in to her and said, 'Choose the one you want.'

At least, in this, she could have her way.

*

On the day of the college election, most of the students spent the day outside the classroom. Although junior college did not have much to do with these elections, they hung around the corridors in solidarity. The keen competition among the candidates produced a wave of excitement. Everyone wanted their candidate to win. Last year, I had kept studiously away from all this. This time too I kept my distance.

It was now Monday. I was not sure whether I should go to class or not. But after two days of relentless rain, the skies had cleared and my mood improved. When I entered the gate, I felt a different atmosphere lap around me. Students, who had hitherto ignored me, stopped to say hi. It seemed as if others were smiling at me. Some girls seemed to be pointing at me and whispering to each other. I slipped into the washroom to check my clothes: no stains, no marks, no blessings from a crow. Reassured, I was making my way to class when a peon stopped me and asked, 'Vipin Parob?'

'Yes? What is it?'

'The principal has asked to see you.'

'Why?' I asked even as I started walking towards his office. I had not set foot inside the principal's cabin since the time I had taken admission.

The principal was very welcoming. 'Come, come, sit down.'

I had never heard of a student being welcomed in this way.

'You're a brave boy.'

That surprised me. I looked around to see if there were someone else in the room. Was this sarcasm? It didn't seem like it.

'Sir, what have I done?'

'What have you done? You have made us proud, my boy!' And so saying he pressed the bell on his table. A peon came in. 'Call Fatima here. And bring three teas.'

I had no idea what was going on. Who was Fatima? And why three teas?

'Sir, may I come in?'

'Please come in. Let's hear what happened from Fatima.'

The girl came in.

The principal pointed at me and said, 'This is the one, right? Your saviour?'

'Yes, sir.'

Oh gosh! It was the girl from Saturday.

*

On Saturday I had left the library around five thirty. The rain was pelting down. Since I hadn't brought an umbrella, I thought I might wait it out. When it seemed to be easing, I made a run for the bus stop. Of course, it started coming down again. I stopped under a tree on the way. There I had to decide whether the drops falling from the leaves were more or less of a threat than the rain. As I was debating this, I saw a girl in a chudidar and salwar with her odhni over her head, hurrying towards the bus stop. I decided to make a run for the bus stop which would afford better shelter. I had started off when a Maruti van came down the road and stopped near the girl. As I neared the van, I realized that something sinister was afoot. Two men jumped out of the van. They ran up to the girl, grabbed her arms and began to drag her to the van. And then without knowing it, I had moved and blocked the door to the van.

'Get lost!' one of them said to me. But my feet would not move.

'Get out of the way or else...' said the other and flashed the knife.

A line I had read somewhere surfaced: 'He who conquers fear, wins over death'. I had no idea what death would be like and nothing had happened thus far to frighten me. Even at that point, I felt no urge to run. I pulled my bag off my shoulder and threw it on the ground. Involuntarily, I found I had raised my fists to fight.

But the knife-waving had only been a hollow threat. The driver of the van started the engine and the van began to move away. It hadn't gone more than a metre when the two would-be abductors lost heart. They turned to look at the departing van and taking advantage of their distraction, the young woman broke free of them and began to run. In turn, the two failed kidnappers ran to the Maruti van, jumped in and it drove off.

At which point, my bus arrived. Drenched, I picked up my bag and went home.

*

I had not even seen the girl's face that day. All things considered, I had not done really much. I just happened to be there. All I did was to stand in the way and face them down when they had waved a knife at me.

'Well done, Vipin. Fatima wants to thank you.'

Fatima's eyes were full of tears.

'Thank you,' she managed to get the words out somehow. And then a sob broke from her. Before the principal told her to sit down, she collapsed into a chair. The principal got up and poured her a glass of water and pushed it into her hand. He asked, 'Are you okay?'

Fatima nodded. The peon returned with three cups of teas. The principal took a cup from him and gave it to me. Fatima waved it away. The principal said, 'Don't say no. Because of Vipin, you got out of an unpleasant situation. In honour of that, have a cup of tea.'

He sat down again. 'Tell me, Vipin, who were those hooligans? Do you know them? Would you be able to recognize them again?'

I thought for a moment and said, 'I don't know who they were. But I think I'll be able to recognize them if I see them again.' And then I added, 'Or maybe I won't.'

'We will take care of this. We will not allow anything like this to happen again. But Fatima, I am asking you now. Do you or your family members think we should make a police complaint?'

'No, sir,' Fatima said.

'Are you sure?'

'Yes, sir.'

Then the principal asked me, 'You were the one threatened. Do you want to make a complaint?'

I said no.

Fatima took a sip of tea and that seemed to calm her down enough to allow her to speak again. She turned to look at me with gratitude and said, 'Thank you! If you had not been there that day...' her voice began to tremble again. 'Anyone else would have just run away but you frightened them off and they ran. Thank you.'

I found the tea was way better than what was served in the canteen.

*

When we came out, Fatima said, 'My brother, Aslambhai, would like to meet you. He's coming here tomorrow.'

'Why?'

'To thank you.'

'Look, Fatima, I really did nothing. They turned and ran. That's all. No one needs to thank me.'

'Please, Vipin, tomorrow at nine o'clock...At the gate.'

I really wanted to refuse again. She turned to go and then the question that had been bothering me came to mind. 'Wait, Fatima. I want to ask you something. I don't know you. And I don't think anyone knows me. So who told you my name?'

'Chitra told me. She saw you.'

I didn't know who this Chitra was but didn't think it necessary to ask. When I got to class, students who had ignored me came up to shake my hand. I didn't want to sit in the class any longer and went outside. But many of the students were hanging around the canteen because of the election. There seemed no escape so I decided to go home. Amrut Patel was at the door handing out leaflets. He said, 'Hi buddy, you're the hero of the day.'

The students began to gather. I got Amrut by the hand and pulled him aside: 'I'm going home. I can't stand this.'

'What? Look, Parob, tomorrow there's going to be a rally to felicitate you for your daring.'

'Really, I'm telling you, Amrut. I did nothing. Please don't...

'Did you or didn't you fight off those goondas?'

'That's what I'm saying. I did nothing of the kind. I simply stood my ground and they ran away.'

'Were they or were they not threatening you with a knife?'

'Was I supposed to be scared because they were waving a knife around? They came at me and I prepared to defend myself. That's all.'

Amrut put both his hands on my shoulders and said, 'That's pretty awesome, buddy. So many people try to take credit for things they haven't done. And here you're downplaying what you really did. That's not on. We will have a felicitation tomorrow.'

*

I got onto the bus as usual. I got home as usual. But it seemed as if the atmosphere had changed somehow. It was raining when I got off the bus but I did not open my umbrella. I turned my face up to the blank grey sky and let the rain come down on me. Is this what happiness felt like? I could not tell but I did know that unintentionally I had done something special.

I began to feel some of the things that I had only read about in books and experienced vicariously. This was not my ordinary state. One part of my mind was saying to the other: This is your right, this belongs to you, it is yours. Where had this other part of my mind been hiding all this time? Is this real or imaginary?

But a new wind was blowing and that wind carried me home.

*

Noon. Daddy was snoring in an armchair in the living room. He spent most of his time at home now. But then where was he to go? He had never enjoyed reading. He didn't even read the newspapers. When I suggested it, he said, 'When I was working, I didn't read a paper. Now what am I going to do with the news?' Was it because Ma enjoyed television so much that he had taken a dislike to it? He was of the opinion that housework was a woman's responsibility and anything to do with the garden or surroundings was to be handled by hired labour. So, all he did was go to the market in the morning and in the evening. The rest of the time he would spend dozing. Or he would start a quarrel or an argument with Ma.

In the last two-and-a-half months, his weight had increased by two-and-a-half kilos. This was a matter of great satisfaction for him.

I dropped my bag and went into the kitchen, drawn by

the need for tea. I felt that the surge of excitement I had experienced earlier would be magnified in some way by the first sip. Then it occurred to me that preparations for lunch had not even begun.

'Are you making tea?' Ma asked from the kitchen door. 'I'd like a cup too.'

'Ma, nothing's on for lunch? What's going on?'

'I couldn't manage anything today, son...'

Ever since Daddy took VRS, she had become lazy about cooking.

'Isn't Daddy at home?'

'He makes my life hell, you know that. I told him to wash the rice and put it on the fire. Then I could have started grinding the masala for a curry in the mixer. But do you know what he said? "That's women's work and the woman of the house should do it." His usual.' Then she added, 'Good thing you're home. You can run over to Vasudev's restaurant and get two loaves and some batata vadas. The two of us can manage on that.'

'And Daddy?'

'I heard him ordering biryani for himself on the phone. When he wants something, he has money to spend. But ask him for something for us and he says he has no money,' she said and settled down, waiting for a cup of tea.

I made the tea and poured us both a cup. And at that moment, a huge thump like a chair falling over. I rushed out and saw that it was Daddy who had fallen over, taking the chair with him. I reached down to give him a hand and discovered that he was in the throes of a fit.

'Ma,' I shouted as I ran back to the kitchen. 'Has Daddy ever had fits?'

She said he hadn't and I called Dr Costabir. Luckily, he picked up immediately.

'Daddy is having a fit, Doctor. His whole body is stiff. What should I do?'

'It will pass. Don't do anything until he gets back to normal. Just stay by him and keep watch.'

Ma came in and said, 'Throw some water on his face.' I paid no heed. After a while, Daddy opened his eyes. I offered him a hand and said, 'Get up, Daddy. Get up and sit down.'

Daddy rested his entire weight on me. He tried several times to hoist himself up. Finally, I asked, 'Want to wait a little while?'

Daddy opened his mouth but it looked twisted and I could not understand anything he said. That was when I began to worry.

'Daddy, try and raise your hand?'

He didn't seem to be able to move it.

'What is happening to you, Daddy? Can you tell me?'

But looking at his face, I knew. I called Dr Costabir again. He said, 'Call 108 or an ambulance and take him to the hospital immediately. It's an emergency.'

As I phoned for the ambulance Ma came there, carrying the two cups of tea I had made. But I had no interest in tea at that moment.

Then the bell rang. I thought it was the ambulance and ran outside. But it was the biryani that Daddy had ordered. Before I could say anything, Ma came out and swooped down on the biryani.

*

I had heard many bad things about Goa Medical College. But my experience with them was very good. Daddy was quickly taken into the ICU. After a while, the doctor came out and said, 'TIA.'

In other words: a stroke. Daddy had had what was called a Transient Ischemic Attack. 'You got here in time so it won't be so bad. Now go get these medicines.'

'Right now?' I didn't have any money with me.

'Don't worry. We've started treatment already. But don't wait too long.'

I rushed home. There was Ma sitting in Daddy's easy chair and finishing up the biryani.

'How is he?'

'Do you really want to know?'

'Why would I ask otherwise? You think worry kills hunger or something?'

I rifled through Daddy's belongings. I found his passbook and his cheque book and ran to the bank. I had to give them a letter. The bank sent an employee with me to the hospital. At the hospital, we met the doctor and he signed behind the cheque.

Then we got it stamped by the hospital. We got Daddy's thumb impression attested by the bank official. After that I got hold of ten thousand rupees and could buy medicines.

Then the doctor arrived with another diagnosis. 'Hemiplegia. There's no hope of total recovery. But if you people take care, some improvement can be expected.'

Daddy's left side was completely paralysed. His left eye did not open. His left arm lolled lifelessly. His left leg had no sensation. His tongue was heavy. But because the doctors and nurses were always on hand, I didn't have to do much for him. On the third day, he was brought into the ward.

That evening Martin Sir came to the hospital to meet me. He said Dr Costabir had told him what happened. He brought a packet of cream crackers with him. I returned it to him saying, 'Sir, he can't eat anything yet.'

Pushing it back into my hands, he said, 'Then you eat it.'

He sat with me for a while. As he left, he asked, 'Do you have enough money? If you need anything just let me know.'

I would go home from time to time, carrying roti-bhaaji or rice and curry from the hospital canteen for Ma. On the third day she said she wanted pulao. Two days later, chicken.

Daddy remained in the hospital for ten days. During that time, I had to make two more trips to the bank. The medicines seemed to be doing him some good. Within eight days, he could sit up in bed. Only I could understand what he said but that was because I knew his habits of old and made educated guesses about what he wanted to say.

The day before he was discharged the senior doctor came to see him. Daddy tried to ask him something but he could not follow what Daddy wanted to ask. He was pointing at me and asking, 'When will he become a doctor?'

'What is he saying?' the doctor asked me.

I didn't want to tell him but finally I did. The doctor looked at me. 'Are you studying medicine?' he asked.

'I'm in the twelfth standard,' I said.

The doctor smiled. 'Let him study. He'll become a doctor.'

Daddy began to mumble again. 'He will heal me!' It was not clear whether he was asking this or saying it.

'I can't understand what he says, sometimes, Doctor,' I said to cover this up.

The doctor had moved on already to another topic. 'Just because we are discharging him doesn't mean he's made a complete recovery. You have to take good care of him. He will need rehabilitation therapy. But only after he's recovered some energy. Come back in a week and meet the physiotherapist. He will explain everything in detail.'

As long as Daddy was in the hospital, I had no idea what it meant to look after someone who had only control over half his body. When he came home, I soon found out. I had to make his food soft and feed him, spoon by spoon. I had to clean him up when he shat and pissed. And that succeeded in killing my hunger almost completely. The only thing I felt like drinking was tea.

11

Hand of Velvet

It took two days to settle Daddy at home. In all this I missed twelve days of class and two sets of practicals. During that time, I had not even thought about college; then suddenly it all came back. The whole thing seemed so long ago: the contretemps at the bus stop, the meeting with the Principal, Amrut threatening to have a rally. Had it happened? Fatima's brother had wanted to meet me. He had probably come, waited a while and then left. As for the wave of happiness that had broken over me, I could not tell when it receded.

I had been in the habit of coming home and making notes on every topic taught in class after doing some research on the Net. But between taking care of Daddy and looking after the house, I had precious little time. Then I thought of Swami Vivekananda's line, 'Never say, "I can't." I made up my mind that I was not going to miss a single class.

After I had cleaned up Daddy's shit and piss, soaked toast in tea and fed it to him, given him a bath, changed his clothes and his bed clothes, I ate some toast and got ready. When I told Ma to keep an eye on him, she began to mumble, 'Let me tell you right now. I can't manage anything. I have my own health issues. If I have to look after him you may have to take me to the hospital tomorrow.'

I refused to let her defeat my new determination. I simply walked out and went to college.

*

I reached college five minutes late. Professor Namshikar's biology class was going on.

'Sir, may I?'

Namshikar gave me a twisted smile. 'Oh, please do come in.' As soon as I sat down, he had a question for me: 'So are you preparing for the twelfth standard or the thirteenth day shraadha meal?' Some students laughed obligingly. Encouraged by this, he continued, 'So how many days have you missed? I have been counting. Have you?'

'Twelve. Today is the thirteenth.'

The same students laughed again. They were regulars at his tuition class.

'So where were you all these days? We finished genetically engineered insulin. It's a guaranteed question this year. How do you plan to catch up? Tuitions?'

He looked at me measuringly and I realized what the problem was: he was afraid I had joined John Sir's tuition class.

I said nothing.

'Your father had told me to teach you well so that you could become a doctor. He said that he wanted you to become a doctor. And here you are running about protecting people's daughters.'

I took a long breath and remained silent.

'Tell your father to come and meet me. Will you do that or do I have to?'

'I will tell him nothing of the kind nor will you. And he's not coming here anyway.'

I picked up my bag and walked out of the class, not sparing a glance at Namshikar. I went to the canteen instead. I hadn't had canteen tea for a very long time and suddenly I wanted some. I got myself a cup of tea and sat down at an empty table. The first gulp brought me to my senses. What was I doing? Had I come to attend class or to drink tea? I could have drunk tea at home. But on balance, I was not sorry. I was filled with a new energy. Was it because I was in college again? Or was it because I had just escaped a home filled with the stink of sickness?

My meditations were interrupted by a new voice.

'Mind if I sit here?' a girl asked even as she set her coffee cup down on the table.

'Feel free. It's not my table. You don't need my permission.' My voice sounded cold even to my own ears.

She pulled the chair closer and said, 'Quite right. Anyone can sit at this table. What I meant was, may I sit with you?'

'I have no problem. But I'm not a chatty person. I'm not given to small talk.'

'That's fine. I am a chatty soul. So, I'll fill up the gaps,' she said and laughed heartily. She looked pretty when she laughed. I felt a little confused. I felt as if her laughter had invaded me, getting into a place I had reserved for myself.

'Hi Vipin. I'm Chitra,' she said and put out her hand. This disconcerted me further. I wanted to run away but my feet seemed stuck.

'C'mon, aren't you happy I introduced myself?' She was obviously a straight talker. Was there a hint of hurt in her voice? If I stayed silent for a little while longer it seemed likely that she might get up and leave.

I didn't want that to happen. So, I took the hand that she offered and was immediately reminded of the velvety texture of some of the flowers that I had planted.

'Hello,' she said, not completely appeased. 'I'm Chitra.'

'You said. Hello Chitra.'

'Thanks.' She shook my hand a little and let it go. 'Pleased to meet you, Vipin.'

'How do you know my name?'

'It's not rocket science. Your name is on the muster, right? Vipin Parob?'

After that she went on talking. She told me she was in the twelfth standard too but in the arts section. After the twelfth standard, she hoped to do Fine Arts at MS University, Baroda.

'What about you, Vipin?'

I had not thought of that and so I did not answer. I kept listening to her. 'You were on the SSC merit list, weren't you?'

'Nothing of the sort. I just topped the school and the village. That's all.'

'And here you topped the eleventh too, great. What do you want to do, medical or engineering?'

I shrugged. 'I thought about doing medicine but...'

'But what?'

'I just changed my mind.' I wondered if I had said too much. I took a sip of tea.

'You know I was so excited about studying arts but all the interest drained out of me in a year. There seemed to be no relationship between this course and the world of art. It's completely misnamed.'

'Well, you study literature, don't you? That's a form of art.'

'You're right but...'

'Don't you like reading?'

'Love it.'

'Then you're set. If you don't like what you're studying, just keep reading. You'll learn more.'

I was surprised at how much I was talking.

Chitra asked, 'I suspect you like literature, right?'

'How do you know?'

'Fiction, offbeat classics?'

She laughed at my expression. 'No, I'm not stalking you. I just happened to see you in the library issuing an Albert Camus novel. It was an odd choice for a science student, that's all.'

'I am a science student but I enjoy fiction. The surreal, the absurd. I suppose, anything that's different.'

'We have similar tastes then. I love Albert Camus. I remember when I read The *Myth of Sisyphus,* I was so inspired, I did two paintings. Should I bring them to show you?'

Before I could say yes or no, she went on, 'Tomorrow?'

The next day Dr Costabir was to come to monitor Daddy's blood pressure. I felt as if someone had clipped my wings. How was Daddy managing? Was Ma taking care of him? I had no idea what the next day would bring.

'I can't say. My father is ill.'

'No problem, Vipin. Give me your number. If I don't see you, I'll call.'

She was pinning me down and I wasn't sure whether I liked it or not. And this was our first meeting. Only it did seem as if we had known each other for a long time.

I looked at my watch. It had been an hour since I entered the canteen.

'Vipin, how about another round?'

She got up and I rose too and said, 'You sit down, I'll get it.'

'No, please. I suggested it so this round is on me. You get the next one.'

She started to walk away.

'Tea for me.'

'I know.'

When she returned, she set down my tea and said, 'You know, Vipin, I love coffee.'

I picked up my cup.

'Tea is my poison,' I said.

'You remember that famous line from Camus?'

'Which one?'

'That famous line: Should I kill myself or have a cup of coffee?'

I suppose my version would be: Kill myself or have tea.

I should read Camus again.

*

Meeting Chitra brought back the wave of elation that I had experienced the last time. It was not as if I had tried to drive her away. I had enjoyed our conversation. I had read about such feelings in books, but they had seemed unreal, hollow. I believed that these were literary inventions. But today I felt that same wave of pleasure lapping around my ankles.

I knew that once I got home, I would have to attend to Daddy. I had no hope that Ma would have cooked anything. In that moment, I realized that I had freed myself from Daddy's ambition for me, and I was not going to study medicine. Was this the freedom of the mind that Martin Sir had talked about? Riding this wave, I went to Vasudev's restaurant and ordered takeaway rice and curry. As I waited, I swigged a cup of tea.

'How's your father now?' Vasudev asked. He must have

heard the news from Costabir. I gave him the short version though he probably knew that already. He patted me on the shoulder and said, 'Look Babu, eating restaurant food every day is not a good idea. Why don't you get someone to work for you?'

Now why hadn't that occurred to me? Perhaps it was because these decisions had always been my father's province. I suddenly understood that they were now my responsibility. When I got home with food, I found my mother sitting in the armchair in front of my father, eating an apple. And Daddy, stuck in his bed, was looking on helplessly.

'Ma, where did you get those apples?'

'Your uncle, the lawyer. He came to enquire after your father's health. He brought some.'

I was glad. The doctor had suggested we give Daddy stewed apples once in a while.

'Where are they?'

I thought I could give him some before we ate.

'What?'

'The apples he brought...'

'They are over. I ate them,' Ma said coolly.

'You ate the lot?'

'He hadn't brought a basket full, you know. Just four or five. And it was lunch time. Am I not allowed to feel hungry now?'

'Here I brought food for all of us.'

'Oh good. You can't fill your stomach with apples, can you? One needs a bit of rice...'

And so saying Ma heaved herself out of her chair.

This was my reality, no wings, no waves. I thought I would go and see Martin Sir. But first, Daddy's medicines. So I arrived there late in the evening. It seemed that there was a celebration going on. When Martin Sir saw me, he said, 'It's our Stella's birthday.'

Stella came out to see who had come. She seemed a bit disappointed to see me. Perhaps she had been waiting for someone who had not turned up yet. I wished her happy birthday, from where I was. She came forward, offered me a hand to shake and said thank you. At which point her mother arrived. She said, 'Today we have a small party at our place for Stella and her friends, you must join us.'

I was empty handed but that wasn't the only reason I couldn't stay. 'Sir, you know what it's like. Daddy's been brought home. He can't even get up on his own and then he has to be given his medicines at the right time. I can't stay.'

Martin Sir took me by the arm and drew into an inner room, his library. There were three large glass-fronted cupboards, stuffed with books, many of which I had read. Most of the available surfaces were covered with books. Unconsciously I began to read the titles.

'Do you have anyone at home to look after him?' I thought of what Vasudev had said earlier: 'Why don't you keep someone?'

Martin Sir continued, 'If you keep on like this handling all the housework and looking after Daddy, when will you get the time to study?'

I wanted to tell him that I had given up the idea of medicine but for some reason I did not. He must have had some notion that Ma was not much help at home. He had also seen what Daddy's temperament was like when he came to enquire about my absence on the first day of the prelims. He was worried about how I would navigate through all this.

'And Babu, have you any idea what it will cost? His medicines, physiotherapy, all of it?'

I had no idea.

'When I went to the hospital I had made some enquiries,' Martin Sir said.

I did not even know what Daddy's job was or even where he worked. I had told Martin Sir that he had taken voluntary retirement. Now he said, 'You will think me a rumourmonger but you should know this. Your father was a filing clerk in a mining company. When the mines were closed down, they conducted a thorough audit and found discrepancies in the accounts. The needle of suspicion pointed at your father. The company considered taking penal action against him. But they held off because of his years of faithful service and gave him a pre-retirement package and set him home. So, all this VRS talk was eye wash. My cousin's wife works in the head office of that company. She told me that the company had given him a handsome package. With his provident fund and gratuity, that package must have amounted to about six lakhs. That may sound like a lot of money but I don't know if it will cover your costs. You have to think about all this.'

I nodded.

'You also have to think about your future. Studying medicine is not that easy. You have to be completely focused to get into medical college and then it takes a minimum of five years. If you want to do a post-graduation, that's another two to three years. How will you manage?'

He waited a while and then added, 'Think about it, Vipin. If you ask me, you need a nurse to look after your father. Part-time male nurses are available. But if you can find a woman, she might even be able to help with the cooking. It's all going to cost a lot. You'll have to consider your financial circumstances and then decide.'

At that moment, Stella came in with some cake. I took a slice but forgot to say thank you. Stella left and Martin Sir continued, 'Eat your cake. I don't mean to frighten you by telling you all this. But you have to brace for it.' He waited while I absorbed all this. 'I know you will overcome this. Please remember: I'm right here if you need anything. You can count on me.' The feeling that I had stepped into the pages of a novel became acute again. First Chitra and now Martin Sir. When I left, it was beginning to drizzle. I had not brought an umbrella.

'Wait, I'll get you an umbrella,' Martin Sir said.

'No, thank you, sir.' I wanted to add, 'Up to now everything in my life has seemed a bit hollow. Today I want to get drenched in the rain.'

I walked on, aware that Martin Sir was watching me. The rain came down gently. And somewhere again I felt the stirring of elation...

12

Meursault and Me

The next day Dr Costabir came at twelve thirty before going to his clinic. By that time, I had given Daddy a sponge bath, changed his bed clothes, fed him some mush and given him his medicines. Around ten thirty the phone rang. This was the first time anyone had ever called me barring of course my father and sometimes my uncle.

'What happened, Vipin? You didn't show up?' It was Chitra.

'I told you, no? My father is ill.'

'No problem. I get it. I hadn't brought the painting either. How's your father now?'

Chitra must have thought Daddy had a cold or cough or something.

'He's okay but it will take him some time to recover completely. I don't know if I can make it tomorrow either.'

'Great. Oh shoot! That's not what I meant. What I meant was: I can't make it tomorrow either. My father called to say my mother isn't well. I'm going to Canacona. I'm leaving in the morning. I thought you were coming so I stayed back. Let's try for Saturday then? Or maybe even Sunday?'

I nodded. But how could she see that?

'I know you're not the talkative kind. So let me say it. Saturday, nine thirty in the canteen. Okay? By the way, we have a problem. I don't get range in Canacona. Though I know you're not going to try and call me, I'm just telling you because I won't be able to call either.'

I said 'No problem' in much the same manner that she did.

When I put down the phone Ma wanted to know who had called. What was I to say? If I just said 'Chitra', she would say 'Chitra' who? And what would I say then? So I just said, 'From the college.'

'What about?'

'About my missing class.'

That satisfied Ma. But Daddy must have also heard this. I was not sure whether he could hear in his left ear or not. But his right ear was doing okay. He used his right hand to beckon me close. In his halting and slurred voice, he said, 'I have to get better. Before you become a doctor I want to be getting around again. Once you're a doctor, I'll be fit and fine...So you better study. You...Doctor...'

'Daddy, go to sleep now. You'll be fine very soon, just you see.' But he grabbed my hand and held on to it.

'Don't worry about money. There's money in the bank. Don't touch the FDs. Take it out of the account.'

'How? The account is in your name.'

'Withdraw. I'll sign.'

Daddy began to gasp. I thought it best to stop and said, 'We'll talk later.'

When Dr Costabir had come and gone, Ma said, 'Babu, get us something to eat. But please not from that Vasudev's. I'm tired of his food. How about some biryani?'

I said, 'Yeah, I'm sick of it too. Let's make something at home.'

Ma frowned. 'You know I would if I could...'

'Don't worry yourself. I'll do it. You just direct operations.'

So I put the cooker on the fire and made some rice. I boiled the dal and added haldi, chilli, tamarind and salt on Ma's instructions. There was no freshly grated coconut which started Ma off. I managed to crack a coconut open but scraping it was another matter. Somehow, I managed to get some coconut milk out of it. I put some kokum, salt, chilli, jaggery and hing and dished up a curry of sorts. And for me the smell of rice, the taste of dal and this scratch curry seemed far tastier than anything we'd eaten from Vasudev's restaurant. Ma had psyched herself up for biryani so she kept finding fault but she ate well too.

When we had eaten, I made an inspection of the kitchen. Supplies were low. I made a list and went to the market that evening and stocked up on onions, potatoes, rawa, wheat flour, oil, salt, chilli, haldi, cumin, sugar and jaggery. When I went to buy tea powder, the shop-keeper asked me, 'What kind?'

I had no idea there were different varieties. I said, 'Give me a good one.'

He said, 'You'll take it strong, no?' And so I bought the one he suggested. That night, I made Daddy a rawa porridge and spiked it with hing and chilli for the two of us. I fed Daddy the porridge since his mouth was still twisted after the stroke.

I could not tell whether he liked it or not. When I went into the kitchen, Ma was finishing the rawa I had kept for myself. She only said, 'If you were going to all this trouble, you should have made sheera and I would have eaten it happily.'

*

That night the memories of Chitra which had been playing hide-and-seek with me all day surfaced. She came and sat down by my side. This time she did not even ask, 'May I sit here?'

In the morning, I went to Vasudev's hotel to buy bread. The first rush having receded, he was hanging around in the gully outside. I bought some poyi and was about to go home when he stopped me 'Hold on, Babu. Have a tea on me.' I accepted a cup. It was good. And it gave me a chance to broach the subject.

Earlier I used to call Vasudev Bappa because his son Sandeep did. When Sandeep got into college, he shifted from Bappa to Pappa. And so I shifted to the name by which he was known in the village. 'Vasudev, you know you were talking about hiring someone for the housework? I think...'

'Glad you bought it up,' he interrupted. 'You know our Krishna, no?'

This was a young man who had worked at Vasudev's restaurant for the past five years, since the age of twelve. But he had told Vasudev he wanted to look for other work and would leave at the end of the month. But even before that, Vasudev had found another worker.

'Krishna is a trustworthy boy,' he said. 'He does whatever you ask him to. I won't stand in his way if he can get another job which will help him come up in the world. And to my good luck, I do have someone else. So I want to hand him a month's salary and wish him well. So I thought...'

I thought of all the extra work I had had to do ever since Daddy began physiotherapy. I had seen Krishna around for the last five years but I knew nothing about him nor had I thought it necessary to find out.

'He is a very nice boy. After working all day, he's got up

to the eighth standard by studying at night. Now he wants to study and finish his SSC. I've spoken to him. I paid him five thousand rupees and his meals. If you can match that, it should do.'

'But is he willing to do it?'

'Yes, but on one condition.'

'Condition?'

'Not about the work. Not even about timings. He wants to study and he wants someone to teach him. But why not talk to him yourself? Should I send him to you?'

*

By the time I had made tea, Krishna was at the door. I divided the tea I had made into three portions and handed one to Krishna. I told him to sit down but he simply would not. He stood respectfully and quietly while I drank my tea. Then I heard a moan from Daddy and got up. He had soiled himself. I cleaned him up. I changed his clothes and the bed clothes too. It was time for his breakfast so I fed him porridge. Krishna watched all this attentively.

Then I sat down to chat with him. He lived with his parents. He had been born in Goa though their family was from Dandeli in Karnataka. Since the family was poor, he had not been put in school. But he had taught himself to read and write.

I told him the unvarnished truth.

'This is not like working in a restaurant. My mother does not keep well. She can't handle the housework. You'll have to cook. And look after Daddy. You'll have to do everything for him. When I go to college, he will be your responsibility.'

'Sir, I will do all of it. Only...' he stopped.

'Vasudev was saying you had a condition?'

'Not a condition, a request, sir.'

'I have one too. Don't call me 'sir'. Everyone calls me Babu. You can call me that.'

'But, sir!'

'Again sir?'

'Sorry, sir!' I frowned. He looked confused.

'Okay, okay, Babu sir.'

'Not Babu sir, just Babu.'

He said: 'Can I make my request? Can you teach me? I'll do all the work. You just have to teach me.'

'What do I teach you?'

'Konkani and English, sir, sorry, Babu.'

I thought then of Amrut Patel and how keen he had been to learn Konkani. Here was another boy who had come from outside Goa who wanted to study while the people of Goa ignored the language.

'But you speak reasonably good Konkani,' I said.

'I can speak it,' he said. 'I want to learn how to write as well.'

'And English?'

'I understand it but I can't speak it.' I admired his clarity; he knew what he wanted to study.

'You would like to get another job then?'

'I want to but more than that I want to learn.' He told me that he had taken the job at Vasudev's in the belief that Sandeep would teach him. And for the first two years, he had.

Later, Sandeep had begun to make excuses. And so Krishna had come to me.

I took him into the kitchen and showed him where things were kept. Even as he listened, he washed the tea cups. When I took him to meet Ma, he bowed low. As I introduced him to Ma, he went about putting the room to rights.

When I asked him about his salary, he said: 'That doesn't matter; just teach me, sir.'

I hoped he'd get out of the 'sir' habit as time passed and ignored it. When I asked him about his timings, he said: 'Your father is ill. Your mother's not well. I'll stay here all day. Only, you fix the time for our studies, sir.'

'Okay,' I said. 'When can you start?'

'Today,' he said. 'Right now.'

And so saying, he went into the kitchen.

*

Saturday morning, I left early for college. I didn't want any repeat performances so I reached before nine. Krishna's coming had taken some of the load off my shoulders. Getting Daddy up, helping him into a sitting position, feeding him mush, cleaning his shit and piss...Krishna had watched me and learned how to do it all in the past one-and-a-half days. He made sure Ma got her tea and her meals on time. And today, he had presented himself before the clock struck eight. When I handed him two hundred rupees to buy fish and left the house, I felt a burden shift from my shoulders on to his willing ones.

Although, I knew I was early, I was walking fast out of habit. Class had begun but I had no intention of attending. I had one interest: to find out more about Chitra. Had I come to college only to meet her? What did we have in common that I should be drawn to her? I was a science student; she was studying arts. She wanted to be a painter; I wanted to be a doctor...no, I had wanted to be a doctor up until a few days ago. I had no idea what I wanted to be now but even that represented another difference. She knew she wanted to be a painter and would go on wanting to be one, as far as

I could see. She was talkative; I was not. She liked coffee; I liked tea. Nothing common. Or was there? She liked Camus. I had never met a classmate who had read and enjoyed Camus, Kafka or Murakami. It was Martin Sir who had introduced me to these writers. But I had never wanted to talk about these books with him; I did with Chitra. She had an interesting and unusual way of looking at the universe. And it was certainly a valid way of looking. Most other people accept the common consensus without bothering to think things through. When, for instance, we are told that Ahilya has been made impure, we all nod our heads. But we don't have much to say about the being who made her impure, why he's Indra and Indra is a god. Kunti had to bear sons as a royal wife; the gods impregnated her thus making it all right. Might Kunti not have enjoyed these encounters, they being with the very gods themselves? The texts are silent about this. We accept what Vyasa writes, ignoring the very real physical pleasure of the orgasm.

In *The Outsider*, Meursault is an extraordinary person but because he doesn't fit into the categories we have constructed, we label him an anti-hero. Camus calls him *The Stranger*, who cannot be recognized, who is not like the rest of us. And since he wished to murder, he kills the Arab. How do we make sense of him? He must pay by going to the gallows. Meursault tells us he is ready for this. If someone has a different way of looking at their own life, that's not their problem, it's ours.

If my father were to die tomorrow, who is to decide whether I should grieve, how much I should grieve and in what fashion? Am I to make that decision or is society? Can I look at myself independently as Meursault does? And if I can, why am I here today to meet Chitra? Why not Amrut?

Think of the Devil. Amrut. If I had seen him earlier, I would have avoided him.

'Hi buddy. Got a kick out of ditching all of us?'

I wondered whether they were really upset that I had skipped their rally. Were they angry?

'Maybe it was all for the best. There was no rally. Fatima didn't want to make a big thing of it. So we dropped the idea.'

'Thank you,' I managed.

'By the way, that day when Namshikar got after you? He was lucky I wasn't in class or I'd have...'

'Forget it.'

'Forget it? How can I forget about it? I'm the class rep. I'll teach him a lesson. How dare he talk to our Phantom like that?'

He put out a hand and took me by the shoulder. I slipped out of his grasp and said, 'Never mind. Really. I have some stuff to do. See you around.'

'Off to the library, I suppose. Carry on, scholar,' he said and he went off.

It was 9:20. I wanted a quick shot of canteen tea.

Tea or Chitra? Or get a cup of tea and a cup of coffee and wait for her at a table? I was not one of those who decided whether to drink tea or not depending on what others were doing. But this time I put my yen for a cup of tea on hold until Chitra's arrival.

Just before nine thirty, I saw Fatima coming. I began to hide my face. I did not feel like meeting her now. My instinct was to duck out of sight but she headed straight for me as if she had been looking for me.

'Hey Vipin,' Fatima said as if we had known each other for ages and pulled up a chair and sat down. There was nothing to do but twist my face into the semblance of a smile.

'You didn't show up that day? Aslambhai waited for a while and then he left,' Fatima said.

'Sorry. I just couldn't manage.'

She was looking even prettier today. Her odhni was draped over her head, around her neck and the ends flowed down her back.

'He came the next day too. And the next.'

Before she could count off all the days, I said:

'Daddy was very sick.'

'I know. Chitra told me.'

'Do you know Chitra?'

'Of course. We are coffee mates.'

'Classmates?'

'No, no. Coffee mates. I'm in degree college. But we meet every day for coffee.'

I thought I should ask but didn't know how.

Fatima smiled: 'Go on then. Ask.'

'What?'

'Why Chitra hasn't showed up yet.'

I had no idea it was known to all and sundry that Chitra and I were going to meet.

'How did you know?'

'She sent me. She had to go back to Canacona suddenly. Her mother's taken ill. She tried calling you but couldn't get through. So here I am.'

What a song-and-dance about a simple message. Now I wanted some more tea. Fatima was still sitting there. Did she have anything more to say?

'I want some tea,' I said and headed to the counter.

'Make mine a coffee.'

That day she had seemed like a frightened calf; today she was a frisky deer.

'Chitra warned me,' she said.

'About what?'

'That if I were to meet you, I'd have to do all the talking.'

What else had Chitra told her about me?

'What else did she say?'

Fatima smiled. 'Oh, lots of things. I think you should hear them from her.'

Seeing that I had finished my tea, she drank the last of her coffee.

'You didn't even ask when she's coming back,' Fatima noted.

Why would I ask? We didn't have enough of a relationship.

'If you don't want to know, why should I tell you?' Fatima said teasingly as she rose to her feet. This seemed like a new facet to her personality.

'Enough of that. Tell me.'

'Chitra said you didn't seem the kind who read his messages. She was bang on.'

I took out my mobile. There *was* a message: 'Monday, same time, same place.'

Fatima was getting late for class but she stopped me outside the canteen. 'You know Vipin, I enjoy dancing. Chitra loves painting so we have only a few things we both like. But of the two main ones, one is...'

'Coffee?'

'Correct. And the other is you.'

*

I walked away in something of a daze. Behind me, the clip-clip of feet sounded. Then I heard a voice calling, 'Parob!'

I stopped. It was Professor Namshikar's son. He was in my class. 'I've been looking for you for four days,' he said, 'You know me?'

'Namshikar,' I said.

'Please, not that name. I'm sick of that name. Sarvesh.'

'Why were you looking for me?' I said even as I continued walking. I wanted to get out of there.

'I wanted to say sorry. For the way he spoke to you that day. I was damn ashamed of my Dad. And angry,' he said, matching steps with me.

'Why are you saying sorry?'

'Unfortunately, he's my father,' Sarvesh continued. Although I was in a hurry, I felt I should not stop him. He wanted to unburden himself about his father's attitude.

'You know, Parob, I also have an ambition of my own. I want to be a chef. I enjoy cooking. When my mother cooks, I learn from her. I like trying things out. Mom supports me. I want to become a chef but Dad simply ignored me. He mocks me. You want to be a cook, a bottle-washer? He wants me to become a doctor. He couldn't become one, no? So now I have to become one.'

Weird. His situation and mine were not very different.

'I admire you, Parob. You have guts. You saved that Muslim girl from those thugs and you walked out of class when Daddy tried to come over all sarcastic on you...I wish I had your guts.'

We were at the bus-stop. He brought a package out of his bag and gave it to me.

'This is Sarvesca. My invention. It's a bit like bebinca and so Sarvesca. Please take it. I dedicate it to you.' I could not bear his diffidence and took the box.

'Thank you, Parob. I wanted to ask another question. Can we be friends?'

Just then the bus swooped down. I jumped in and his question remained unanswered.

*

Meanwhile, at home.

The doors and the windows were thrown open. The light, the air, thus far denied, had leapt joyfully into every room. There was a new energy in the house. Krishna, unaware of Daddy's rules, had simply broken them and threw the house open to the elements

For the first time, lunch was ready before I stepped into the kitchen to make it and without having to order it from outside. There was a shellfish hooman; the modso slices I had bought in the market had been turned into what Krishna no doubt referred to as a 'rawa fry'. The warm aromas filtering in from the kitchen awoke my hunger. And Ma, who had always found the trek from her room to the dining table too difficult was now sitting there, waiting to be served. When Krishna asked if I were going to eat, I said, 'Let Ma finish and then we can sit down.' If Krishna had not set aside two slices, they would not have escaped Ma's ravenous paws. With a series of satisfied burps, Ma returned to her room and by the time I was at the table, she was offering a background score of snores. It was obvious she had eaten rather too well.

Poor Daddy. When raw mangoes were in the market, just such a hooman paired with Vasudev's rawa fry had been one of his favourites. The same aromas must be reaching his nostrils as he lay in his room.

When Krishna served me, he placed a single thali on the table. I said, 'Come Krishna, sit with me.'

'No, sir, I'll eat later.'

'Right then. I won't eat either,' I said briskly and got up. And so, somewhat reluctantly, he came and sat down too. I don't remember saying much to anyone at the table until then other than, 'No thank you' or 'Yes, I'll have some more' but this time Krishna and I talked.

I asked him about his desire to study. Perhaps he had wanted to share this with someone for he began to talk and tell me the story of his life. His father had told him that no one becomes a good human being unless they study.

'How much had Appa studied?'

'He didn't get a chance to. But he says he did not succeed in life because he didn't study.'

'So what does Appa think you should study?'

'He wants me to finish school. And if I can, he wants me to go further.'

'To college.'

'I did up to the eighth standard in night school. But there are no night colleges, no?'

'If you want to do it and you have the determination, anything is possible.'

'I want to become a cook,' Krishna's voice was full of certainty.

'Then why leave Vasudev's restaurant?'

'Not that kind of cook, sir. I want to be a cook in a big restaurant. They call them chefs, no? And I need to write Konkani and speak English well for that. Which is why I am here.'

He was only seventeen years old but he knew what he wanted to do. And he was willing to do whatever it took to get where he wanted to go. And I? I had no idea what I wanted to do or what I wanted to become.

When we had finished eating, I said: 'Get your books. Let's get to work.'

'Give me half an hour, sir,' he said. And in that half-hour, he had washed the dishes, put the vessels to soak and loaded the washing machine. When he did sit down with me, he proved to have a mind as quick and able as his hands.

At home, his parents spoke Kannada to each other and Konkani with him. His father thought his own Konkani uncouth and would send him to do odd jobs to the neighbours so he might pick up a better variant of the language.

His father had worked his way up to becoming a mechanic in a garage and his mother had worked as a household help. But then his father told his mother to stop working. He put his son in the primary school but the teacher had him cast as a ghaati and would ask him to do the teacher's household chores. When Krishna was in the fifth standard, his father went to jail, taking the fall for his boss. The owner of the garage had stolen a new stepney from a car that had come in for servicing. When the car owner found out, the garage owner asked Krishna's father to take the blame and promised he would get him out soon. And so Appa went to the police station, a lamb to the slaughter. The owner kept his word, bribed the police and got Appa out but then he sacked Appa too. With no breadwinner, Krishna went to work at Vasudev's restaurant. Now his father started his own repair works, handling two-wheelers on the road to the Goa University at Bambolim. They were beginning life from scratch. But Appa wanted Krishna to pass his tenth standard board examinations. 'Take tuitions,' he had said. 'Don't worry about the money,'

That evening I went with Krishna to his home. It being Sunday, his father was at home. They lived in an out-house that belonged to a landowner and paid five thousand rupees rent for two small rooms. They had to do some chores as and when their landlord had need of it. They were often called ghaati because they were 'outsiders', a term Appa hated. He figured that it was the way that he spoke Konkani that gave him away. He wanted his son had to speak good Konkani to pass as a local.

Krishna's mother brought me tea. Krishna looked embarrassed and said, 'Sorry, sir, very little milk in that.'

Appreciative of their desire to become as Goan as possible, I smacked my lips over the tea.

13

The Night's Darkness

'Monday. Same place. Same time.'

I got there on time. With Krishna at home to look after my parents, I could please myself. I took out my mobile just to check.

A message: 'Sorry'.

When I looked up, there was Fatima with two cups in her hands. She set my tea down and sat down herself. 'Chitra says she's sorry,' I said hoping to forestall questions. Another thought: had Chitra sent Fatima? Or had Fatima dissuaded Chitra from coming so she might be alone with me? And here I was, waiting like a silly simpleton. I wanted to get up and leave. I almost rose—'Your tea will get cold. Drink it and go,' said Fatima, obviously a mind-reader. I remembered what she had said at our last meeting—their two common likes. I studied Fatima intently as I sipped my tea. She had her odhni over her head; was this to cover her hair or to provide a fitting frame for her face? And that face. She seemed to be fresh out of a beauty parlour. The hair tendrils that escaped—artfully?—from her odhni, the eyebrows, the cheeks, the lips, her eyes lined with kaajal... Fatima seemed embarrassed by my staring.

Perhaps to conceal this, she raised her coffee cup to her lips. The pink nail varnish flashed. Fatima was quite beautiful! And Chitra? I had only met her once. I hadn't paid her that much attention. But I remembered that she had not used lipstick. Her hair was not done up in any particular style. I couldn't remember whether she had had nail polish on. I had no idea why but Chitra reminded me of Saratchandra's *Rajlakshmi*.

Gosh, why was I comparing the two? Perhaps it was because of what she had said yesterday. They had a common liking: me.

'Can I ask you something, Vipin?'

I raised my eyebrows.

'Do you sleep in the dark?'

'What's it to you?'

'Tell me, anyway, na?'

'Yes, I like the darkness.'

'That's it. Chitra said he must like the dark, his eyes are so dark it's as if he uses kaajal. It's the night's darkness that has made his eyes like that.'

Suddenly Chitra was back. I became uncomfortable.

'And you haven't even asked yet.'

My eyebrows raised in a question as I sipped my tea. I knew what she was talking about: I had not yet asked about Chitra. But couldn't she just have told me?

Her face darkened a little. 'Chitra's mother is very ill. She won't come back for a week at least.' She paused for a moment and then asked, 'Why didn't you call even once?'

I was confused. It was true that I hadn't called but then neither had she.

'It's okay. Even if you had tried, you wouldn't have got through. Coverage is pretty bad there.'

'I'm wasting my time,' I said and rose.

'Listen. I'm going to bunk tomorrow and go there.'

'Why are you telling me?' I asked, annoyed.

'To Canacona. To see Chitra. She's worried about her mother, poor thing.'

That struck me. In my head she was the Chitra of our first meeting, full of energy and enthusiasm. A Chitra who was worried and concerned?

'Come with me? She'd like that. And I'd have company.'

Did I agree because I felt Chitra would appreciate a visit?

Or because I wanted to keep Fatima company? I couldn't tell but we agreed to meet the next morning at the Kadamba Bus Stand.

*

When I realized that a male nurse would charge fifteen thousand rupees a month, I could not help feeling that paying Krishna only five thousand was not fair. Martin Sir had given me some inkling of Daddy's financial situation. Daddy's passbook said he had one lakh in the bank. Already about forty thousand rupees had been withdrawn for medicines and the hospital bills. I would need his signatures for further withdrawals. Since his right side was functional, he could sign. Now that things seemed under control, it was time for me to understand our financial condition.

First, I asked Ma but she said that she had no idea. I was not surprised but then she asked after her gold, the ornaments she had brought with her at the time of her marriage. She had handed them over to Daddy. The last time she had worn them was when Uncle Junior got married. After that, they had vanished. Daddy said he had put them in a bank locker but she had no faith in him.

'You ask your Daddy about my gold,' she said and trotted after me to his bedside. I had never had any reason to talk to Daddy about money. The old fears, planted in childhood, were still inside me. But at this moment, with Daddy confined to his bed, I found it easy to ask him about money matters. He objected to Ma standing there, all ears. He kept gesturing for her to go away until she could no longer ignore it and went off, muttering angrily to herself.

I brought my ear to his lips and managed to decipher what he was mumbling.

'When will I get well?' he asked.

'Your treatment is going on, Daddy. You will recover soon.' I knew that this was what one said in these cases.

When I asked him about money, he said, 'When I get well, I'll give it to you. Don't worry about money. Study hard. You must become a doctor. I have money.'

'But we need it now to spend.'

'Take the money in the drawer,' he managed before collapsing, exhausted. I wanted to tell him that the money in the drawer was long gone. But then he would have demanded accounts. The doctor had told us that we should try to keep his blood pressure normal by making sure he avoided any tension or anxiety. I got up and came away. That night after he closed his dispensary for the day, Dr Costabir came to check Daddy's blood pressure.

'Normal,' he pronounced and I followed him to the door and stopped him to explain my situation. He knew Daddy of old. He turned right round and went back to Daddy's bedside. 'Mr Parob, I have been treating you but have not been paid for my visits over the last fortnight.

'Babu spent a lot of money and so you were saved. And there are more expenses coming up. If he doesn't have money, how will he manage?'

This worked its magic. As soon as he left, Daddy called me to his side and asked me to bring him his cheque book. I got him into a sitting position and supported by pillows, he signed a cheque. Then he warned me: 'It's a bearer cheque. Don't let it out of your sight. Go to the bank yourself. Take out only how much you need.'

Then he added, 'You should be the joint holder in the account. Tell the manager.'

I knew there were fixed deposits in the bank. When I asked him about Ma's jewellery, he got agitated and this made his speech even more incoherent. I could make out that he was blaming Ma. She had not allowed him to come close to her and so there had been expenses. I decided not to think too much about this. I put the cheque away safely and went to call Krishna, who was folding clothes, so that we might get down to his studies.

14

Window Seat

Fatima of the first year of degree college looked like a puppy next to me, the Man Mountain from the twelfth standard. The two of us were on a seat meant for three but then the bus filled up. Since Fatima was at the window seat, I was the filling in the sandwich. It was early in the morning and the air was still damp. The sun poked a hesitant head from behind masses of clouds. Its rays poured down, a liquid gold benison on grateful greenery.

Fatima sighed: 'If Chitra had been here, she would have hopped off right now to paint this.'

'Did you call her?'

'She managed to get through. She said her mother's a little better. I told her we were coming today.' Changing the subject she said, 'This is my first long bus journey, Vipin, and I'm so happy it's happening with you.' She pinched my arm gently. I had made no such excursions either, I realized. Just to my mother's home when my grandfather died and that visit to all our gods, and that had been in a taxi.

Before we hit the ghats, it began to rain. The window near Fatima refused to close. I got up to try some brute force and just then the bus driver hit the brakes and I lurched into

Fatima. I said, 'Sorry' and sat down again. But the window was still half open and every so often, a gust of rain would blow through it. Fatima would shrink away from it, into me. I tried to keep a courteous distance between us but that meant invading the space of the third passenger, seated on the other side of me. Fatima, meanwhile, seemed to be experiencing no discomfort. Finally, she said: 'Put your arm around my shoulder. That'll make it easier.'

And until the rain ended, my arm remained there.

'You go gymming?' she asked. I shook my head. The surya namaskars were enough for me. She said nothing more so I asked: 'Why do you ask?' She pushed her neck back against my arm and squeezed the bicep. 'Your muscles.'

I removed the arm from around her shoulders.

*

Everyone seemed to know Chitra's home. When we got down, two villagers cheerfully went with us to show us the way. A wooden fence surrounded a fine, large compound. Inside, an even more beautiful garden. A garage to one side with a jeep and an SUV; between them an Enfield bike. Behind the garage, a cow shed. From the outside, you could tell it was a traditional house built around a chowk.

As we began to climb the steps, we heard a voice raised in anger. 'Didn't I say that you shouldn't? Must you insist? Don't you get anything I tell you?' I was used to the sound of raised voices. Daddy often shouted at Ma. His shouting was lined by the threat of violence. But this raised voice was veined with love.

It had all the threat of a lover's pillow fight.

We stopped on the stairs, nonetheless. And a white dog came yipping and skipping from somewhere inside. Scared,

Fatima grabbed my arm again. The dog came to a sudden halt, his bark had the same warmth as the scolding.

'Pakhlo, come here. Friends, Pakhlo, friends,' Chitra said.

'Meet my best friend,' Chitra said as she scratched the dog's head.The dog began to wag his tail. We went inside where she introduced us to her father. In his shorts and white t-shirt, he looked like a retired film star.

'Be with you in a minute,' he said and went in.

'So handsome!' Fatima sighed and then gave me a mischievous poke in the side. 'Like you.'

Chitra took us to her mother's room. Mamma was reclining in an easy chair and knitting. She showed all the signs of having been a great beauty but there were lines of pain etched around her dull eyes which told us of her illness. Fatima approached to look admiringly at the knitting.

'Mamma, this is Fatima.'

'She's the one who sent us biryani on Eid, right? My mouth still waters at the memory.'

Fatima was delighted.

'How beautifully you knit, Mamma. Will you teach me?' Fatima asked.

'I would have loved to, darling. But it's too late now. I don't have that much time left.'

'Mamma, don't talk rot. You promised to knit booties, bonnets and sweaters for my babies, remember?' Chitra scolded her affectionately and then added, 'This is Vipin. You know him, right?'

'The one you wanted to invite over? That brave one? The smart and silent type?'

Her father entered the room and added, 'The one who should have been an arts student but studies science, right?'

I was truly embarrassed by all this.

'Come along, breakfast is ready,' he said, pointing at an inner room. 'You come too, darling. We can drink our tea together.' He gently helped her to her feet. 'I've made your favourite mint chutney.'

There were ghaavan made of rice to eat with mint chutney. I gorged myself and then sat back. There were kettles, I saw, on the gas range. Chitra poured me a cup. 'Try Pappa's tea. Made with milk from our own cows.' She poured him one too. 'He's one of your tribe: a tea drinker.'

'What about me?' Fatima asked.

'Coffee for us,' Chitra said and picked up the other kettle.

'And here I was, gritting my teeth and getting ready to drink tea.'

'Would I ask such a sacrifice in a coffee mate? No, we stick to our tenets.'

'The tenets of coffee?' Her father asked, mildly satirical.

'Of course. We love our coffee.'

Her mother intervened.

'But remember this, Chitra. There's always room for compromise. He drinks tea. I like coffee. But once in a while, I have a cup of tea with him. Or he has coffee with me. And then we set those differences aside.'

'That's right,' said Pappa and he and Fatima exchanged a high five, as if they were old friends. It was a revelation to me. There were fathers like this. And mothers! Who were cheerful even though they were ill.

But when Chitra walked us back to the bus stop, it was a different Chitra from the one who smiled and laughed at home. I had felt she had been putting a brave face on it but when we were alone, she dropped the mask.

'Pappa and I keep up this double act. Mamma can barely

manage anything but she tries to do the housework. Then Pappa shouts at her. We both keep trying to make sure she rests. The medicines seem to be making her even more tired.'

'What is the matter?' Fatima asked the question uppermost in our minds.

'Cancer.'

I hoped frantically a bus would turn up and whisk us away. I couldn't bear the sight of Chitra's woebegone face. Then finally the bus came into view.

'Thank you, Vipin, for coming. I was so glad you made it,' said Chitra, taking my hand.

'Oh wow, what about me?' Fatima pretended to be hurt to lighten the tone.

'How can I ever thank you? You're the one who got Vipin to come,' she said and hugged Fatima. Was she looking at me out of the corner of her eye?

I felt as if her lips had brushed my cheek, not Fatima's, as I climbed into the bus.

*

We didn't speak much through the long trip back to Panjim. At the bus stand, she asked: 'When do we meet now?'

I shrugged. She smiled. 'I could have guessed your answer.'

'What?'

'When Chitra comes back, right?'

I shrugged again.

'But I want to meet you. I owe you,' she said seriously. The passengers began to ease themselves out of the bus.

'What?'

'You remember Chitra gave me a kiss on the cheek when we left?'

'What of it?'

'Don't you know? She said it wasn't for me.'

'So?' I got up to get down.

'You're a little slow,' she said. Her gaze flickered away and she said, 'I was told to pass it on to you.'

And Fatima went off, never looking back.

15

Brutally Honest

Over the next fifteen days I did not go to college. Chitra sent a message: she wouldn't be coming to college either, not until Diwali. Fatima called twice. I didn't answer because I did not feel like talking to anyone.

Daddy's physiotherapy sessions began. For the first few days, Krishna and I took him to the hospital. Then the physiotherapist said, 'No need for you to come. Krishna can manage. You study.' Daddy only instructed me to hurry up and become a doctor. He said he wanted to live a hundred years.

By the time I got to college, there was one day before the Diwali vacation began.

*

Generally, students welcome the vacations. I wasn't like that: going to college or studying at home were pretty much the same. But this time there was a hollowness somewhere. It was then that my laptop came to my aid. I studied everything that I had missed from the various websites devoted to this. At the last lecture of Namshikar's that I had attended, he had asked how I was going to catch up, specially since he had finished with genetically engineered insulin. He had made it sound formidable.

When I looked it up, it turned out to be quite easy. I got the syllabus from Amrut. And if I could study it all at home, I need only attend the practicals.

One day, I had finished with my work on my laptop. Lunch was done and Krishna and I had gone over some work together. Ma was immersed in one of her endless serials. I was sitting alone in my room. Now that Krishna was in charge of the household, all the windows and doors were open. But this was a day of such interior darkness that even the faint light coming through the windows hurt the eyes. I closed the windows. I was empty inside. I remembered a line I had heard somewhere: 'If you feel lonely when you are alone, you are in bad company.' I became even more agitated.

Why did I feel that if Chitra were around she would have been able to get me out of this mood? Why not someone else? Only after fumbling around for a while did I think of Martin Sir.

*

The afternoon wore on. I waited until it was about four o'clock and then called on Martin Sir. He was at home.

'I was just thinking about you but thought you must be in the middle of the preparation for the festival. Tomorrow is Diwali, no?'

Tomorrow? Diwali? Probably. Someone would have had to tell me.

'I've heard good things about the staff at your higher secondary. Are you happy?'

I said, 'Yes' because he clearly expected it.

'Made some new friends?'

This time I nodded but I didn't know what I would say if he asked their names. I changed the subject. 'Sir, I don't think I want to study science now. I think arts...'

'What?' I had never seen him so surprised.

But no more than I was. Where had this come from? Had I come here to talk about this? I did not remember consciously planning it.

'You were going to do medicine, right?'

I was silent.

'Have you discussed this with Daddy?'

'No, sir. But I will finish the twelfth standard exam.'

'Look, my boy, you've started out to China and halfway there, you're changing direction for France.'

I was. Why was I? Was it because Chitra was doing arts? I had decided to abandon the idea of becoming a doctor, it was true, but why abandon science too?

'You should have taken arts in the first place. I thought you would become a writer or a philosopher. But now it would be good if this is an independent decision and your resolve is firm. All I would say is: think well before you make up your mind. But remember this: You won't be the first person to do that. Somerset Maugham studied medicine and he became a writer.'

I had gone hoping for answers but I got more questions. It was as if I were being drenched in a gush of dirty water. Instead of going home directly I began to walk. It was dusk when I got home. Krishna had finished work and was waiting for me.

'I'll be a little late tomorrow, sir. It's Diwali, na?'

I felt no desire to eat. I closed the doors and windows. But my mind kept returning to its unease, examining it, inspecting it. Finally, I pulled my pants down to my knees and masturbated, hoping to distract myself.

In the morning when I woke up, I threw open the windows and let the morning light and the clean air blow the cobwebs away.

*

'Happy Diwali, Vipin.'

Chitra's voice brought joy in the morning.

'Thank you.'

'Won't you wish me?' she asked.

I did not care for formalities much. I had never understood why people said, 'Happy Diwali' to each other. I knew enough to say 'Thank you' when someone said it to me. That was, I knew, a formality too.

'Sorry, I'm no good at formalities.'

I could not remember having said anything in so straightforward manner. Was this the first time?

'No problem. I think that's what I like about you.'

I understood what it was to feel a burst of pleasure.

'Have you had your bath?' she asked.

'I rose and bathed in the early light and the fresh breeze of the morning.'

Where were these words coming from?

'Wow. You're waxing eloquent! Or even poetic. This must be the result of hanging out with Fatima.'

The doorbell rang as Chitra asked, 'What pohe have been made today?'

Krishna appeared at the door with a dabba in his hand.

'Amma sent pohe, sir,' he said.

'What kind?' I asked him. Chitra thought I had addressed this to her.

'How would I know?' she asked.

'Fodni poha,' said Krishna.

'Come over,' said Chitra. 'You'll get ten types of poha here. Mamma made poha with milk and I made it with curds. Come on, we'd all be so happy to see you.' She seemed sincere.

'I would but for the distance,' I said. 'Keep some for me.'

'Did you wish Fatima?'

I didn't like this turn in the conversation.

'She's very annoyed with you. She says you don't take her calls.'

I said nothing.

'She is a good girl, Vipin. And my best friend. You're not to hurt her, you hear? Do you know how much she values you as a friend?'

How would I tell her that while she said Fatima valued me as a friend, Fatima said she liked me? Just then Chitra's father called her and she hung up.

A moment later, Fatima called. I answered. I thought she would start with the usual 'Happy Diwali!' but instead, she said:

'Chalo baba, thank you.'

'For what?'

'You took my call. And now, mubaraq baat: Happy Diwali. You were waiting for my call, right?'

'No,' I said instinctively.

'Come on, that hurt. You were waiting to call me, weren't you?'

'Why lie?'

'Oh Vipin, you're so brutally honest. Couldn't you have lied just to please me?' I did not answer so she continued, 'Chitra must have called you this morning, no? Did you talk to her the way you talk to me? I'm sure not.'

'Don't mix things up, Fatima.'

'Oh well. Before you hang up, I'll ask: When do I see you again?'

'Wait and watch,' I said and hung up.

*

That day, I gave Krishna his salary.

He seemed surprised. 'Vasudev Kaka said it would be five thousand.'

'You work for me now. Not for him.'

'Seven thousand?' he touched the money to his forehead. 'But what about your tuition fee?'

He tried to return some money.

I pushed it back into his hands.

'I cut it already.'

*

I could not help but admire Krishna's dedication to education and his appetite for work. One day I asked him: 'How old are you?'

The next day he brought his birth certificate along.

'You've done the eighth standard. Why not sit for the tenth now?'

'This year?'

'Yes. You're old enough.'

He was game so I began to coach him in all the subjects, from mathematics and science to history and geography and the languages. Since we were leapfrogging from the eighth to the tenth, he now took time to grasp concepts but once he had them fixed in his head, they stayed there. He recited well and he was willing to work hard.

In a matter of a month, I could see his self-confidence

improving. He went and got the forms he would need to sit as an external student.

And somewhere along the way, Fatima called.

'*Hum Aapke Hain Koun...?*' she said.

'Why ask me?' I asked, confused.

'Matinee show. Come, na, with me?' she wheedled. I could not tell whether she was truly asking or just teasing.

'You didn't find anyone else to tease?' I asked.

'If Chitra were here, would I be asking you?'

'Do I smell some emotional blackmail?'

'Call it what you want but come.'

Had she really expected me to give in?

I said, 'Sorry,' and ended the call.

But all day her face, childish and affectionate face haunted me. And so eventually I did something unprecedented. I watched *Hum Aapke Hain Koun...?* on my laptop.

16

Two's Company, Three's a Crowd

Before the holidays ended, I often thought of calling Chitra and asking after her mother. But a mocking voice in my head would ask: What do you care about Chitra's mother's health? Why not just call her and ask when you can come, when you can meet?

But then Chitra called and told me when she was coming and when we could meet.

I waited for the day she named as one waits for the results of an examination. As I walked in to the canteen, I could hear my heartbeat thundering in my ears. Chitra was already there. Her hair was tied back. She was wearing a white salwar with a black odhni. On her lips a smile, in her eyes, energy.

'I hate to have to say this but I'm here too,' said a voice. Fatima was sitting next to her. 'It's the age of "'Buy one, get one free". So here's Chitra with Fatima free.'

I didn't care for the comment but Chitra and Fatima exchanged a high five.

'Did you bring the paintings?' I asked Chitra in order to start a conversation.

'I brought Chitra with me,' said Fatima.

'Chitra? Painting? Get it?'

'You...' I didn't know how to complete the sentence. 'Enough of these jokes.'

'What's wrong with a joke or two? I love her sense of humour. Faces blossom when a joke is told,' Chitra said.

Fatima would not be Fatima if she were to let things go. 'And a day without a smile is a day wasted.'

They high fived each other again. 'One might say that there are those amongst us whose days are all wasted.'

'Let it go, girl. If he doesn't smile at you, that's your problem. His smile...'

Fatima interrupted: 'Have you seen him smile?'

'Of course. I forgot to show it to you when you came to Canacona. Hold on.'

She pulled out her mobile and showed us a picture of an incomplete canvas.

'When it's done, I'll show it to you.'

A painting of me. Possibly. All the bits and pieces were there.

'Good sketch. But I don't see that elusive smile.' Fatima pursed her lips.

'You have to know how to look,' Chitra said, her eyes filled with self-confidence. I looked at it again.

Her shading was interesting. Those eyes. Was there a smile lurking in them?

'I'll get tea,' I said and stood up.

'Coffee,' Chitra reminded me. I returned with a tray on which there were two cups of coffee and my tea.

'Come on, Vipin. You could have kept us company and had coffee today,' Chitra said with pretended anger.

'I wouldn't drink something I don't like just to make someone else happy.'

Was it wrong to say that? For they exchanged glances and changed the subject.

'What did you do in the holidays?' Chitra asked.

What had I done? Nothing worth recounting.

'Shall I tell you what he did? He watched a film,' Fatima said, wrinkling her nose.

'Really? Which one?'

'*Hum Aapke Hain Koun...?*' Fatima winked. 'We went for a matinee show.'

I was uncomfortable with the possibility that Chitra might take this to be true.

'Without me?' Chitra raised her eyebrows.

'She's pulling your leg. I saw it on my laptop. Ask her who she saw it with.'

The tone of my voice must have shown that I wanted this to be cleared up.

'Let it go, man. I've seen it three times already,' Chitra said, her voice in turn suggesting that we find another topic.

Fatima finished her coffee and picked up her bag. 'Time flies when you're with friends but I have a lecture to go to and the prof has her eagle eye on every empty seat.'

We rose too.

'Take a stroll with me, Vipin?' Chitra asked as we stepped out.

'No one asked me or I might even have joined you,' said Fatima, hovering expectantly.

Chitra waved her off. 'Two's company, three's a crowd.'

'Okay, bye Vipin. *The crowd* is off to class. Enjoy the company.'

Fatima tossed this barb over her shoulder and ran off.

'She's so lovely. I really have a lot of time for her.'

And then Chitra stopped for a minute and gave me a poke in the ribs. 'And she for you.'

'She's just too much sometimes,' I blurted out.

'You may have a point. But that's why she's misunderstood. You will not believe it but she is scared of boys.'

'And yet with me she...'

'That's what I'm saying. I think she really likes you. Perhaps because you're different.'

Chitra seemed to have a single topic to talk about: Fatima.

'She loves poetry. Urdu, Hindi, Konkani. She really recites it well too.'

By this time, we had reached the street. A scooter came up and stopped near us.

'Hello, Chitra. No sign of your tail today?'

'Just gone to class,' she said and pointing to me she said, 'Aslambhai this is that very Vipin.'

'Oh! Vipin Parob! How long I waited for you that day. But we didn't make contact. Anyway, I wanted to thank you. We are all grateful to you. You saved Fatima's honour. Thank you so much.'

He extended his hand and I shook it. I was eager to see him off so I said nothing. He left and Chitra said, 'You know who that was, no? Fatima's brother.'

I didn't want to talk about Fatima while walking with Chitra. 'You were going to show me those paintings?'

'Yes, the Sisyphus Series. Next time. Look, I'm still an amateur. You could call me self-taught. I don't have the courage to show them to people. Do you know why I offered them to show to you?'

'Why?'

'To get a chance to meet you again.'

'So the paintings don't exist?'

The idea that she might have lied about the paintings gave a certain edge to my voice.

'Of course, the paintings exist. They're here, with my uncle. And I really would like to show them to you. Tell me when? Tomorrow?'

*

The next day she actually brought the picture. And an easel too. I thought there was something familiar about Sisyphus.

'You know,' she said. 'I think I may have modelled Sisyphus on you.'

That startled me. She added, 'It's not just the physical thing? Look at the expression on his face? Impassive. Innocent. Adamantine. The determination that come what may I will move that stone.' How could she have intended to do this?

'These paintings were done before I met you. Which is why you looked familiar when I saw you the first time. That's why I wanted to talk to you.'

'But I don't...'

'You have to look at yourself through my eyes. And even so there's something in this picture that I didn't see in you.'

'And that is?'

'I'm sorry to say this. But the determination that Albert Camus assigns to his character and that confidence is missing in you.'

And Chitra began to pack the painting away.

I had felt from childhood that there were many deficits in my personality. No, the deficits were pointed out to me. And yet, I had managed to get this far. I believed that I was never going to overcome them. I had never, however, said these aloud. The belief lay inside me as a stratum in the sedimentary rock of my personality. Chitra had unwittingly evoked that belief. Now I really needed a cup of tea.

'Canteen? I need tea.'

'Sure. But I have a request. You must speak freely with me.'

Chitra's request disconcerted me. The need for tea began to trouble me. But I still didn't want to leave her company.

'Don't I always?' I had to say though that I had not had much experience talking to people. And yet I felt I had spoken a great deal to her. 'What do you want me to talk about?'

'About yourself. Your home, your people, your childhood, your reading habits...'

'I can't just talk like that. But if you ask questions, I will try to answer them.'

Which is what happened. For the next two hours, we warmed the chairs of the canteen. It was only when I got home that I remembered that I had not asked after her mother.

17

The Sound of the Television

I made a timetable for Krishna. From seven thirty to nine thirty, he was to study maths and science. From three to four, history and geography. And from four to five, the languages. Since the days were now drawing in, he would return home and revise what he had studied. If he found that he hadn't understood something, he would ask the next day. There was something inspiring about his determination and his dedication.

Daddy could now sit with some help. But he needed someone to get him to the toilet as one foot still dragged.

Having Krishna around made Ma's life much easier. Yet she avoided anything to do with Daddy. I tried to increase Daddy's range of motion. When Krishna left for home, he would sit Daddy in the easy chair. Ma would lumber off to her room to watch television and I would take over, having finished my studies for the day. That was our routine.

One day I was on my laptop, making notes. Dusk had gathered. Krishna had left. Ma never missed her seven o'clock serial. That day I finished early and when I closed the laptop, I heard Ma's voice talking to someone outside. When I came to his room, I found Daddy lying in bed and

Ma, sitting in the easy chair across from him, talking to him. Since her back was to me, she could not see me. I might have thought this was a good thing, Ma choosing to talk to Daddy, but then I heard her voice and it was full of venom. When I came close, Ma was in full flow. I stood there listening.

'What you're going through is the fruit of your karma...I should have stayed single...I would have had a better chance at happiness...I married you and was thrown into hell. You loved torturing me, didn't you? Now suffer! You'd say a woman should do what is woman's work...so what was I, a maid servant? You made me do everything...and yes, I didn't want a maid in the house...And you know why. When I had delivered, the woman who was brought to help me, do you think I didn't know how often you banged her?...And then that Durgamma? That's the reason why I didn't want any maid in my home. But did you ever bother about me? You had ants in your pants...Okay I said I didn't want a maid so you could have kept a man servant. But you thought I would have something to do with him. My father gave me fifty tolas of gold...so that I might live well...but you kept it for your happiness. Who did you give my gold to? Did I not want a good time too? You came to me when you wanted. You would force yourself on me when the mood took you, as if I didn't know you were bringing some woman's leftovers for me to eat...Now see who will be there for you. Let me tell you this, I'm not going to do a thing for you.'

Daddy was listening. His right hand and right leg were trembling. His body had shrunk into itself.

I could see that he was trying to say something but the words fell from a thick and disobedient tongue. Ma ranted on: 'I know you don't like listening to this. When you were well, I got no chance to speak. I just had to listen. Now it's your turn. So, listen and listen well. You'll never get well again. Don't think you're going to get better tomorrow and teach me a lesson. This is how it's going to be for the rest of your life. A cripple, who can't speak or take a shit himself.'

She began to laugh, an ugly laugh with no joy or humour in the sound.

'Ma, enough of that now, go inside,' I said. I thought her behaviour reprehensible but I also felt sorry for her. When she heard my voice, she got up and walked away as if nothing had happened. A few minutes later, she switched the television on and the sound spread through the house. When Daddy had been well, she had kept the volume down to a whisper.

*

When I woke up in the morning, Daddy was lying in bed, but his body was twisted and bent out of shape. Experience had taught me a thing or two and so I called 108 instead of disturbing Dr Costabir. At the hospital, Dr Misquita said, 'He survived this one. But he can't have his BP shooting up like this.'

This time I didn't have to run about as much. The nurses in the hospital took care of everything. I didn't have to spend the day there either. I made a daily trip with gruel and whatever medicines were prescribed.

Krishna now had less work to do at home so I made him study for longer hours. One day when I was getting ready to go to the hospital by bus he said, 'Daddy's scooter is just lying there. Why not use it?'

Why hadn't this occurred to me?

'But I don't have a licence.'

'I don't have one either. Doesn't stop me. Appa will repair the bike.'

He called his father and though it had been lying unused for four months it took him only an hour to get the scooter going again. Krishna tried it out and then I mounted.

'Babu, you know how to ride, no?'

It was true that I never actually ridden a bike before. But I had seen how it was done. I took my first round staying close to the house. I remembered Chitra's disparaging remark: 'I do not see any self-confidence in you.'

I decided that I would take the bike the next time I went to meet her. When I came home, I found that Ma had set Krishna to the task of pressing her feet. She said, 'But he's finished his homework!' From that day on I began to set him additional homework.

*

In the morning, on the way to the hospital, my phone rang.

Fatima. I was in no mood for her raillery. I rejected the call. It began to ring again. I stopped the bike and answered.

'Vipin, bad news.'

'Enough of your jokes...'

'Listen to me, Vipin. Chitra's mother passed last night. Chitra's gone to Canacona.'

I didn't know what to say.

'I'm on my way there. Aslambhai is driving me. Are you coming?' She was assuming that I would.

'No. Daddy's in hospital. Tell Chitra...' But I didn't know what I wanted to tell Chitra.

'I will. You take care.'

How did Fatima know what I wanted to say?

*

In the hospital parking lot, Martin Sir's scooter came and stopped besides mine.

'What are you doing here?' Martin Sir asked me.

He had come to see a relative of his who was in hospital and now he came with me to see Daddy. Then he began to talk about something else altogether.

'I know this is not the time to think about it, but this is also the only time you have to think about it which is why I'm asking. I hope and pray your father gets well soon. But, God forbid, if something happens, I hope all his documents are in order.'

He could see that I didn't know what he was talking about and so he explained everything in detail.

In the fifteen days that Daddy was in the hospital I transferred the bank account, the fixed deposits, the house and the scooter into my name. I later realized how much Martin Sir's pragmatic attitude had helped make my life easier. I also put in an application for a driver's licence.

*

Up to the Christmas holidays, I did not go to college except for the practicals.

On Goa Liberation Day, Fatima called. I answered immediately as if I had been waiting for her call. Before I could even say 'Hello', Fatima had started speaking, 'I know you won't ask, but I'm going to tell you anyways. That day I went for Chitra's mother's funeral. You know how strong Chitra's father looked? He seemed devastated. Chitra looked very composed. What am I saying? They didn't bury her. They cremated her in Canacona itself. Chitra was in charge of everything because her father simply wouldn't have been able to manage. She even lit the pyre. Very courageous of her I thought.'

Immediately an image of a calm Chitra lighting her mother's pyre appeared before my eyes.

'Hello, can you hear me, Vipin? I think we should meet. Will you come tomorrow to Panjim? To the Campal? The Kala Akademi canteen? Around five?'

I did go. Fatima was already there with a cup of coffee for her and a cup of tea for me.

'Have your tea when it is hot,' she said. 'I just brought it when I saw you coming in.'

Until the cups were empty, we said nothing. The normally exuberant Fatima was quiet and serious today. Finally, she said, 'Chitra called yesterday. She asked how your father was doing. I think you should phone and tell her.'

Only then did it strike me: in her moment of sorrow, I had not had the guts to call up Chitra and condole with her. The thought ran a cold finger down my spine.

'Shall we go for a walk?' I asked. Fatima rose immediately. We walked on the grass towards the Mandovi Jetty through the car park and onto the footpath.

'I know that you would not have come just because I asked you to. It was because we were going to talk about Chitra, that's why you came,' she said and laughed sadly. What could I say? It was the truth. Without thinking, our feet began to take us to Miramar.

'So what else was Chitra saying?' I asked, to break the silence.

'She said that she was sure you would have come if your father had been well.'

'I don't know.' It was only the truth.

Fatima nodded. 'Even I could not face her that day. When I think of her, my heart breaks,' Fatima said and took my hand. Her fingers were cool. We walked like that for a while. There were busloads of tourists all over the beach. I began to look for a spot where we might be able to sit on the sand. On one side a group of about ten to fifteen people seemed to be celebrating something, going by the laughter, the roars and the hugging. One of them was playing a guitar, another was singing. Since their mood was so diametrically opposed to ours, we chose to sit a little distance away. We watched the passing show of all the different kinds of people who had chosen to visit Miramar that evening. We spoke little; long stretches of silence.

The sun was setting. Fatima watched its slow descent. Then, as if speaking to herself she said, 'Hey Ol' Sol! Take Chitra's sorrows as you set and bury them deep in the sea.'

Then she fell into a reverie until the light faded.

'Shall we? The sun's almost set,' I said. 'We have to go back to Kala Akademi to get my bike.'

I got up and dusted the sand from my trousers.

'Gosh, you're right. I have to get home before it's dark.'

She took the hand I proffered and pulled herself up. At that moment, five or six men came and surrounded us.

'Hey, what are you guys up to here?' one of them shouted.

'I think they're eloping...'

'What religion are you?' another asked in an aggressive tone.

'The chick looks Muslim and he's Hindu,' a third said.

'Pull down his pants and check!' At this they all laughed loudly. I felt my temples grow hot. My jaw set.

Who were these people?

What did they have to do with us? What gave them the right to ask questions? And why should I tolerate this? I took Fatima's hand and pulled her closer to me. They began to close in on us.

'I'm telling you nicely. Keep your distance,' I warned them.

Fatima grabbed my arm with both her hands. My warning caused them to back off a little. Then one of them said, 'He speaks Konkani, he's a Goan.'

'So what of that? Should we tolerate these people who smear our religion?'

This was a skinny fellow, making up for his size with a show of bravado.

'What do you guys want? And who are you?'

This was a challenge to their authority.

'We will show you right now who we are.' He said and thumped his arms. 'The Hindu Watchdog Committee. Have you heard of us?'

They were acting as if this ugly parochial organization was some huge revolutionary force. I felt my hackles rise. I ran at him and threw myself upon him.

My weight simply bowled him over. The others reacted. Fatima shouted, 'He's got a knife!' And then the group that had been celebrating, suddenly turned up and surrounded us.

'Hey, what's going on here? What's all this shit?' One of them roared. There was a command in his voice.

'We have just come to give him a warning. He started this fight,' one of the watchdogs said in a quiet voice.

'What do you want?'

'Look, the girl is Muslim, the boy is Hindu. We will not tolerate these things. We are the Hindu Watchdog Committee. They only...' the skinny boy began and his voice started rising with excitement.

'What are you going to do?' asked the man from the celebrating group. He grabbed him by the collar and shouted to the rest. 'Come on, all of you. Let's circumcise all of them. Let's show them what we think of this shit.' Seeing the sudden change in energy, the watchdogs decided that they had better move on. They scattered. The group waited with us until we heard the sound of motorcycles revving up and they were gone.

'Okay, you lot,' said someone from the group. 'I think we've seen the last of them.'

And they went back to their celebration as if nothing had happened and they hadn't saved us from indignity.

'Let's go,' I said to Fatima, taking her hand and turning in the direction from which we had come.

'Were you frightened?'

'Not with you around,' she said and pressed my hand. I could see that she was returning to her normal self.

'Look at what they do and then claim it is a religious thing,' I said, disgusted.

'Oh, there are lots of those around,' she said. 'You find them in every religion. Our mosque has this new Imam who's trying to change our way of living. But there are also people like that in the world: the ones who came to our help.'

She began to walk to the bus-stand.

'Hold on,' I said. 'I'll get my scooter and reach you home.'

'No need for that,' she said. 'I was nervous for a moment. But do you think that would be enough to scare me? They were the cowards. All their courage came from the mob. No one has any time for them in Goa.'

When she saw the bus drawing near, she pressed my hand and said, 'But frankly I'm happy to see your concern, saying you would reach me home and all that. When I call you, you must come over.'

The bus left. I walked back to the beach. The group of

young people was still having fun. They were now dancing to music, played over their phones. On my approach, two of them detached themselves. They looked familiar but for a moment I could not place them. Then light dawned. Of course, I had seen them before.

'A reversal of roles, right?'

My question took them by surprise. They had probably thought I was coming to thank them.

'We thought you hadn't recognized us.'

Another man detached himself from the group and wandered over: 'Is he one of us?'

'No such luck. We'll catch up with you guys. We'll just get a cup of tea and come.'

'Tea? On a night that calls for champagne?' He laughed and went back to the group.

I wanted tea too. We crossed the road to a stall and drank tea in a paper cup, sitting on a bench.

'You're right, you know. Today our roles were reversed but we wanted to thank you.'

And then they told me their story.

They said they were partners. However, they had also developed an addiction to weed. When their money ran out and the craze was upon them, they were willing to do anything for money. One day they hatched a plan to kidnap Fatima and demand a lakh of rupees as a ransom. Fatima's father was a businessman. They gambled on the belief that he would not go to the police for such a small amount. But I had intervened and their plan had failed.

'But why are you thanking me?' I asked.

They had an answer to that as well. After their unsuccessful attempt at kidnapping, they were terrified that Fatima's family would lodge a complaint, I would stand witness, the college would make an issue of it and a police warrant might be issued in their names. So for the next ten days they went underground. That was a form of cold turkey. After ten days when everything calmed down and no complaints seemed to have been made, they came out of hiding and discovered that they were no longer addicted. After that, they had stayed clean.

'But you would have ruined the girl. What about that?'

'You mean would we rape her? No way, man. Don't you get it? We are gay.'

That was when I saw the light. It was only yesterday that the courts had shut down Section 377 of the Indian Penal Code that criminalised homosexuality and that was why this group had been celebrating on the beach.

'Okay, but I still have to thank you guys. If you hadn't come when you did things could have worked out differently. Thank you.'

'That makes us even!' One of them said and we shook hands, all around. 'By the way, we didn't know she was your girlfriend. Good choice. Give her our best wishes too, will you?'

And they ran off back to the group.

I didn't think I was going to mention this to Fatima. I'd never hear the end of it.

18

A Problem with Cognition

Exams had never worried me. When Daddy was well, he would get after me to study. All he wanted was for me to score enough marks to get into medical college. I was fairly sure that I could manage to do that. And I still felt that I should respect his expectations of me. But having given up the idea of studying medicine raised the burden off my shoulders. I had no idea what I would do afterwards nor did I feel the need to. I kept on studying anyway, depending on books I took from the library and my laptop. Most of my time I spent at home and when I ran short of time during the day I studied at night.

I was teaching Krishna when Fatima called.

'Chitra is coming tomorrow.'

'I know.'

'She told me when we talked yesterday that she had been planning to come after Sankranti. Her Pappa reminded her that her mother would have said that the day after Sankranti is an inauspicious day. So she is coming on the sixteenth.'

She waited and said, 'You don't have anything you want to say to me?'

'Tomorrow, we'll...'

'Not tomorrow. Today.'

'What am I supposed to say?' I asked.

'Will I have to tell you that too? It's my birthday!'

'Oh, happy birthday then. Happy now?'

*

When I got to the canteen the next day, they were both sitting there talking seriously over their cups of coffee.

'There. You can ask him yourself,' Fatima said.

I got myself tea and sat down near them.

Fatima said, 'Chitra is in a dilemma. To be or not to be?'

'Have done, silly Billy. Have you even read Shakespeare?'

Chitra explained what she was thinking about. Since the time her mother had fallen ill, she had not had much time to study. And after her mother died, her father had been moping at home. This meant, she had missed classes and had not studied at all. So now she was wondering whether she should sit for the exams or not.

'What do you think, Vipin?'

I had no answer.

'I don't even think anyone will take me on for tuitions. The exams are just two months away. If I don't get someone to help me, I'm going to plug. But...'

'Tell him honestly what you wanted to say. She thinks I could help her,' said Fatima. 'But only I know how I studied for the twelfth standard. Even then I would have said yes but I haven't studied much either. My father will have my guts if I don't pass.'

I drank the last of my tea and shook my head. I needed another cup.

'Give me a moment,' I said. 'I'll think of something.'

I went and got myself a cup of tea and as I drank it, I said, 'Shall I teach you?'

Both stared at me dumbfounded. Then Chitra recovered and said, 'Hello, you do remember I'm doing arts?'

'Let me try. Tell me what you're supposed to be studying. Tell me what your difficulties are. I'll need your textbooks, of course.' It was difficult for them to believe the confidence my voice was showing.

'Okay, let's even say you can do this. But don't you have exams too?'

'Don't worry. Just leave both exams to me.' I thought I should explain. 'I'm not trying for medicine any longer. I know you want to try for Fine Arts and you'll have to focus entirely on it. That's up to you...'

'That's the spirit,' said Fatima releasing the breath that she had been holding. 'What confidence!'

She raised her hand for me to give her a high five but when mine did not move from the table she clapped her hand down on the table instead.

'I admire you, Vipin,' Chitra said but the lines on her forehead were still there. 'But I have to warn you it's going to take a lot of time...'

'I told you, right? Leave that to me.'

'Well, if you insist. Now let me explain the magnitude of what you've taken on.'

She said she could manage English, Konkani and history. She needed help in geography and economics. Also a few chapters in psychology.

Fatima was waiting for this conversation to end.

'All settled? Now can we have cake?' she said and took out slices of cake and gave them to us.

As I ate, I remembered what Chitra had said about January 15 being inauspicious.

'Chitra, is it true? January 15 is considered a bad day?'

Before Chitra could say anything Fatima chipped in: 'Right, I'm a bad girl. Which may explain why I like you. Bad boys like bad girls, wouldn't you say, Chitra?'

Chitra laughed.

The days up to the examinations were completely packed. I had to work all the time. There was Krishna to be taught, Chitra's subjects to be read and understood and then explained to her and what was left of my time, I used for my studies. I focused most on Chitra's subjects. I was lucky to have the scooter licence which saved time on travel. Somewhere in between Fatima called, 'Sir, I'm having difficulties with a subject. Would you be able to help, please?'

I thought this was one of her usual jokes and snapped: 'Fatima, please leave me alone. Let the exams end. Then you can start up again.'

'No, really I'm asking.'

'You're my senior.'

'In name only. Please help me the way you work with Chitra.'

I realized that she really had a problem. So I looked up cognition on the internet and then explained it to her.

By the time we got our hall tickets I had covered all of Chitra's portion. Revising it was up to her and she took care of that. There was time for Fatima's semester exams. Krishna's SSC was going to start after the twelfth standard ended so I could leave Daddy's care to him. My first paper was English, common to arts and science. Chitra and I also had the same examination centre. When I came out at the end of the paper, Chitra was waiting for me. Her face was alight.

'Well begun,' she said.

'So half done,' I replied.

None of our next papers coincided with each other. Chitra's last paper was four days after my last examination. Since mine had gone well, I was happy. Chitra had told us she would go back to Canacona immediately after her last paper to be with her father. I thought we would not be able to meet. But when I finished my last paper and came out, she was waiting for me.

'Surprised?' she said.

'I thought you were off to Canacona.'

'Didn't go. I told Pappa I'd come after four days. But first, your news. How did they go?

'I'm just glad they're over,' I said.

'They must have gone well. Mine did.'

We arrived at my scooter.

'So when do we meet?'

'What's wrong with today?'

'Today?'

'Yeah, right now.'

I had no chance to refuse. I kick-started the bike. It occurred to me: 'Let's go to Miramar, they have some great tea there.'

'Not at all.' She punched me on the back. 'There's no coffee there. Dona Paula is where it's at.'

With a wind blowing in my face and Chitra holding on to me, I discovered for the first time how beautiful the road to Dona Paula was. We turned into a restaurant and I took a sniff of the tea and wrinkled my nose. She took a sip of her coffee and grinned.

'The coffee is great. Wanna try it?'

'No, thanks. Bad tea over good coffee for me.'

She turned serious. 'Really Vipin, you saved me a year.'

I was embarrassed. 'Don't talk rot. I took the horse to the water.'

'Sure, but this horse had no idea where the water was. You're simply brilliant. I don't think you even know your own potential. Take some time off and get to know yourself.'

Perhaps it was the heat or the exams but there were few tourists around. The hotel staff kept hovering around us and this annoyed me. 'Let's go for a walk.' We strolled to the bottom of the hill. Chitra read the signboard which offered some information about Dona Paula. 'I don't know if this is right or wrong but I don't like the story.'

'Then dismiss it as a legend.'

'Legends should inspire people. I don't approve of this glorification of suicide.'

'But if someone no longer wants to live, why force them to?'

I had never paid much attention to this. So I had no idea where this thought came from. It was as if being with Chitra uncovered hidden thoughts.

'But I do like the statue,' she said as we climbed the stairs and although there were people coming and going, we found a place to sit. There was a mountain of clouds in the sky making a vain attempt to hide the sun.

'Vipin, what do you think the clouds are saying to me?'

'That the rains are approaching?'

'I think they're asking me to put them into a painting.'

At which point, the clouds parted and the sunlight poured through. Her eyes were now being dazzled by it. I said, 'Why don't you sit with your back to the sun?' She turned around so we were facing each other. She stared at me with an intensity that left me slightly embarrassed.

'Why are you looking at me like that?' I asked.

'Do you remember once I told you that I didn't see the self-confidence of Sisyphus in you?'

How could I forget?

She went on. 'I was partly wrong. There is something in you which is very different from the rest of the world. It's a sort of challenge to me as an aspiring painter. I'd like to find out what that is. In a painting, I mean.'

She was speaking to me but really I felt as if she were talking to herself.

'The first time I saw you was in the library. That was when I knew there was something different about you. I asked the librarian and she said that you had borrowed a book by Camus. I thought I should get to know you better. When you left the library, I actually followed you. But you walked so fast and with such determination that I could not keep up. Then the rain increased and you stopped under a tree. I thought I should offer you my umbrella but immediately after that...what a drama! That van came to a halt and those boys jumped out and tried to grab Fatima. You stood there like a rock. I can still see it even today. That was when I knew that only you could have done that.'

For a while she did not say anything and remained lost in thought. Then she shook her head and said, 'Wow. Six thirty. And the sun is setting. Shall we?'

She must have seen my expression for she asked quizzically, 'What were you thinking?'

I was remembering something that happened to me in the fourth standard. The geography teacher had said, 'The Earth spins around the sun. The sun stays in place.' Later when Daddy said to me, 'You think the sun shines out of your backside,' I said to him, 'That's not true, Daddy. The sun stays in one place, it's the Earth that moves.' Daddy got really angry and said, 'Don't try your school learning here. It won't work with me.' I didn't ask him too many questions but that day I did ask Daddy, 'We say the sun rises and sets as if it is moving. Isn't that wrong?' At which he grabbed my ear and twisted it until my eyes filled with tears and said, 'Don't try all this book talk with me. What we say comes from our ancestors and it cannot be wrong. What you study in school is for you to write in your exam papers. Nothing more than that. Do you understand me? *Do you understand me?*' He did not get the expected 'yes' from me and so I got a slap across my face...How had this memory, buried for so many years, suddenly surfaced? It seemed odd so I told Chitra about it. She said, 'You know Fatima says you never smile.'

'And what do you say?'

She ignored my question and continued, 'She likes you very much. But you seem to take no notice of her. She thinks you don't like her. I told her...'

'What did you say?'

'She likes you and you don't know that.'

'And you?'

'That's for me to know and you to find out.'

When we were returning, Chitra sat even closer to me. 'Drive slowly,' she said. 'We will get more time together.'

At her uncle's house, she got off the bike and said, 'Tomorrow I'm going home. Call me when you can. And if you don't get through, leave a message with Fatima.'

That day, I got home late. Krishna had waited for me to return and although night had fallen, I decided right then that until his exams happened, he should have finished his entire revision. I made a new timetable. I took a lot of Daddy's work upon myself. And still interruptions kept happening mainly from the two of them. First Chitra called, 'Dad wants to meet you. When can you make it?'

'Me?' I was a bit startled.

'Yes, you. I told him so much about you.'

I wondered what she had said. Finally, I had to say, 'I'm really sorry I don't think it will be possible.'

'But the exams are over. Your father is in a stable condition now. So what's the problem?'

'Krishna's exams are close...' I told her about our endeavour.

'One more thing for Dad to admire. Wait a moment...'

She spoke to her father and then came back.

'He says if you can't make it here, he'll come to meet you. He's asking when he should come.'

There seemed no way out. Finally, I said I would go.

'How about Sunday? See if you can stay over.'

I told her Daddy was still bedridden and she softened at that.

'Okay then just come for lunch. I'll see you on Sunday.'

'Sunday will be difficult,' I said. 'Krishna won't be here and I can't go out when he's not around. How's Monday for you?'

'We are vegetarian on Mondays.'

'Makes no difference to me.'

'But makes a difference to us Canaconians. Come on Tuesday then.'

*

And as if that was not enough immediately afterwards, Fatima called. 'I want to meet you,' she said.

'Why?' I asked.

'Can't study.'

'What can I do about that?'

'You're supposed to help me.'

'Sorry.'

'If I fail, you'll be sorry. Wouldn't it be better if we just met?'

I wanted to say no but somehow couldn't.

'When?'

'You can't make it on Sunday.' She must have spoken to Chitra. 'And on Mondays, you are vegetarian.'

'Don't talk nonsense. I don't believe in all this.'

'I have a yen for the biryani at Sher-e-Punjab. Why don't we have something there together and you can help with my problems as we eat?'

I began to smell a rat again but she must have suspected this for her voice turned serious.

'Please, I'm not joking.'

'Never mind.'

I put down the phone. The phone rang again.

'Sorry, sorry. Look, I'm really sorry. This evening five o'clock. You'll bring your scooter, right? I'll meet you at the Mandovi Hotel corner.'

Before I could say yes or no, she had hung up. Were the two of them playing some kind of game here?

*

Fatima was standing on the street watching for me at five o'clock. Her clothes were different: jeans and t-shirt. She swung a leg over the scooter and asked, 'How do I look?'

'Like Fatima,' I said, starting the scooter.

'Don't you see anything different?' When I began to turn the scooter, she shouted in my ear. 'Where are you taking me?'

'To the library.'

'No, no. Somewhere else. Take me for a ride.'

'And what about those difficulties you had?'

'That's the difficulty. I wanted to learn how to sit pillion on your scooter.'

What was I to say to that? I drove on.

'Not Miramar, okay? Those watchdogs might be there again.'

'Are you scared of them?'

'Not a bit. But they were threatening to take off your pants, na? And I didn't want to see any of that. So let's go to Dona Paula.'

She wound her arms around me and held me tight. She said, 'Ride fast. I love speed.'

'Sorry, I will drive at my own speed.'

'That's what I'm saying. Your speed is my speed. You see, we'll get there together.'

We went back to the same restaurant and I got tea for myself and coffee for Fatima.

'I was ready to drink tea with you. Don't you remember that day in the Principal's cabin I drank tea? So why do you insist on getting me coffee?'

This seemed unanswerable so I said nothing. She answered herself.

'I know why. Because you care for me.'

Was she trying to disconcert me or was I getting disconcerted? She finished her coffee and said, 'Let's go for a walk. I enjoy walking with you.'

She took my hand in hers. When we got to the bottom of the hill, she looked up and said, 'Not up there. Let's go somewhere else. Anywhere else.'

I had begun to realize that Chitra and Fatima had no secrets from each other. But then I thought this was quite a sensible way to conduct a friendship. I didn't like concealment either. She turned us towards the jetty. There was an empty bench on which she sat down and sat me down as well. She asked, 'Do you like poetry?'

'No.'

'Music?'

'No.'

'Dance?'

'No.'

'What are you, a zombie?' she looked at me, a little hurt. 'Why do I never see you smile? Chitra says she sees a smile in your eyes. I feel jealous of her. Please, Vipin, smile just a little for me.'

'Fatima, ask me for what I have.'

'Have you no friends at all?'

If I had said 'No', it would've offended both her and Chitra.

'To tell the truth, not really. Not until I met Chitra and you.'

'Thank you, but we practically forced our friendship on you. But you could expand your circle further, you know. You never look for friends. Try it, Vipin. There are many people in the world, some likeable, some just for hi-hello.'

I looked at my watch.

'I have to go back soon, Fatima. Let's leave.'

'You won't change. You keep building walls. And I'm telling you to build bridges.'

'Bridges have to be built from both banks.'

'That's as may be. But open your eyes and take a good look around, Vipin. If you need help you have to ask. I'm here. So is Chitra. But you have to ask.'

She took my hand in hers again.

'Do you both have some kind of plan for me?' I asked.

'Maybe. Chitra's an artist. She's trying to understand your interior landscape.'

'And you?'

'I have to do something about the blasted heath I see inside you.'

'Enough already. You do know your exams are close, right?'

'I do have a test to pass but it isn't the one you're imagining. The day I see you laughing wholeheartedly, that's when I'll celebrate my success.'

It was really getting late now. I thought of Krishna waiting for me. I got up.

'Wait, I've written a poem. This is it. It's called "Heaven's Light". It's based on a Yeats poem. I have reworked it a bit.'

She dug about in her purse and pulled out a piece of paper. She gave it to me and said, 'I know you'll read it and say nothing. But that's all right. Read it anyway. That will be enough for me.'

On the way back, she sat close to me again and said, 'When I sit like this I feel as if there's something, an inspiration, a current of power passing into my body. Do you feel it too?'

Truth to tell, I was aroused. In that moment I could believe in what Fatima was saying. I didn't find nothing put on. When she got down, she said, 'Every morning when you wake up, look in the mirror and think of me. Then try and smile. When the smile seems natural and happy, call me and let me know. We will celebrate then.'

And fool that I am, I began looking in the mirror in the morning.

*

Krishna had told me that he would not come to work on Monday but he turned up on Tuesday as usual. Daddy was not doing very well. Since no one could understand what he was saying, he had given up speaking. He opened his mouth only when a spoon was brought close to it. He was clinging stubbornly to the belief that his son would become a doctor, heal him, and earn loads of money. He could no longer tell us when he needed to use the bathroom and so he wore adult diapers all the time. Krishna had been trained how to change them. Ma was getting her meals without having to move a finger. She simply told Krishna what she would like to eat and she got it.

When I left to go to Canacona, I felt guilty. But as soon as I had closed the door behind me and stepped into the clear bright, spring morning, I perked up considerably. The trees I had planted and the ones I hadn't planted were all covered in flowers. I thought of plucking some for Chitra but then almost as soon as the idea came to my mind, I gave it up. The flowers looked better on the tree. As I kickstarted the scooter, a butterfly fluttered by, the kind you see in pictures. I thought of Chitra and of Fatima.

I had warned Krishna that I might be late and left for the Kadamba Bus Stand where I parked my scooter and took a bus.

*

Pakhlo came running up, barking and wagging his tail. It was close to ten o'clock but Chitra had waited to have breakfast with me. There was another elder of their family present.

Chitra's father said, 'This is my cousin Visu, or rather Vishwanath. Chitra calls him Vishwappa.'

'You can call me Visu,' said the man cheerfully.

'Vishwappa was about to leave but Pappa told him so much about you that he felt he had to stay and meet the paragon,' said Chitra.

'First, we eat. We have made heet-ros for you,' said her father, leading the way in. Chitra added, 'I told him you get idli sambhar everywhere. But this idli made with coconut milk is part of Goa's traditional foods which people have forgotten. Have you ever eaten it?'

And where would I have? When Ma was feeling chatty, she would talk about how heet-ros was made in her home on certain auspicious days. But if she knew how to make it, she had never demonstrated her skill. So that was the first time I ever ate it. Through breakfast her father sang a paean of praise to me. My intervention when Fatima was about to be abducted, how I had helped Chitra with her studies, how I had condoled over the phone when his wife died—all that I had done and some things I had not done got glowing mentions. His cousin listened patiently but finally he could bear it no longer and burst out: 'He really seems to be a paragon of perfection.'

I said nothing because I could not detect any sarcasm under his compliment. When Chitra went in to get tea, he began his interrogation. Where did I live? Where were my roots? What did my father do? And my mother? No one had asked me so many questions before. But I kept answering as well as I could. Finally he asked my surname. When I said it was Parob, he said, 'That means you're a Prabhu, right?'

I was silent.

'Or did you say Parab?' His voice changed slightly as he mentioned the lower caste name. I said, 'I see no difference.'

Then he asked me where my mother came from.

At which point Chitra came out with the tea. She must

have heard some of this for she said, 'Why this interrogation, Vishwappa? You're not thinking of him as a potential son-in-law, are you?'

Vishwappa was slightly embarrassed by this. Chitra added, 'You haven't asked him who the family deity is?'

Vishwappa sensed Chitra's annoyance and settled down to drinking his tea in a somewhat shame-faced manner.

'Let it go, Chitra,' I said. 'I really can't tell you who the family deity is anyway.'

And that was true. I thought of the temple we had visited when my tenth standard results had come out and Daddy wanted to propitiate the gods to get me into a good college. But I couldn't remember who the deity in the temple was.

'You know, Pappa, we're such good friends and he still hasn't asked me what my surname is?'

And turning to me she challenged, 'Go on then, Vipin. Do you know? I don't think he knows that Fatima is Muslim. These things just don't matter to him.'

'I don't think Vishu believes in them either. He was just trying to locate him.' Her father tried to smooth things over. 'Have we every taught you to bother about these things?'

'No, not at all. But you know these differences exist. Vipin doesn't even know that. That's one of the reasons I like him so much.'

I was warmed by how these things could be discussed so openly between father and daughter.

Vishwappa finished his tea and got up, 'I'm off. If I get the Karwar bus, I'll get home soon.' Pappa saw him to the door and when he came back, he said to me, 'I hope you weren't offended by Vishu?'

I said no and he looked relieved. 'This is the age at which people shape themselves. I like the fact that you think independently. It's familiar in a way because our Chitra is like that. She has no faith in rituals and traditions. But I think she won't interfere with someone else's beliefs.'

'Pappa, I know where this is going. Now you're going to ask him about the existence of God,' Chitra said with a wry smile.

'And is there any harm in asking?' He turned to me and said, 'So? Believer? Atheist?'

I had never thought seriously about this.

'I don't know,' I said.

'Swami Vivekananda says that those who don't believe in God do not believe in themselves,' said Pappa, looking at me searchingly.

'I have complete faith in myself. And doesn't Swami Vivekananda say, "If a man has complete faith in himself, he is a believer"? I believe Vivekananda was against hypocrisy and in that we think alike.'

'See Pappa, you've been cherry-picking your Vivekananda.'

'When someone of your generation thinks about these things seriously, regardless of what they think, it pleases me,' he said and seemed to mean it too.

We rose and came outside.

'Why don't you show him around our place?' he suggested.

Chitra seemed to be waiting for this and came out into the sun. The house was large; and so were the grounds around it.

'If you're ready for a walk, we can go down to the sea?' Chitra asked and without waiting for an answer, she set off at a brisk pace.

There seemed no need to talk. We startled a sow and her piglets who scattered. Cows lowed somewhere.

'Who does the housework when you're not around?' I asked.

'We have a family that looks after things—the garden, the cattle, the grounds and the house. When Mamma was well, she would cook. Pappa likes to cook too. But now we have a woman who comes in to do that. Pappa will get on okay without me, I think. But now that Mamma isn't here, I worry a little about him.'

What would Daddy have done if Ma had died? Would I have been worried about how he would manage? Daddy had never moved so much as a finger when it came to cooking and cleaning. I would have had to do all of it. It was a good thing I had listened to Martin Sir's advice. Daddy would have never spent on himself even though he had the money.

'May I ask you a question?' Chitra asked, 'Are you an atheist or an agnostic?'

I shrugged. 'What about you?'

'I have no time for organized religion. But I do believe that the one who initiated everything is around here some place.'

'If he invented it all, shouldn't he be outside it?'

'Why do you say that?'

'If you paint a picture, you're outside it, right?'

Chitra grinned. 'How can you say that? If you look at a painting from the eyes of a painter, you'll see the artist in it.'

I thought then of a Manoharrai Sardessai poem I had read a while ago.

Tu joglaat, tu vaaadlaat.
Tooch ujyaant jaltaa
Saglyaan bheetar aasoon tu
Saglyaan baheer urta.

You're in the lightning and the storm.
You burn in the fire.
Even as you are within it all,
You remain outside it too.

Now the roar of the sea came to our ears. Chitra seemed lost in thought.Then she said: 'You know, when we were young, our relations would come to visit us in May for their annual sea baths. Pappa was a bit short on relatives but he had a sister by acknowledgment. She would come for a sea bath every year. She would bring her children with her. We would all come down to the sea in the morning. The women would sit in the sea, letting the water lap around their legs all morning. Then they would lie down in the shacks and rest. We kids would romp about in the sand. Our lunch would come down to us. And then we'd collapse for a siesta. In the evening, the women would go back down into the water and we'd be back on the sand. Since my aunt had some pain in the joints, she would sit at the edge of the sea, her legs splayed out and we would slap wet sand down over her legs, burying them nicely. We'd build sand-castles and decorate them with shells and conches. My aunt would show me how to make collages with my treasures. I think that's where my art journey began.'

Chitra's face was soft with nostalgia.

'You know, looking at you brings back the memory of a butterfly I saw this morning.'

'Really? Why?'

'Maybe its colour...'

'Or its carefree attitude?'

She was right as always.

Then she spoke about how her father had encouraged

her to think for herself, how he had given her the love of reading and how her mother had introduced her to the magic of form and colour.

The sun was now overhead. We dabbled our toes in the warm water and then turned to go back.

'You see how I take advantage of your silences? It's your turn to talk now. Say something about yourself.'

What could I tell her? Far from building sand-castles by the sea, I had not even played with children outside my own home. Could I tell her the story of how I won some marbles and how Daddy had confiscated them? My father's rage when I had refused the judges' special prize when I had won the race? Or his contorted face when he saw that Bible stories book the priest had given me? The tea that Ma had made for Daddy at 2 a.m.?

What did I have to tell that had not left me plagued by questions?

'But then I suppose a garrulous lass like me gets a chance to talk with someone as laconic as you,' she said and began to laugh. For some reason this reminded her of Fatima. 'Fatima should have been here. What fun we would have had!' I would no doubt have been the butt of their jokes. But suddenly I was reminded of the paper she had handed me. I pulled it out of my pocket. 'She wrote a poem...'

Had I the heaven's embroidered cloths
Dawn-ray light and mothwing soft.
I should wrap those cloths around you.
And keep you warm when the winds blow cold.
But how can I make so bold
As to hope that you might let me fold
You and my own broken soul
Into all that a mothwing dawn-ray might hold?

Chitra read it and sighed and turned to me.

'When did she give this to you? Last evening? She read it to me yesterday.'

'You know about it then?'

'Yes. It's based on that Yeats poem. She likes that sort of reworking. Such a madcap!' she said fondly.

*

By the time we got back to the house, the heet-ros were a pleasant memory. Chitra's Pappa went off to organize lunch and Chitra took me to her room to show me her paintings. I did not understand them but it seemed like there was a maturity to them. I had the feeling that she would make her mark one day.

'So what did he say?' her father asked when he came into the room.

'I haven't shown him that one. I've left that for the last,' she said and hoisted a new canvas up for me to see.

I could not tell how I knew that this was a portrait of me but I did and it did seem as if my eyes had laughter hidden in them. Perhaps I was looking with an artist's eyes—with Chitra's eyes.

*

I could not remember anyone having cooked specially for me, not even Ma. I had never seen such a variety of dishes on a single banana leaf. Of course, I had been to Flavia's wedding feast but that was a buffet, lots of the food the general public were supposed to like. How could it compare?

Here was a wild boar xacuti and wade to go with it. I had eaten wade at my uncle's wedding but I hadn't liked them much; these went extraordinarily well with the spicy xacuti. There was unpolished rice with a hooman of backwater fish. And then, Chitra set down a fried shevta, the length of a man's span, before me. It was delicious fish.

'In Canacona, we call it the gajni shevta,' her father told me. This was followed by a saasav. I had often eaten this since Ma liked it and cooked it too. But I had not eaten it cooked so well. I ate until I was stuffed. At home, no one encouraged you to eat more over your protests. And when one went to a restaurant, one was served and one ate. It did not occur to me that here one would have one's plate refilled until one covered it protectively with one's hands and refused all further food. So how could they guess how stuffed I was? After I had finished, I made ready to leave when Chitra's father said that no one left without having a farewell cup of tea.

As we were sipping our tea, he said, 'Chitra's mother has left me to worry about her.'

'Why would you worry?' I asked.

'How could I not? I'm ready to pay for her education, but a daughter is always a cause for concern, no?'

I could see what he meant but Chitra was having none of it. She said clearly: 'You do want to see me happy, don't you Pappa? Then please don't start planning any marriages for me. I want to live as an artist and for that I must have my independence. You remember Mamma promised me that, right?'

When Chitra went inside with her empty cup, her father sighed and said, 'I really would like her to find a suitable someone and settle down but she's adamant about these things.'

I left wondering why her father had thought it right to bring this up in front of me.

*

The next morning, I did glance in the mirror, and following Fatima's suggestion, I tried to smile but it seemed forced. Just as I was beginning to wonder how come she hadn't called, the phone rang.

'I knew it. You were waiting for me to call.'

I found that I did not like it when someone guessed my state of mind. 'Right.'

'Thank you. I like the idea of you pining away by the phone,' she said with a giggle bubbling through her voice.

'Nothing of the kind. You're just green that I went to see Chitra yesterday.'

'Ah, but I heard all about it. I hear everything. I called to say that since you asked me when we were going to meet again, I thought we might set a date.'

'When did I say that?'

'All of twice. Once when you offered to drop me home. And the other time when you said it was getting late, let's go, we can meet again. Have you forgotten so soon?'

'Look Fatima, don't put words in my mouth. And now you should concentrate on your exams, okay?'

'Wait, wait, wait,' she pleaded. 'There are fifteen days to the exam. We can meet in between…'

'No chance. Exams first.'

'Okay boss. As you say. But afterwards don't go back on your word.'

'What word?' I asked, annoyed.

'Your promise. That we'll meet after the exams.'

'When did I promise that?'

'My Lord, you said and I quote, "'Exams first." That implies a "next" and so I shall wait.'

So she liked to tease. But why did I let her tease me?

*

I had read about the Twelfth Standard Syndrome. The pressure to achieve outstanding marks at this level led to many psychological and behavioural changes in young people. Madan had taken his life because of it. I didn't think I was about to fall prey but I did notice some changes in my behaviour too. It seemed as if everything was changing rapidly. Why did I now feel as if I had known nothing until the end of the eleventh standard? It seemed as if my childhood had ended. I had always been given all the necessities of life without even having to ask for them. My food, my clothes, my footwear, were all produced without me having to ask. But then it was also true that I could not ask for anything. Once I had asked for a pair of boots and my father decided to take that literally. To give someone 'boot' was also to heat an iron rod and burn an infection out of someone. That was what Daddy did when I asked for boots. I had never forgotten that lesson. I did not cry and Ma thought that it had not hurt me. She told me about the time her mother had given her the same treatment. Once Ma had made ghaavan. When I ate one and asked for another, I got a crack on my knuckles with the hot spatula. Like Oliver Twist, I learned not to ask for more.

When my grandfather died, Ma had taken me to their home in Mapusa. There one day, one of her brothers had asked her: 'How come your house doesn't feel like a home?' So I asked Ma later, 'What's the difference between a house and a home?' She said, 'A home is where husband and wife care for each other.' After that wherever I went I tried to decide whether I was visiting a house or a home.

Ravi's home, for instance, a hut in the fields, in danger of being demolished. I wondered if that could happen to our home but Ma assured me that we were in no danger of that happening and my heartbeat returned to normal.

For I did feel safe in that house. Nothing ever happened there. No festivals disrupted our lives. No guests came, no friends visited, no special dishes were cooked. All that was asked of me was that I should never do anything I liked. What Daddy bought was to be eaten, what Daddy said was to be done. Since the doors and windows were closed, the outside did not intrude upon us. But there were times when the village drunkard Samvlo would lurch from one side of the road to the other as he walked home. By the time he had crossed from one side to the other, he had spat out a series of inventive expletives. Ma seemed unaffected; she would listen attentively to the abuse. When I asked her who he was abusing, she said he was just shouting empty curses. This reassured me that we were not on the receiving end of these insults. I let them flow past me. The first dramatic shift in my life had been when I went to school. I had never experienced such an environment of freedom. I remembered the one time Daddy had sat me up on the back of his bike and we had gone to the market together.

The rush of cool air across my face made me feel good but I know this was not something he had done for me; it was only because he wanted to go. When I went to school, the openness of the compound brought back that excitement. But there I found I was not to be left alone. Although the other students had kept their distance because I had been put into school late and was strapping even as a child, they began to draw close. One of them, thinking that I was a defenceless child, stabbed me with a pencil. When I complained to Daddy, he did not sympathise. 'Why tell me?' he demanded. 'Don't you have hands of your own?' The next day I went up to the boy and hit him solidly in the stomach. After that, the other students began to keep away from me. Once the teacher described me as a good student. When I came home and told my mother this, she said, 'We sent you to school to be a good student.'

When I stood first in the class and came home and told my father, he took hold of my ear and twisted it, saying, 'School stuff stays in school, you hear me? Let me hear one peep about you from your teachers and you'll see what I'm made of.' I wondered then what he was made of and how he planned to show it to me but nothing like that ever happened again as I told him nothing about school. I was content with my home, my school and myself. And so it seemed as if without any effort on my part, things happened, life went on and I was whirled along in the current. The first change was brought about by Martin Sir. But I did not allow that to interfere with the way my home was run.

It was only after my tenth standard results came out that Daddy changed. I had accepted the superficial changes that had happened. Our school uniform became long trousers in the ninth standard. In the tenth standard, I was given an allowance: every Monday a hundred rupees. Every Sunday I had to account for that sum. None of these cosmetic changes had any effect on my interior landscape.

Even today that house is my comfort zone. Small changes can make me uncomfortable. Staying within it keeps me happy. Indications came from the outside of change.

Often these came from books. I found the worlds in those books strange, but I knew that they were different. I had no relationship to them. When I visited the worlds of Franz Kafka or Albert Camus or Kazuo Ishiguro, I accepted them. But I saw them as different and I kept their worlds hermetically sealed inside myself. When I watched the news of a riot or a football match or even scenes from a film, I felt like an outsider. But over the last few months, things had happened that left me confused. I could no longer maintain my by-stander status; things were beginning to affect me internally.

Daddy's stroke, my academic success, meeting Chitra and Fatima, Namshikar's sarcastic jibes, helping Krishna with his studies, hearing Ma's savage verbal attacks on Daddy, the scooter I had appropriated...I had not willed any of this to happen nor had I any hand in it. It was as if Ma's saying, 'Que Sera Sera' was right. I had accepted things as they came, going with the flow. But now after this visit to Chitra's home, I began to feel that I could no longer sit on the fence. The things that were happening began to touch me deeply.

Why had I felt the need to read up on economics just so that I might be able to help Chitra? I could contextualise my desire to help Krishna. It was my need for his help and the condition he had set down for taking on the work. I had had little choice in the matter. Even the laptop had been given to me, it was not as if I had wanted one, I had got it without having to ask.

And when Fatima had told Chitra we went to a matinee show together, why had I been so frazzled? Why did I have to insist on exposing what was really a harmless lie, a little fib? When I had heard of Madan's death, I had not gone to his funeral, nor had I paid a condolence visit. So why did I feel guilty that I had not gone to Chitra's mother's last rites?

What was this attraction to Chitra? And Fatima? She seemed sweet but she was a bit of a hanger-on too. Why did I take her affectionate teasing? Why had I enjoyed the way she had held me tight on the back of my scooter? It was not as if I were averse to any of this. It was as if I could see objectively that my passivity was dangerous. All this unsettled me and it was only when I drank my first draught of a good strong cup of tea that I felt myself again.

*

Krishna's first exam. I called his father. He was setting out for the centre with his son. He gave his son the phone. I told Krishna not to take any books with him to the centre. If he had taken any, he was to send them back with his father. I told him that he should take two pens. After finishing his writing, he should read his papers again to see if there were any mistakes he wanted to correct.

I made tea and took some to Ma. As I began to sip my own, I heard Daddy moaning. I thought it was his usual sounds but then I heard a rumbling sound that sounded like farting. I went to see what might be the matter and found that his diaper had overflowed with the shit and piss of the night. As soon as I cleaned him up, another burst of shit. Diarrhoea then? And right now?

It never rains but it pours, and now the shit was pouring out of Daddy. I put down my tea and set about cleaning him up. At least, he had an oil cloth under him. By the time this was done, the tea had gone cold. I warmed it up again but as I raised the cup to my lips, the odours seemed to be clinging to my fingers still. I washed my hands again and once again, the tea had cooled. Anyway, I no longer felt the need for any.

I phoned Dr Costabir. He must have been examining a patient. Since he was not answering, I got the scooter out, stopped for a quick tea at Vasudev's and then brought Dr Costabir back on my bike. He examined Daddy and said it might be wise to have him admitted.

The hospital was now Daddy's second home. I also

found the hospital an oddly peaceful place. When I took Dr Costabir back to his dispensary, he said: 'Babu, I don't think he'll make it. Maybe four or five days.'

Daddy managed eight. On the ninth morning, Daddy died. Even as the doctor drew the sheet over his head, Krishna called: 'Babu, it's the last paper. Social sciences. All the kids are saying there's going to be a question on the Boston Tea Party. Can you run over it with me?'

Even as I dealt with the paperwork and the bills, I delivered a potted lecture on 'No taxation without representation' and afterwards, went to the canteen and drank a double chai.

*

My elder uncle brought a priest with him. When he began to explain the pandit's rates and tariffs, I could see that he had a vested interest: he was to get a commission. I told the priest clearly, 'I have no intention of guaranteeing my father a place in heaven. If my uncle wants, he can organize ceremonies for the thirteenth day, the month-end ceremonies and whatever else he is willing to pay for. I am not going to do any of this.' Uncle Senior was incensed. 'Did you ask what your mother wants?' I asked her in front of him and she told her brother:

'Babu is the man of the house now. He decides.'

When I pushed a thousand rupees into the priest's disappointed hands and sent him off, there were only five of us, including me, standing around the pyre. Vasudev, who never left his till unattended, had handed over charge to his staff in order to attend. Hoping perhaps for a drink, Samvlo hovered around.

Appa turned up to carry the body, having heard the news over the bush telegraph. 'Come on, get it over with,' my uncle kept saying but he stayed till the skull cracked. As he left, he said: 'You are an adult now, Babu. You have to look after your mother.' Having acquitted himself of all responsibility, he left. Appa took Vasudev pillion and he left too. Samvlo looked at me hopefully, scratching his head. I gave him a fifty-rupee note and sent him on his way. I waited in the heat for a pilot. With both hands on the motorcycle driver's shoulders, I tried to cool off as we went home. When I got in, Ma asked: 'Didn't you bring any food?' I turned to find Appa at the door with two tiffin carriers in his hands.

'Vasudev sent this,' he said.

'I've had a bath,' Ma said. 'Go and clean up.'

I was hot and sticky, my hair full of the smoke and ash from the pyre. The water out of the taps was cold and I scrubbed myself down thoroughly. I found as I dried myself that what I wanted most was a cup of tea. But it was lunch time. When I went into the kitchen, I found that Ma had made things easier. I ate what she had left and set the kettle on.

*

When I had called Ma from the hospital, she had said: 'Free at last.' Then she added, 'All of us.' I had no idea why she felt that way. But in one way she was right. Had Daddy begun to recover, I would have had to run about for medicines and rehab; his death brought an end to all that.

No one seemed to notice Daddy's passing. No one came to visit or condole. Only Krishna showed up after his last paper. Uncle Senior had said at the cremation grounds: 'We should put a notice in the papers.' I knew what he wanted was the pleasure of reading his name in the newspapers.

'Go ahead,' I said.

'It'll cost a couple of thousands,' he said.

I said nothing. If he were willing to spend that kind of money, why should I refuse?

'Can I have the money?' he asked finally.

I said: 'I don't want to see my name in the papers. And I don't think there'll be many people complaining that they were not informed about his death.'

Of the uncles, the younger one, the lawyer, had a court date. The elder was unemployed. He came. His son, Kalpesh, was not present, on the grounds that his father was still alive. The younger aunt was menstruating and could not come. This meant that my elder aunt had to do all the housework so she could not come either. That was about all the relatives I knew of. Daddy's side was a line of single children. For three generations, there had been only one son in the family. So I had no paternal relatives at all. Daddy seemed to have no friends and he had always been hostile with our neighbours. But when his dead body came home, Pascoal did come to condole with us.

Until Krishna came over in the evening, no one in the house had so much as shed a tear. But Krishna wept. 'Were you crying over Daddy?' I asked. He shook his head. It seemed he was thinking about my loss. Then he went inside to meet Ma. He did not weep with her.

When he went into the kitchen to start on the dinner, I stopped him and told him to get us something from the restaurant.

It was only when he left that I realized I had forgotten to ask him how his papers had gone.

*

When I woke the next morning, my room was in darkness. I wanted to stay like that, to leave the doors and windows closed and float in the darkness. There was nothing I had to do for Daddy. Ma would manage on last night's leftovers. I did not expect any further visits. There was no reason to get up. The urge to lie still and simply experience this darkness was seductive. Yesterday had been an inflection point but that did not mean I had to jump right out of bed this morning. Then the phone rang. I reached out and picked it up.

'What is wrong with you? How I waited for your call! You do remember my exams start tomorrow?'

I had only thought to tell my uncles about my father's death. Now I wondered: should I have informed Chitra and Fatima as well? But what could they have done? Come to the cremation? Added some wood to the pyre?

'What kind of friend are you? I have to come and ask you for wishes?'

My silence spoke to Fatima.

'What happened, Vipin?'

'Nothing.'

'No. Something has happened. Tell me, Vipin.'

'Daddy died.'

The call ended there. Had I ended it? Had she?

The doorbell rang. Ma would not bestir herself, expecting me to get it so I went and found Krishna there.

He should be on holiday.

'What are you doing here?'

'Ma said I should come to work from today.'

And I got a cup of good strong tea a la Krishna.

'How did the exams go?'

'I should pass, I think,' he said with a big grin. He collected my empty cup and said: 'Should we leave the door open today? People might visit...'

'Never mind. No one's likely to come.'

But there I was wrong. Martin Sir came to condole. He hugged me briefly and sat for a while. Krishna brought him a cup of tea. He took it but raised his eyebrows.

'I thought it was your custom not to serve anything to those who come to condole?'

'Is it? I had no idea. But since I drink tea, I offer it too.'

He finished his tea and handed me the book he was carrying. *The Year of Magical Thinking* by Joan Didion.

'This is one of the finest books about grieving that I have read,' he said.

I wanted to ask: 'Sir, do you think I am grieving?' Perhaps he guessed what I was thinking, for he said, 'I thought you might want to know how other people handle loss. Try to relate to it.'

The lawyer uncle found time to visit. He patted my back briskly and having done his bit to help me deal with the grief at losing a father, he proceeded briskly to Ma's room. When Daddy was alive, he had always had a frightened look. Today he was sitting there as if he were waiting for a client. Krishna did not serve him tea.

'You should have his photo in a frame on your table,' he said for want of something meaningful to say.

'I would if we had one in the house,' Ma said.

'Did he have insurance?' he asked as if the thought had just struck him.

'No idea,' I said.

But Ma's eyes lit up.

'Oh yes, he must have invested in some insurance.'

'Do you have the policy papers somewhere safe?' the lawyer asked.

'Babu, would you go and look? They should be in the drawer in his cupboard.'

I wasn't particularly interested. But the lawyer was. 'Come on, let's have a look.'

I had never touched that drawer. We looked but found no policies but we did find Daddy's engagement ring. My uncle could barely conceal his curiosity and greed with a show of impersonal interest. As I was trying to close the cupboard, he said: 'Just a minute, just a minute. What's that bundle wrapped up there?' It looked to me like old documents, birth certificates and the like but I pulled it out. When we opened it, it was bundles of five-hundred-rupee notes.

My uncle's eyes bulged.

'Take them all out. Let's count. Let's find out how much it is.'

'Never mind. What good will counting do?' I tied up the bundle again and put it back.

'You'll need it now. You might have to pay off...'

'Do you have to pay off someone Daddy owes money?'

'No, but...' He took a deep breath. 'Never mind now. Let it go. Close the door properly.' Then he put a hand on my shoulder and murmured confidentially in my ear. 'That's the money. I know all about this. This was what he got, you know, over and above. His salary wasn't much either. Well, what's a man to do?'

Of course, he had to go and tell Ma all about this. She had been lying down but shot up to sit upright in bed.

I went to my room and read the book Martin Sir had loaned me.

*

Did anyone at all miss Daddy? Yet two neighbours, one male and one female, came to condole. Two of my classmates,

Ignatius and Raymond, came home. Then one afternoon, around twelve thirty, an Innova stopped in front of the house. A man in starched white clothes and dark glasses with an enormous pot belly preceding him descended from it and a fifty-year-old bald man in a brown safari suit followed. This man who had a diary under his arm and a demeanour that declared him to be a secretary said, 'This is the house.'

'Are you the son?' the man asked. Had he come to recover some money Daddy had borrowed? When I nodded, he put out his hand. 'Terrible, terrible. A fine man.'

I was silent. This was the first time I had heard my father so described.

'Don't you recognize me?' he asked, seeming surprised.

'Who are you?' I asked and the question seemed to really surprise him.

'Don't you know?' The secretary could not believe it. 'He's our MLA.'

Did he think I should prostrate myself? At which point Pascoal came huffing and puffing. It had taken him a little while to put on a new shirt after he saw the MLA's car.

'Come in, sir. Please sit down,' Pascoal said, pulling up a chair and doing the honours as if it were his home. 'Sir, I'm Pascoal. I live in the house next door.'

'How many people here?' asked the MLA. The secretary looked in his diary and said: 'There were three. Two now.' He was obviously counting votes.

'Sir, can I get you something to drink?' Pasocal was all but kneeling in deference.

'No,' he said, ignoring Pascoal and focusing on me. 'Now listen, young man, you're not to worry about a thing. Anything you want, you come straight to me, hear? Are you in service?'

'Studying, sir, he's studying,' said Pascoal.

'When you have finished, come and meet me. We'll find you a job,' he said.'Our condolences to your dear mother. And remember next year, we go to the polls again. All good men to the aid of the party, haan? I need you to help me.'

He made an almost imperceptible gesture to the secretary. The secretary drew two five-hundred rupee notes out of his pocket and proffered them. The MLA turned ostentatiously away to leave. Seeing my cold reception of this, the secretary put the money back in his pocket and trotted out after the hon'ble representative.

'Arre Babu, why didn't you take it? That Baldy is now going to take it himself.'

Lamenting my folly, Pascoal left too.

Krishna was getting to know me well. He brought me tea before I even asked.

*

When I finished the book, I was deeply appreciative of Joan Didion's honesty and the beauty of her writing but nowhere had I felt any resonance with my own state.

In the morning, Ma said: 'It's the third day. No one will come today.' I needed some air so I went for a walk. I got to Vasudev's and thought to pay for the food he had sent but he said that Appa had already paid. I ordered four batata vadas, Ma's favourite, but he clicked his tongue. The vadas had onion, forbidden to us during this period. I thought I'd order some fish but remembered in time that it was also forbidden. After I got to the school, I turned back. At home, Ma was in a tizzy. 'Have you put that money away safely?'

I made no reply and she said, sotto voce: 'He's been near that cupboard twice already. Go see if it's all there.'

I hated her casting doubt on Krishna like that. 'No harm will have come to it,' I said briskly. I turned away but she stopped me, saying in a worried voice: 'Why don't you lock it up well and bring the keys to me?'

If I had offered to bring the bundle and tuck it under her pillow, she would have been delighted.

*

After lunch, I browsed the Net. Was grief different for the North American and the Nigerian? It seemed not. Only the cultural expression was different. And what about us? I thought of Shenoy Goembab's story. 'Mhaji Ba Khainy Geli?' (Where did my Mother Go?) Our teacher had told us how she had wept after reading the story of the little boy wandering disconsolately to the altar to find his mother. I read it now to see its effect on me. I found that the story made me angry. Perhaps Babulya's mother had been a different kind of woman, loving, sensitive, whatever.

But the ploy of telling the child that his mother has gone to God and having the boy follow her there made me angry. I felt manipulated. I downloaded several books on my laptop. Then I thought of a short story I had once read: 'Practice' by Chiara Barzini, an American writer. I felt some connection there. I read it again.

> With her husband at death's door, a wife awaits her freedom. She takes out all the items he would use regularly his wig, his watch, his cigarette case, his hat, his trousers—and scatters them across the floor. Then she gets dressed and goes for a long walk. When she returns, she acts surprised by the things she finds on the floor. She sorts them out. This wig:

how can he go out without it? His watch: how will he keep track of the time? His hat: he goes nowhere without it.

She is content now. Her rehearsal is complete. Then she remembers her grandmother's death when she was a girl. Other deaths followed. And now her husband. She must be ready for that. She has rehearsed. The sorrow that must follow will be easier to handle.

I found the story of a woman preparing for her husband's death as fascinating as when I had first read it.

And I dreamt that I too were preparing for my own death.

*

Since I had not expected any visitors, I had left the door closed. Krishna opened it when Chitra and Fatima arrived. When we were in the Principal's cabin, I had wondered how Fatima had found out my name. Today I wondered how they had found out my address.

Since no one seemed to know what to say, we sat for a while in silence. Then Chitra pulled her chair forward and asked, 'Was it painful?'

'For whom?' I asked without thinking and then realized that she probably meant Daddy.

'Daddy couldn't tell us what he was going through. At home, he may have been in pain. But in the hospital, they had him on painkillers. There must not have been too much pain.'

'I was shocked when you told me. I wanted to come immediately but how could I come alone? Chitra was in Canacona. We are both very sorry for you.'

She wanted to sound like she was condoling but couldn't pull it off. Her gaze fell on the Didion book. I said, 'Martin Sir lent it to me. To understand the process of grieving, I suppose...'

'Any good?' Chitra asked.

'She's on the side of William Faulkner. "Between grief and nothing, I will take grief." You have to live through it.'

'And what would you choose?'

'Nothing.'

Then something reminded me. 'Fatima, don't your exams start today?'

'Yes. My first paper was this morning. I answered it and came here.'

'What was the need for all this?'

'It was my duty...' she said, her voice demonstrating that she took her duty seriously, a duty arising out of her feeling for me.

'Where's Ma?' Chitra asked, changing the subject. She wanted to condole. I could only hope Ma would not raise some point of order such as, 'Don't you know you're not supposed to come on the third day?'

I took them to see Ma and went into the kitchen. Krishna was making tea. I told him to make coffee but of course there was no coffee powder in the house. I sent him off for some and went back to Ma's room where interrogations were in progress. She must have already discovered Chitra's name. When she heard Fatima's name, she said: 'Christian?'

They were both uncomfortable. Chitra said: 'She's Vipin's friend.'

'Oh!' Ma was surprised. 'I had no idea that Vipin had any friends.' It was nothing less than the truth.

'We are both his friends,' Chitra said.

'Let's sit outside,' I said.

But before we could get to the living room, Chitra asked: 'Which is your room?'

I pointed it out but she said she wanted to see it.

'So dark?'

'I like the darkness,' I said and put on a light.

'I like dispelling the darkness with light, just as you did.'

In the living room, Krishna had served two cups of coffee and tea for me.

'It must have been awful to see a family member die. I feel really sorry for you.' Fatima said with a shiver. I did not want hurt her so I made no reply.

'But you're looking at the whole thing objectively,' Chitra said.

'I like that. That's the spirit. After all, Vivekananda says, "Death is but a change of garment."'

'Easy to say. Remember how terrible you felt when your Mamma died?' Fatima said.

'Yes, it was awful. But I knew I would overcome that sorrow. What I was worried about was Pappa. He had to manage on his own. But he has adjusted. Which reminds me, Vipin, Pappa sends his condolences too.'

There was nothing left to say. They got up and shook my hand. Fatima pressed my hand, just a little too tightly.

*

'It was the third day so we didn't come yesterday,' said Uncle Senior as he made an entrance with Kalpesh in tow. Uncle Senior went and sat with Ma. That left me with Kalpesh. I had nothing to say to him but he didn't notice for he had a lot to say to me.

He told me had struck up a fine friendship with a

Mumbai-Goa bus driver. He had gone to Mumbai twice on that bus. He said this with the air of someone announcing that he had scored two goals in the World Cup. And a taxi driver had taught him how to drive a car. Although his uncle had a car, the lawyer would not let him touch it. But as soon as the money was arranged, his father was going to get him a car.

Meanwhile he told me of two young men out of Mumbai, who had brought a bar girl to Goa for some fun. They loved the new Palm Farm at Valpoi. There they had their first taste of uraco.

They liked it so much that they got themselves two bottles and went back to the resort. They settled down with the bottles and sent the bargirl off with Kalpesh.

When he began to describe what happened next, salivating at the lubricious memories, I got up and went to ask Krishna to make tea.

'Let me tell you, Babu, that if you have money, you can have all the fun you want. But you must have money,' he said. He drank his tea and putting down the cup, he came to the point. 'Did you count the money? How much is it?' My elder uncle must have heard this for he stormed into the room and snarled at his son, 'Didn't I tell you not to bring that up? Dimwit!'

Then he asked me to accompany him to Ma's room. 'Now, Babu, listen to what I'm going to say and listen well. The pundit said that your father passed away at an inauspicious hour. We need to do some rituals for that.'

'What if we don't?'

'That's what I want to tell you. Your life will be in danger.'

'I'm willing to take that risk. I want no rituals.'

But there was another subject he wanted to broach: the money in the cupboard.

'He must have meant that money for his wife. You're still very young. You can ask your mother for your expenses. Let her have the money.'

'Uncle, two days ago you were telling me that I was a grown man. Today you're telling me I'm too young to handle money. You should make up your mind first.'

I went out and found Kalpesh waiting to tell me all the many things that such money would buy.

*

Just when I thought no one else could possibly be expected, Amrut and Sarvesh turned up. The poor fellows had no idea what to say. They pumped my hand and sat down, visibly uncomfortable. Since I could see that the lengthening silence was making them even more uncomfortable, I volunteered some information.

'It was a paralysis attack. He was in the hospital. He died four days ago.'

'Sorry for your loss,' Sarvesh muttered. If Namshikar were to die, would Sarvesh grieve?

'But at least, it happened after the exams,' Amrut said.

Would it have mattered if Daddy had died during the exams?

'How did your exams go? Just asking because you didn't attend classes.'

'Pretty good. You guys?'

'Not bad. I don't want to do medicine. No engineering for me either. But I should pass,' said Amrut.

'I did okay,' said Sarvesh. 'Daddy says I should get 80 per cent. It's the GCET he really cares about. Everything depends on that.'

He actually wanted to know whether I was preparing for the engineering examinations.

I put him out of his misery, 'Best of luck, Sarvesh. I'm not sitting for the entrance.'

'Oh bugger,' said Sarvesh. 'I was hoping you would be. Then you could have helped me with all the stuff I can't get.'

This came from the heart, I could tell.

And when they left, there were no further condolence callers.

*

Daddy was free. And as Ma had rightly pointed out, his death had freed her too. But she had not been freed from the idea that one might be able to calm a troubled soul with an appropriate ritual. I did not have the heart to refuse and taking my uncle's advice, we had the twelfth day ritual performed at the holy teerth of Harwale, thus making the priest richer by seven thousand rupees and providing my father's soul with spiritual peace.

19

Saramago and Sorpotel

'An idle mind is the devil's workshop', the saying goes. I did not have an idle mind. Even when I was sitting in my room, in the dark, with the doors and windows closed, my mind was active. But when there was nothing to do, I began to get restless. Then I would go out into the garden or go to the library or take a long walk...the rest of the time I spent on my laptop or reading books. Then there were e-books and e-magazines too.

As long as Daddy was alive, I did not have to buy anything. I was not allowed to ask for anything either. He would bring things home and I would receive them. Now I was the Giver and the Recipient as well. I got myself a new model mobile phone. I ordered an iPad on Amazon. I bought the books I wanted to read and stored them on the iPad. Now I was the buyer and I was the reader as well. But every so often I felt my hands tremble at my own daring.

One day, I walked by the Goa University near Bambolim and found myself passing Krishna's father's repair stand. I had nothing better to do so I stopped to watch him work. His dexterity, as he dismantled and repaired a scooter, astonished me. With no formal technical education, he managed the job neatly and precisely.

On my way home, I bought the tools I would need to service my scooter: spanners, screwdrivers, grease and machine oil.

The next day, I sat down and began to open up the scooter. I dismantled the engine completely, separating it into individual parts. Krishna rushed to help but I told him to deal with the housework. I operated by instinct.

Then it was time for lunch so I stopped to eat. But when I had finished, I went back to work. Krishna brought me the oil. I made him set it down and sent him off again. I changed the oil myself.

Just as I was greasing up the back wheel, the phone rang. My hands were smeared with grease so I ignored it. But Krishna came and picked it up and said, 'It's some Chitra, sir.'

I could not tell him to answer it nor could I ignore it. He understood my dilemma and held the phone to my ear.

'Congrats, Vipin!' Chitra's voice was vibrant with excitement. And then I remembered that the results were expected that day.

'Are they out?'

'You haven't checked? I did! You crossed ninety.'

I was silent. What was there to say? Oh, perhaps 'Thank you' might have been appropriate.

'Why so silent? You ought to be congratulating me too. Guess what I got?'

'Tell me.'

'And to think I didn't even want to sit for the exams. If it hadn't been for you…'

'What did you score?'

'Seventy-seven. I didn't even believe it.'

Since she had given me notice that she expected to be congratulated, I did so.

'I'm coming to Panjim tomorrow. Let's catch up.'

Krishna switched off the phone. It promptly rang again.

'It's Fatima. Bring it here.'

He glanced at the phone and saw that I had guessed right. He brought it to my ear.

'Thank you, Fatima,' I said, anticipating her.

'Hey, let me congratulate you first.'

'Consider it said.'

'And there you were looking downcast at how badly your papers went. Chhupa rustam!'

'Are you done? May I hang up?'

'No. Hold on. One moment. We must meet now. Not over the phone. I want to shake your hand.'

'Both my hands are greasy. I'm repairing the scooter.'

'What's a little grease between friends? At least I get to hold your hand.'

'That will not be possible today. Sorry.'

And all the while I was aware of Krishna's presence, holding the phone.

'Not today? Okay, but tomorrow for sure. I'll call in the morning. And I'll tell Chitra.'

Krishna had heard the results. He was as delighted as if the marks were his. He rushed in to tell Ma. By the time I was done with scooter and had scrubbed the grease off, Ma was in the kitchen, holding the sugar jar in her hands. 'Babu, you got good marks. Come, sweeten your mouth.'

I took a pinch of sugar. Ma walloped a handful.

When I logged in, I discovered that I had scored ninety-three per cent. There weren't many people I wanted to tell. Martin Sir had always been at the top of the list. But now my desire to meet Chitra was so strong, I suspected he had slipped to the second position. No, this would never do. If

I had achieved anything, if anyone had kindled my spirit, it had been Martin Sir.

I told Krishna where I was going and went out. Halfway there, Martin Sir called.

'Congratulations, Babu! We are so happy. Not of course that we weren't expecting it.'

I thanked him but he continued: 'So what are your plans today?'

I couldn't tell why he was asking.

'Agnes wants you to come over for dinner. We'd love to have you. Come by seven thirty?'

I turned back so that I could go there later. I had learnt the rules of punctuality from Martin Sir and arrived at 7:30 p.m. The door was open as it usually was. Martin Sir was watching the news on television. When he heard my footsteps, he looked up: 'Congratulations, Babu. You made me proud.' He hugged me. He called Stella and she and Agnes Aunty came out. Both wished me with such genuine delight that I was left covered in embarrassment.

'Ninety-three per cent means you can try for medicine,' said Stella but Martin Sir said almost before she had finished: 'But he must want to do medicine, right?'

'So what's your blueprint for the future?' Agnes Aunty asked.

What could I say? I found myself blank. Martin Sir came to my rescue:

'Ladies, ladies. Let the poor boy sit down first. We'll talk about his plans over dinner, shall we?'

'What will you have? Whiskey or beer?' Agnes Aunty asked. I shook my head.

'Don't feel shy. Your Martin Sir isn't going to say anything.'

Agnes Aunty seemed in a very good mood.

Sir smiled. 'You know, he doesn't drink. But you can make an exception today. Let's say: a beer?'

As she went off, Martin Sir followed her with affection in his gaze. I could not imagine a husband looking at his wife like that.

'Agnes is in high spirits today. Do you know why?'

Sir was looking at his daughter as he spoke. I didn't understand why she ran off inside. 'Stella is getting married. She found someone herself. A gem of a boy. We fixed the wedding date today. May 12. We even have a hall booked. Now do I have to tell you that you must be there?'

Stella returned with the beer, foaming over the sides of the glass. She handed it to me with a quick, 'Sorry.'

'Don't bother, dear,' Martin Sir said. 'It's overflowing. In much the same manner as her heart is overflowing with joy.'

This time Stella did not seem embarrassed. She picked up the bottle and as she was going inside, she turned and asked her father, 'As if you and Mamma can control your happiness!'

I should have congratulated Stella but the moment passed. Sir raised his glass and I brought the cold bitter liquid to my lips. 'Have you been reading anything new?' sir asked. Then he corrected himself. 'Oh sorry. Your exams followed by your father's death. Where would you have had the time?'

'I read your Joan Didion.'

'I know you probably couldn't relate to it. But it is part of the range of human experience and I wanted you to experience that.'

He brought out a gift-wrapped book and said: 'A gift for you. I'm sure you'll like it. Take it.'

Blindness by Jose Saramago.

I had heard the name before.

'My favourite author,' said Martin Sir. '*The Gospel According to Jesus Christ* is my all-time favourite. There is no attempt to deify Jesus. Saramago chooses to present him as a man. It is a highly philosophical book but of course, the Catholic right wingers condemned it.'

I picked up the book and sir said, 'In this one a pandemic of blindness suddenly begins to rage. No one can find a cure and the panicky responses are delineated well. It is a magnificent flight of the imagination.' At that point Agnes entered the room. 'What's this? His glass is untouched. And here I was coming to ask if you guys need refills. Anyway, dinner is ready. It shouldn't get cold.'

As she turned to leave, sir said, 'I think Kipling once said something about how he could not be everywhere, looking after everyone, and so God invented mothers. I look at Agnes and think this is true.' I thought of my mother but it did not feel it was the right time to argue the point.

Stella came in to hurry us along. 'Come on, Daddy. Mamma is waiting for you.'

Martin Sir drained his beer. I took three or four gulps and rose too.

*

The table was laid for four with the food in the centre. 'Now you must eat well,' Agnes Aunty said, opening the serving dishes. 'This is ambot-tik. This is chicken xacuti. Chonak fried. Prawn pulao and those are sanna.'

This was the first time I had eaten at a Christian home. I had heard that they were big on formality and etiquette which made me a little tense. But this didn't seem to be the case here. Martin Sir urged me to serve myself. Agnes Aunty was a good cook. I ate and enjoyed everything I tasted. There was one serving bowl which remained covered. Sir opened it and served himself.

Then he said, 'This is sorpotel. Will you have some?'

I had heard of it of course but never eaten it.

'It's pork. If you don't want to eat it, it's fine.' If they were eating it, why shouldn't I? Agnes Aunty thought I was hesitating and said, 'I know Hindus generally don't. I shouldn't have even put it on the table but Stella loves it so...'

I reached for the dish and served myself. I didn't think it was because I wanted to please them. Nor had I any well thought out reasons not to eat pork. But how was I to know whether I liked it or not unless I tried it. It was rich and piquant so I took another serving.

Then Stella's phone rang.

'Finish your dinner first,' Agnes Aunty said. But Stella took the call anyway.

'What?' she said and stood up abruptly. She ran into the other room and began talking. After a while she had still not come out and so Agnes Aunty went in to her. When she didn't come out either, Martin Sir got up and said, 'Sorry Babu, please continue. I'll be right back.'

A couple of minutes later, mother and daughter emerged, ready to go out. Martin Sir came and sat down by my side. His face was lined with worry.

'Sir, what happened?' I said and my tone was worried too.

'There's been an accident. Stella's fiancé Ramiro. He's been taken to the hospital.'

'I hope it's nothing serious.' I got up.

Sir said nothing.

'Sir, should I wait?'

'No. We've called Raju's taxi. We are leaving now.'

There seemed like nothing I could do so I left.

All night long, the sorpotel rose like bile inside my throat.

*

In the morning I made tea and gave Ma some.

I looked at my phone and began reading my WhatsApp messages. Fatima had written a poetic message. Chitra wrote: 'All 3 of us did well. We must celebrate each other's successes. This afternoon, 12:30 at Ambil. c u.' My first response was: 'Not today.' But then I wondered whether I had any right to spread my bad mood around.

'Let's have chicken today,' Ma said. 'Krishna really makes it well.'

Ma's appetite had blossomed after Daddy's death. I said nothing. Ma got impatient: 'Aren't you listening, Babu? How about some chicken...?'

'Certainly not.' I snapped and took the cup out again. Memories of last night came back to disturb me. Martin Sir must have returned home. How was Ramiro? Maybe Stella had stayed back at the hospital. What if he had broken a leg or something? They would have to postpone the wedding.

Krishna came and I left without breakfast. Halfway to Panjim, Ignatius flagged my bike down. He said, 'You heard about Stella's fiancé, na? He died on the spot.'

I turned around and went home. There Krishna said, 'You forgot your phone at home.' Two calls had come. I did not take the phone from him. I told Krishna, 'Keep it outside and don't answer if anyone calls.'

I went to my room and closed the door. I didn't feel like paying a condolence visit to Martin Sir and family. I would not have been able to bear looking at Martin Sir's sad face now. I remembered Stella's face, blooming when Martin Sir had told us the good news. Agnes Aunty, that mother whom God had created because he could not be everywhere, how was I to face her? And Ramiro. Death had claimed him before he could say 'I do'. Stella and Ramiro, whom I had not even seen, danced before my eyes in that dark room, a *pas de deux* of death.

Lunch time. Krishna came to call me. I did not feel like eating. I said: 'Go ahead and eat. I'm not hungry.'

To which Krishna said, 'Then I'm not hungry too. I won't eat either.'

I was annoyed at this. But I knew he could be stubborn so I said, 'Serve me something and bring it here. Then you go and eat.' Perhaps the sorpotel had finally been digested for at around three o'clock, I suddenly felt hungry, the pangs perhaps aroused by the aroma of the food. I got up and ate in the darkness. I came out and put my plate to wash, rinsed my mouth. Krishna told me that the same person had called three times. I did not look at my phone and went back into the darkness of my room.

*

Krishna came early the next morning, full of news. Ramiro's funeral was to be at 4 p.m. today. At Taleigaon. A bus was leaving from our village. I did not go. The mobile was cold, its battery dead. I opened *Blindness* and lost myself in the white darkness Saramago was talking about. The protagonist is driving his car and has halted at a signal, waiting for the lights to change. But suddenly he can no longer see anything because a white cloud has obscured his vision. The cars behind start honking angrily but he cannot move. Someone finally gets into the driving seat and takes him home. But then he drives away with his car. His wife puts him in a taxi and takes him to see an eye doctor...

White blindness, it seems, is infectious. He, his wife, the car thief, the eye doctor and anyone who comes in contact with him turns blind. And suddenly it becomes an epidemic. In days, thousands of people are quarantined and suddenly the common decencies are suspended, human beings turn into animals. The doctor is being taken into quarantine when his wife lies that she is blind too so that she may go with him...

At this point Chitra and Fatima arrived at the door, carrying pedas. Krishna opened the door.

'Waah. And here's the young man himself, lost in a book! And there we were all getting worried...'

Fatima interrupted Chitra and said, 'What is it, Vipin? Something is wrong, no?'

'Right. But first sit down.' And I tried to figure out what I was supposed to say to them.

'What happened, Vipin?'

I told them. 'I don't think I could bear to see Martin Sir. Or worse still, Agnes Aunty. Yesterday, she was so happy. And Stella! So many dreams of a life with Ramiro.'

This must have been my longest speech ever and that too an emotional one.

'Did you see him?' Chitra asked.

I shook my head.

It was not our custom to visit people nor were we accustomed to visitors. Curious, Ma came out. 'Who are these young ladies?' she asked. When she got a little closer, she recognized them.

'Oh yes. You've come before, right?'

Ma's attention was drawn by the box in Chitra's hands. 'Did you bring something for Vipin? Krishna, come and take this inside. The ants will get it here.' But before Krishna could obey, she took the box and went inside herself.

In a soft voice Chitra said, 'Wild! You didn't get so senti even when your Daddy died. And all this for your teacher's prospective son-in-law who you haven't even seen...'

Krishna came in with tea and coffee and Chitra left her thought incomplete.

'I envy him his death, Chitra.' Fatima said, holding her cup of coffee and looking straight at me. 'If it were I who had died, Vipin would have felt just this much pain for me, don't you think, Chitra?'

'Shut up, Fatima.' The words burst out of my mouth and to stop them I raised my tea cup to my lips.

'What are you reading?' Chitra put out a hand for the book.

'Saramago's *Blindness*.'

'Oh yes. I've read it,' she said, returning the book to me. 'So beautiful, but also so disturbing. The complete spectrum of what humankind can be—their virtues and vices, hatred, greed, compassion—it's all there in this book. You'll find yourself in it. And your mother, Fatima too, and me as well. I think it's also about how an epidemic can evoke humanity and also such selfish behaviour.'

'May we never live through something like that!' Fatima said, putting her hand on her breast.

'Not that we have any say in it,' Chitra said. When they got up to leave, Fatima said, 'Yesterday's celebration hasn't been cancelled, okay? Just postponed. Aambil is waiting for us. But you decide when we meet.'

When they left, they took the dark clouds with them, leaving the sky a clear blue again.

20

Property Matters

After Daddy died, Uncle Senior had begun to visit us at least once a fortnight. If he had work in Panjim, he would lunch with us. Whether this was because Daddy's death had freed him of fear or because Krishna cooked well, I could not tell. It seemed as if he were now deeply concerned about his sister's present and his nephew's future. When he had finished lunch one day and released a satisfied belch, he brought Ma into my room and I discovered the real reason for his concern.

'The money is safe,' I said, saving him some trouble. 'In case you're worried about it.'

'I'm worried but only on your behalf. Your mother's medicines, your education...'

'I've counted it. No need for you to worry.'

'How much is it?'

'Quite a lot.'

'Give me an approximation, at least?'

His curiosity was out in the open at last.

'Ten lakh thirty thousand so far.'

'And there's more?'

'Oh yes. More than half left. I think it should come to another fifteen or twenty...'

I could practically see him salivating. I added, 'Don't you want to know how much is in the bank? I can't remember really if it's thirteen or twenty-two...'

'Lakhs?' Ma asked, making her brother's work easier.

'Did I tell you how much we are getting from the insurance as well?'

'How much?'

I pretended to count on my fingers.

'My mathematics isn't that good. Can I let you know later?'

My uncle grew a bit annoyed. 'Why tell me? But surely you should tell your mother? Keeping the poor thing in the dark...'

'Is that right, Ma? You want to know?'

My mother was taken aback. 'Well, he says...'

'Arre it's her right to know and surely she should get some pin money...'

'But we haven't talked about Daddy's debts. Surely you want to know about those? According to the bank notices...' I started to count on my fingers again. 'From the Urban Bank, fifteen lakhs with interest. From the State Bank, twelve but two have been returned. The LIC policy is mortgaged too. You could help, Uncle. He left some unpaid bills at Vasudev's and Kistodi's bar. You could pay those off and help your sister. They are really not much. May be ten or eleven thousand.'

'Where would I have such money? We are practically hand to mouth...'

'Oh really? Perhaps you'd like some pin money as well?'

My uncle did not wait to hear anymore.

*

'Is it okay if I take four days leave starting tomorrow?' Krishna asked as he finished up the day's tasks.

'Sure.'

'Don't you want to know why?'

'If you want to tell me.'

'We are going home to our native place.'

'Is there a jatra?'

Krishna seemed to be deciding whether to tell me or not. Finally, he said: 'There's a famine in the village. People are starving. Appa says we should go back and help.'

And how would Krishna, a boy who cannot even afford to study and so would do whatever job was offered, help in such a situation?

'Do you need some money?'

'No, Babu, thank you. But when we come back, I'll let you know if we need some. Appa has some savings; we are taking those. Ammi has bought some rice and wheat on the neighbour's ration card. We'll do what we can with our hands to help them.'

On the way back from the market that afternoon, Vasudev hailed me. He put a cup of special tea in my hands and said, 'I was very happy to hear about your results. What else can I give you? This cup is on me.'

The tea was very good. I told him about Krishna's plan.

'Those who have suffered can understand the suffering of others. When you have known what it is to want, you give with an open hand.'

*

'We couldn't bear to see your crestfallen face that day. How are you now, Vipin?'

Chitra's voice was full of concern.

'Honestly? I felt so much better for your visit.'

'Fatima must have felt it worse than me. She sent me something on WhatsApp yesterday. Her own lines, should I read them to you? You'll see how compassionate she is. Give me a moment to find it?

'How fleet their feet when they come to the feast.
When the heart is dark, friends are the East.'

I remembered Fatima's words: Aambil is waiting for us.

It was my turn to give them the treat.

*

That day Krishna made sugarless cake to celebrate his results so that Ma could eat it. He had scored a respectable sixty-nine per cent. He was delighted.

'Now what are your plans?' I asked, although I knew.

'I want to do catering,' he said.

It seemed that he had already researched the possible courses that he could take.

'Even with such good marks, you still want to do catering?'

My question confused Krishna.

'If you want to become a chef in a five-star hotel, you can't just do a catering course. You have to do a degree in hotel management. But first your twelfth standard.'

I had done some research myself. There were hotel management courses aplenty. But they were all expensive. The certificate courses were cheaper but they offered fewer prospects. 'Perhaps it would be best to do a diploma, a two-year course.'

'What about the fees?'

'I think it would be about two-and-a-half lakhs but don't

worry about the fees right now. First, finish your twelfth standard. Study hard.'

I put a cheque of thirty thousand into his hands. 'This should take you through eleventh and twelfth. If you need some more, you know where to find me. But let your father see his son a chef in a grand hotel.'

'But the diploma course fees...'

'Look, one year ago you didn't think you could get through the tenth standard but here you are. With sixty-nine per cent. And that's how you'll get your diploma.'

I saw his eyes fill with tears and left in a hurry.

Krishna kept coming home and Ma kept ordering him about. The clothes, the cooking, the cleaning all were his responsibility. Then one day I found that Ma had asked him to massage her feet.

I called him aside and told him to focus on his studies. I would handle the housework.

*

'Babu, when you go to the market, get some nice baangdas. Krishna makes them really well with udid-methi.'

'Krishna will no longer be working here.'

That day, we made do with rice, curry and papads.

21

A Smile Poses a Question

Chitra was now in Canacona. She didn't get range there but still she managed to call.

'We must meet today. At five this evening.'

'If it's that important, let's meet right now,' I said eagerly.

'Idiot, I'm in Canacona. I'm leaving now for Panjim.'

*

I got to Miramar about ten minutes early. When I parked the bike, I found Fatima was already waiting. 'I knew that you'd be early because Chitra summoned you.'

It was the holidays and so the beach was crowded. The sun hung low in the sky. Instead of sitting down, we thought it better to stroll about close by.

'Look how our shadows have mingled with each other. You can't tell where I begin and you end.' At least she wasn't spouting poetry. I looked at my watch. Why was Chitra late? 'I'll be happy if Chitra is late. We can spend some more time together,' Fatima said. 'And I got a chance to walk alone with you.'

An auto came to a halt right in front of us. Chitra poked

her head out and said, 'It's too crowded here. Vipin, let's go to Dona Paula. Hop in.'

Fatima clapped her hands. When we were sitting in the auto Chitra said, 'He doesn't want to sit between two girls which is why he's crouched on the edge there. Now this is not about you, okay?'

But Dona Paula was also crowded. We found place to sit somewhere at the base of the hill. 'Why the suspense?' I asked.

Chitra stood up. She took a deep breath as if she were beginning to deliver a lecture. Then she said in one quick breath, 'Tomorrow I'm going to Mumbai. To do Fine Arts. I got a call from Raheja Institute. The interview is on Monday.'

The sun went behind a cloud. The air went dense, or so it seemed.

I got to my feet.

'What happened?' Chitra asked.

'Tea,' I said. I got up and they followed.

'Vipin offered no reaction,' Chitra said. Or was she asking a question?

'*Tumne kisi ki jaan ko jaate huey dekha hai*?' Fatima sang, ignoring the crowds around. Where did she get off, asking, 'Have you ever seen someone lose his life?'

Chitra picked this up. 'You sing beautifully, Fatima, but if you're just doing this to tease, that's not on.'

'Two coffees and a tea,' I placed the order. We were stuck where we were. And then the rain, the damned rain, rain out of time. There were crowds of people all around; and crowds of thoughts inside my head.

'Inspiration strikes!' Chitra said. 'I want to get this down on canvas, these crowds, this energy. Inside the head, maybe?

Ants and worms and other vermin swarming. In one head, a white dove striving for a clear blue sky. If only I had a canvas and paints right here...'

'Stick that inspiration in your backpack and take it out when you need it,' Fatima said. 'And while you're at it, take this rain, this damned rain with you. You might need it when you paint our portrait.'

'Why would I need your pictures with me? I'm carrying them in my heart.'

I had no reply to that.

There was no place to sit. Everything was wet. And so we simply walked around. Chitra could not stop talking. 'First, I thought I'd go to MS University. Then I wanted to join JJ School but their entrance exam was right in the middle of my twelfth standard. So I could not sit for it, but now this has come up.' It seemed as if the rain had let up but when we came out, it was drizzling. I took out a handkerchief and tried to cover Chitra's head.

'Thanks but I like getting wet,' she said. As if waiting for the opportunity, Fatima took it from her and covered her own head.

'Put your odhni over your head,' I said, reclaiming my handkerchief.

'Well, at least you spoke to me because of that,' Fatima exclaimed. Then to Chitra, 'A fine time this will be to catch a cold. Let's turn back.'

Then Chitra went on to talk about how she had persuaded her father to let her go, how a flat her father owned and rented out had suddenly and fortuitously fallen vacant, how it had been decided that now she would stay there, how she had packed the paintings that she was going to take to show at the interview, and how she had included the portrait she had done of me.

'Why take mine?'

'The Mona Lisa. You've heard of it, right? A smile poses a question. I think that's what happens with your portrait too. You can't tell whether you're smiling or sad. Whether there is something going on inside your head or you're blank. Oh dear, I've just gone and compared myself with Leonardo Da Vinci, haven't I? I didn't mean it, I'm just saying that it's the same kind of thing.'

'Enough already,' the rain seemed to say and came pouring down again. We had lost track of the time. We flagged down a rickshaw. They were ready to drop me home but I had left my bike at Miramar. And so we agreed to meet on Sunday and they dropped me back to my bike.

*

The rain forced me to halt by the side of the road for a while. It was already eight o'clock. I had told Ma I would come home and see to dinner. I realized she would be hungry and got back on and rode through the rain. I stopped at Niyaz and bought Ma a biryani. It was 9 p.m. when I reached home. To my surprise I found Ma was already having her dinner.

'You were late so I made myself some poli-bhaaji.'

That settled one thing: if push came to shove, Ma could cook for herself.

*

On Sunday Chitra was catching the Konkan Kanya train from Madgaon. In the morning Fatima called. 'How are you going?'

I had thought of biking down but not with a pillion.

'Nothing settled yet.'

'If you're taking the scooter, you know who's riding pillion.'

'No scooter for me.'

'The train is at six. Chitra says she'll get there early. Shall we meet at three thirty near the Kadamba Shuttle Counter?'

'Make that four.'

'Done. I'll get there by four and buy the tickets.'

*

I thought she would be chattering and joking all the way to Madgaon but she was so quiet that finally I had to ask, 'So silent today?' Then she began to talk about Chitra. Fatima told me how she had isolated herself, how her past haunted her. She had not been able to form any friendships, nor even with girls, never mind boys. And then one day Chitra had asked whether she could take a photo on her mobile. Fatima had refused but Chitra had insisted. Then she said, 'You're so beautiful but your eyes are melancholic. Why is that?'

'I had become introverted and loneliness was becoming something of a habit. It was Chitra who dragged me out of my shell, who helped me overcome my shyness and even deal with my shame. She liked reading and painting and I loved poetry and dance. But I had never read out a poem or danced in public. My poems were for my diary and my dancing was for the mirror in my room. Chitra made me confident about my talents. She made me laugh, she straightened my spine and all this though I was her senior. I began to enjoy being her shadow...'

She was silent for a while and then she murmured, as if she were speaking to Chitra now, 'Earlier you would go home for the vacations but we knew you were coming back. When you came back, it was as if our happiness was doubled. But now the world is going to feel empty and forlorn.'

And Fatima fell silent again. I don't know where I found it in me but I took her hand in mine. Her eyes filled with tears and she turned to look out of the window, wiping her eyes from time to time with a wisp of a handkerchief.

What Fatima had said about Chitra deepened my feelings for her. With Chitra for a friend one would need no others.

When we reached Madgaon Station, the train was not yet on the platform but Chitra and her father were already there. Her father seemed a little downcast too, unlike his normal cheerful self. 'If you had been going with Chitra, I should not have been so worried.'

'Pappa, and what about me? No one seems worried about how I'm going to manage without Chitra,' Fatima said in between sniffles.

'Why are you talking like that?' Chitra said, folding her into a hug. Fatima wiped her eyes. 'Now let's have enough of this. Are you here to make me cry? It's not as if Mumbai is that far away anymore. It's almost the same as me being in Panjim. Now stop worrying about me. I should be worrying about you. Instead here I am resolutely setting off for another city.'

'I'm not really worried, girl, but I can't help what I feel,' her father said.

'I'm not going if I have to hurt anyone. That's settled then. Let's go home. Mumbai cancelled,' Chitra said firmly.

'Who says you're not going?' Fatima did a U-turn.

Chitra looked her straight in the eyes and said, 'I know you won't ask me to stay.' Then in a voice only Fatima and I could hear, she said, 'Because you want me to leave more than you want me to stay, right?'

'Am I such a selfish beast?' Fatima said and hugged her.

The train chugged onto the platform. Pappa gathered up the luggage. Chitra and Fatima were still hugging each other. Over Fatima's shoulder, Chitra beckoned me close. 'I need your word, Vipin. While I'm away you won't avoid Fatima.'

'Why are you saying that? Why would I do anything like that?' Fatima stepped back from the embrace and put a finger on Chitra's lips.

'Fatima feels you will,' Chitra said, moving Fatima's hand away.

*

The train came to a halt. Pappa carried Chitra's bag into her compartment and Chitra boarded the train. In a little while, her father got off. The smoked glass windows made it difficult to look into the train. I got in. Chitra was arranging her luggage. She saw me and said, 'Hey. I was going to come out.' For a moment we stood there looking at each other.

Then Chitra said, 'Right, Vipin. I think the train is going to move now.' There were many things I wanted to say, so many things that I said nothing.

When I got down, I saw that Fatima and Pappa were standing in a disconsolate huddle.

On the way back Fatima said nothing. Through the trip, she stared out of the dusty window. When we reached the Kadamba Bus Stand, her eyes were still wet.

'Should I drop you home?' It was already seven thirty. Fatima shook her head and hailed a rickshaw. Before she got in, she took my hand and squeezed it. 'Please don't stop meeting me just because Chitra isn't around. Please.'

All night long I was haunted by Chitra's wordless gaze in that train compartment and Fatima's imploring voice.

22

The Bitterness of Maat Bhaji

'I met your teacher. He was asking about you,' Krishna said as he entered. He was carrying some freshly prepared vegetables with him. 'Ammi had planted these in a corner of the field. She told me to take you some.'

Ma was not impressed by the maat bhaaji; it had a bitter taste. 'Didn't she plant some cabbage or cauliflower?' she asked.

'All the better for me,' I said, 'I love maat bhaaji.'

Krishna had come to tell me that he had got admission. He had bought some of the textbooks that he needed. 'There is still some time before college starts. Is there anything you want me to do?'

'Nothing at all. If you come, I'll get out of the habit of doing the work. Instead, just drop by when you're free. And if you have a problem, I'm right here.'

Krishna left and I was assailed by a feeling of guilt. Martin Sir was asking after me when I should be asking after him. I resolved to go and see him that very day.

*

As always, I went empty handed. I realized also that I never returned from Martin Sir's house without carrying away something, whether in my heart, in my mind or in my hands. But now I was going to condole with him. What could I possibly take? When he had come to pay his respects after Daddy's death he had brought me a book. What could I take him? I had nothing to give but much to take. I could offer him my support but did he really need that? He was like the zen cup that was already full and needed no addition. By now he would have made his peace with sorrow. But Agnes Aunty? How had she dealt with it? Thinking of her brought back memories of the last meal we had had together. The thought brought back the afterburn I had felt with that first taste of sorpotel. How happy Stella had been, a tree covered with blossoms. She must be deeply depressed now. At the thought of actually shaking her hand or saying something, I wanted to turn back and run home.

But luckily there was no need for that. Sir was at home and he let me into the hall. Agnes Aunty did not appear. Neither did Stella. Then sir told me, 'Stella has gone to Kolkata to become a nun.' This was the way she had chosen to forget her grief over Ramiro. She was hoping to enter the order of the Missionaries of Charity. She preferred to spend her life serving the poorest of the poor rather than moping around, remembering her lost love.

I was stunned. Was this her way of making an offering of herself at the altar of her dead love?

'It was her decision to become a nun,' sir said.

For a moment I thought of him as a saint. But then his feet of clay became apparent.

'How happy we were. We thought our daughter would want for nothing with a boy like Ramiro. We thought we had gained a son. Instead, we've lost our daughter.'

He sighed. 'I have never worried about death. If I

worried about something, it was life. Ramiro's untimely death did leave us grieving. But I know that time will heal the hurt. What I'm worried about is Stella. I hope there's no more sorrow waiting for her.'

I took my leave and as I left the house, I saw a bird flying away from a branch on which it had been perched. The branch shook for a while after the bird's departure. I wondered if it were bidding me farewell.

*

Chitra called. 'Why didn't you go to college today?' This was her second call from Mumbai. The first was a description of the interview, about what the panel head had said about her paintings, how much she liked the Raheja Institute and Bandra...She was also delighted that English Literature was one of the subjects she was taking. 'But I haven't made any real friends yet.'

She sounded a little sad about this and I wondered if I was going to feel jealous of any friend she makes in the future.

'College started yesterday. Forgot?'

'What would I do there? It's just about getting the timetable and that stupid orientation period which I don't need anyway.'

'Didn't you know someone would be waiting for you?'

I said nothing.

'Made your ID card?'

'Yes.'

'And only because Fatima reminded you.'

Chitra seemed to be well up on the news.

'At least go to meet Fatima. You know she has no friends left in college now, right?'

'A good chance for her to make some new ones now.'

She was quiet for a while.

'No chance of that. You know how they say a burnt child fears the fire? This one got singed and now fears the sun.'

'I don't understand.'

'I am sharing a confidence with you because I hope it will help you understand her better. Fatima was molested as a child.'

I did not know what to say so I resorted to silence. Chitra looked closely at me and then nodded, as if she approved of this response.

'She came close to committing suicide. She had even given up on going to school. What had saved her was poetry and dance. Television had taught her to dance. Then Aslambhai had also intervened and somehow persuaded her to go back to school.'

Until she had met Chitra she had lived a cocoon of self-imposed isolation.

'When I told her I was going to Mumbai she said, "Then I'm quitting college too." I nipped that in the bud by saying that Vipin would be lonely. And she agreed that she would have to continue. For you. You see?'

'Yes.'

'Prove it. Call her right now.'

*

Each phone call from Chitra reminded me how far away she was now. I went into the kitchen and made myself a big cup of tea. Even before I finished the last gulp my phone rang. 'Thank you, Vipin. I won my bet.'

'What bet?'

'I just spoke to Chitra. I was supposed to wait ten minutes for your call and if I didn't get one, she wasn't going to phone you again.'

'I was about to call.' I mumbled. 'Classes over?'

'No idea. I'm in the canteen. I'm here with a cup of coffee and a cup of tea. The coffee cup has shrunk to half its size in embarrassment. And the cup of tea is suffering the pangs of rejection. It's saying there's no point waiting for someone who has lost his way.'

'Stay right there. Give me twelve minutes. I'll drink it even if it's cold.'

*

When I joined the college I wondered if I would ever mix with the students there. But the weakness of the higher secondary system and the weakness of my fellow students had become my strength. On the first day I was not the only person who had bunked class but slowly I realized that the majority were in the canteen or outside class.

As I got to know them a little, I found that most of them were there to have fun rather than to study. More than half were smoking. Most of them spent a lot of time partying where all kinds of drugs were being experimented with. One day I even saw two girls smoking on campus. It seemed a little odd. That day for the first time I went and bought myself couple of cigarettes. When I got home, I lit one and spent the next half hour coughing. Later I discovered that there were kids, boys and girls too, who were smoking and drinking and partying all night in our college. I wondered if they did not have parents to control them.

'Do you really think they tell their parents what they

are up to?' Fatima asked. 'And do you think kids we know don't do this? They just do it in hiding.'

Now, they were all experimenting with bigger things.

*

The seniors took the lead in organizing a freshers' party. They came to our class and asked for suggestions.

Someone suggested a theme party. Someone else said, 'Let's have "Who's your superhero?"' Fatima was looking at me. Amrut must have noticed this. He pointed at me and said, 'Phantom.' Everyone applauded and I just wanted to vanish. I picked up my bag and headed for the door. Fatima stopped me, 'Please stay. No one will ask a thing of you.'

And then she put the programme together. Everyone was to come dressed as their favourite superhero and each one would present their talent: dance, singing, jokes, physical feats...whatever. The seniors would take the lead. And since Fatima seemed clearly in command, I thought she would volunteer to recite a poem or present a dance. But she did neither. However, when the names of two seniors were presented to lead this, Fatima's was one of them.

I did not go to college on the day of the party.

'I wanted to present the dance,' Fatima told me later. 'But I didn't. You know why? I knew you'd bunk.'

*

We had different timetables, so meeting was difficult. Last year I had found it difficult to be at peace if I did not meet Fatima and Chitra every day. Even now I was missing them. When I felt lonely, I would call Chitra. Time passed easily, hours flowing by when we were together. Now a phone call lasted five, ten or twenty minutes.

Fatima managed to circumvent our conflicting schedules. Her classes were in the morning. Mine started at two o'clock. So she suggested I come to college a little early and she would wait a while after class. In this way, we could spend half an hour together. Sometimes, finishing the work at home would delay me and I would reach late. On such days, she would sit in the library and wait until my classes got over. One day, she even said: 'You know I'm studying a lot more now.'

She took a book from her bag and showed it to me.

'Mirza Ghalib. One of my favourites. Shall I tell you why I like him?'

'His love poetry, I suppose. What else would you be reading?'

That must have hurt Fatima. 'He's a poet of pain. That's why I love him. I think you'll also like him.'

'We are different people, Fatima.'

'Not really. We have some things in common.'

'Such as?'

'Pain. I hide it. You run from it.'

That night I ran a search on Ghalib. I read some of his ghazals. I read some rubaai and some of his poetry. I ordered Gulzar's book on him.

*

When I met Fatima the next time, I acknowledged that there was some truth in what she had said. 'You were right about him being a poet of pain.'

'And what I said about us being united in pain?'

I paused a moment and then said, 'Maybe.'

*

One day I met Sarvesh in college. 'Parob, got a moment?'

I thought he was going to talk about Namshikar or some problem he was facing with his studies. But this was completely different.

'You're a friend so I'm asking. But keep this between us, okay? You want some stuff? I can get it for you.'

He had lowered his tone and was looking shifty which made it clear to me what 'stuff' he meant. Was he under pressure to do this pushing?

'What's in it for you?' He looked confused as if he wasn't sure whether to tell me or not.

'Are you on commission?' He shook his head.

'If you want, I'll even buy some for you. If you're getting something out of this. But first tell me the truth. How long have you been using?'

That afternoon I took Sarvesh to the beach. He told me everything and I felt rather sorry for him. A week ago, someone had left a packet in the tool box of his bike. He had no idea about this or what the contents of the packet were. As he rode out of the parking lot, two policemen in plainclothes stopped him. They patted him down and said, 'Where's the stuff?' Then they checked his tool box and found the packet. 'This is weed. Come with us to the police station. You must be dealing.' At that point a senior, Mustafa, intervened. He slipped the cops some money and they left. But Mustafa warned Sarvesh that if he did not find them five new clients, the policemen would be back.

'You were scared?'

'Yes.'

'Who were they?'

'I don't know.'

'Who's this Mustafa?'

'He seems to be a senior. I think he's from third year.'

'Will you be able to recognize him? Show him to me?'

Sarvesh looked terrified.

'Then he'll get me. He says he'll tell Daddy.'

I managed to calm him down a little and sent him home.

Later I called Fatima and asked, 'Do you know a senior by the name of Mustafa?'

'Not really, but there is some Mustafa who hangs around the college. I've heard Selena and others say that he can supply you with dope or whatever you want. Why? What happened?'

I gave her some placebo answer.

The next day I met Amrut and told him. I thought he might know Mustafa.

'He hasn't crossed his path with you, right?' he asked.

Then he himself said, 'He's a real lowlife. But don't worry about it. Leave him to me and tell Sarvesh that if Mustafa gives him grief again, he should tell me about it.'

Amrut was on his way into politics, it was clear to see. The Student Council first, then General Secretary then a youth leader, a party ticket…'But I need your support, okay?'

Sarvesh began to park his bike elsewhere.

*

August 15. Flag-hoisting ceremony. I thought I should go. Hardly any students turned up. There were more staff than students. Fatima was there.

'Good to see you. At least you came.'

She explained what she had meant over a cup of coffee in the canteen. She took it personally that so few students had turned up for the flag hoisting. 'I don't think they understand the value of independence,' she said. I wondered why I had thought to come. It was a celebration but I had very little in my life to celebrate. I had no one in my life I thought of as worth saluting; the flag could fill that gap.

In a few days it would be Ganesh Chaturthi and we would have seven days of holidays.

'When do we meet?'

'When college reopens.'

But that didn't happen. On the day of the Chaturthi, I began to miss Chitra. And with Chitra, Fatima. And since I could not meet both of them together, I called Fatima: 'Shall we meet today? Five p.m. at the Kala Akademi canteen?'

*

Krishna had come that morning and brought karanjis and coconut wadis. I handed them over to Ma and asked Krishna, 'Can you make some savoury karanjis?'

Fatima was delighted.

'How did you know I like my karanji spicy?'

'Call it intuition.'

'Thank you, Vipin.'

I did not know what to say to that when she said, 'Aren't you going to ask why I thanked you?'

I shrugged. 'Pretty obvious. Wouldn't you say?'

'You're thinking about the karanjis? Thanking you for that would just be a formality. But today for the first time, you called and asked if we could meet. That's why I'm thanking you.'

Since it was a public holiday, not too many people were around. I went to the counter and said, 'One coffee, one tea, special and double. Lots of milk, please. Make it really special.'

23

The Unicorn and the Pillion

Just when the Diwali holidays were beginning, Ma had a fainting spell. I called Dr Costabir and he checked her blood sugar. 280. However, he didn't think hospitalisation was necessary.

All sweets were forbidden. Also rice. I hid the tins with jaggery and sugar. Costabir prescribed medicines and injections and his bills shot up. He warned me, 'She must move, she must exercise and she has to control her diet. She can't eat sweets just because she likes them. They mean death.' But despite all that, Ma would go foraging in the kitchen.

'Monitoring is essential. If she's alone at home, she could slip into a coma. And if the sugar keeps going up, it could affect her eyes, kidneys and heart.'

I got a glucometer and added one more job to my routine chores. Ma now took the place Daddy had vacated with his death.

'Have you told Veenu? He'd have come running if he had heard,' Ma said, so I called my uncle. He thought it best to advise me over the phone. 'Tell her to control her tongue. Our mother had diabetes. If it's kept under control there's no problem.' I conveyed this free advice from my uncle to Ma.

'Call Krishna. He'll be some help to you.' she said. She had said "you" but she meant "me". I ignored this but I thought I should meet Krishna. Then I remembered that there was a packet of nankhatai at home. I took them with me before Ma could lay her hands on them. Krishna was outside when I arrived. He invited me in but I refused.

'Was there something you wanted, Babu?' he asked, concerned.

'I just wanted to meet you.'

'But why did you think of me suddenly?'

'Arre, Ma had mentioned you and I thought I'd come by and see how you were doing.'

'I haven't seen her in a while. Tell her I'll be there on Sunday.'

'Not Sunday, no. I won't be home.' I kickstarted the scooter but it refused to cooperate. It seemed to be in its last stages, a patient collapsed at the hospital gate. Krishna gave it a try. Then he said, 'I'll show it to Appa when he comes and if he can do something, I'll bring it back tomorrow morning.'

I walked back home.

The next morning, Krishna came without the scooter. 'Appa says it's a gone case. He will repair it but it would be better to get a new one.'

That day I booked a Honda Unicorn. The Unicorn because it had a comfortable pillion seat. For whom?

Chitra? She wasn't even in Goa. Fatima? It was hardly likely that I would meet her regularly.

*

By the time I got to college, classes had started. I decided to skip them, when my mobile buzzed. A WhatsApp message from Fatima: 'In the library.'

When I got there, she was watching the door. She gestured me to wait and came out.

'Thank you.'

'For what?'

'I called and you came.'

She was right. Do I come to college only to meet her? I wasn't the kind to go running when someone called. Or was I changing?

Seeing me silent, Fatima asked, 'Why are you late today? All well I hope?'

I said, 'The scooter is being repaired.'

'Time to get a new one,' she said as a joke.

'I booked one.'

Her face blossomed.

'When is it coming?'

'When it comes.'

'Bags I the first ride. Let's do it this way. Take me along when you get delivery, okay?'

I said nothing when Fatima babbled on, describing the long rides that we would take together. Meanwhile our steps were turning automatically towards the canteen. Everyone seemed to have the same idea; the tables were full.

Someone said, 'Phantom' when we came in. After that fresher's party, I began hearing this. I generally ignored it.

I got Fatima her coffee and me a tea and began to look for a place to sit.

'Arre, Roy, Suraj, come join us here,' someone shouted and Roy and Suraj moved, freeing up a table.

We swooped.

'Have you ever mixed tea and coffee and tried it?'

'No. Sounds like a nightmare,' I said, taking a gulp of my tea.

'Nor have I, but I should. I'm sure I'd like it.'

'What rot you talk!' I changed the topic. 'Do you think Chitra will come down for Diwali?'

'You could try. Call her. She seems to have taken to Bombay in a big way. The college atmosphere suits her just fine. She says she wants to see Diwali in Bombay. And there are art galleries to explore. She said that if she could make it, she would try and come. I told her it was okay with me if she didn't make it for Diwali but she must not skip Eid. Eid is in November. I told her that Vipin is coming too. I invited him. I think he might come. Why don't you tell her too?'

'Why did you say I'm coming?'

'If I invite you, you'll come, won't you?'

'You haven't even mentioned it, let alone invited me.'

'But I've mentioned it and invited you now, no?'

'What if I can't make it that day?'

'I'll celebrate Eid on the day you can make it.'

*

It was as Fatima said it would be. Chitra did come but only after Diwali.

'I've only come for eight days. I want to spend those with my father. Why don't you come here? How about Saturday? I'll ask Fatima as well.'

*

The dealer called. My Unicorn was ready.

'Come on Friday.'

I called Krishna. We went on the old scooter to the showroom. When I got my Unicorn, I handed over the keys of the old scooter to him. 'It's yours now. Until you get a new one.'

I remembered Fatima's words and called her after I had taken delivery. There were two hours left of class but she bunked the last two periods and off we shot to Dona Paula.

'The seat is very comfortable,' Fatima said. I didn't tell her that that was why I had bought the Unicorn; she might read too much into it.

That we could now drive down to Canacona was delighting her. 'Just sixty to seventy minutes from Panjim to Canacona,' I said. She retorted, 'Where's the fire? Let's do it slowly, stretch it out over two hours. All the more time for me to ride pillion.'

*

But our stars were crossed. On Friday evening Ma complained that her feet were hurting. When I offered to massage them, she refused to let me even touch them. She didn't come out for dinner and ate only what I served her. I didn't care to disturb Dr Costabir in the night so I called him only in the morning. But I spent a night reading up on her problem. She had diabetic neuropathy but it was not too far advanced. If we started treatment immediately and she was careful, we could beat this. I sat by her side all night, listening to her moaning. I felt truly sorry for her. She had never known much happiness. I called Costabir in the morning. Then I called Fatima and explained my predicament. 'But you go. Tell Chitra we'll try and meet before she leaves.'

*

When I was at the pharmacy, Chitra called. I thought I'd speak later and did not answer. When I got home, Fatima called.

'Was Chitra mad at me?'

'At both of us. I didn't go either. Just not in the mood. How's your mother now?'

I called Chitra.

'It's Eid on Tuesday. We can go together to Fatima's place. I'll show you the new bike.'

'Sorry Vipin, I've had to cut this trip short. I'm leaving tomorrow. I'm catching the Mangalore Express from Canacona.'

She seemed to be cutting our conversation short too. I didn't feel she was very keen on meeting; there seemed to be no warmth in her voice. Or was I just imagining it?

Fatima was also depressed. 'Your mum is not well. Chitra isn't here. Let's celebrate Eid next year,' she said.

I called on Tuesday morning.

'Eid Mubarak, Fatima!'

'Thank you, Vipin. Are you likely to be in Panjim today?' She seemed in a hurry.

I had to pick up Ma's reports from Lobo Lab at noon.

'We'll meet there then,' she said and before I could warn her that I would not be able to stay too long she hung up.

I didn't want her waiting, so I got there five minutes early. A man at the counter said, 'A young lady had come and left this for you.'

There was a container and a note. The note said: 'Sorry, Vipin, can't meet today. I'll tell you why later.'

I could smell the tantalising aromas of mutton biryani, one of Ma's favourite dishes, but I'd have to eat it in hiding. The next few days left me uncomfortable for many reasons. I felt personally responsible for Ma's worsening condition, for one. And Chitra seemed to be drifting away from us. My invitation for Eid had also been cancelled. All this because Chitra had left or because the new Imam disapproved of

Fatima's socialising? Even though we had agreed to meet at twelve, she had found it difficult to come. I had never felt so lonely before.

Lonely? Being alone had been a condition I was used to. I was alone at home, I studied alone, I played alone. Even if Ma and Daddy were at home, I was alone. I felt as if I were alone now even though Ma was at home with me. So why was solitude weighing on me so heavily? I found that I had to talk to someone.

'Hello, Fatima. Can we meet this evening?'

'All well?'

I could hear the concern in her voice. Warmth spread through me.

'Just feeling lonely.' I had never admitted as much to anyone. Was this weakness on my part? I gave Ma her medicines and when she fell asleep, I left. As I wheeled the bike out, I suddenly found myself worrying that Fatima would cancel suddenly. What was that about? Was I the burned child now who feared the sun?

With Fatima as pillion, I rode to Dona Paula. It was thick with tourists.

'We have to find another place.'

I kept looked at her for a moment. Could she read my mind?

'What?' she asked.

'I was thinking the same thing. We won't get a chance to talk in this crowd.'

'Should we go somewhere else?'

'Next time.'

'Thank you!' she said, taking hold of my arm. The clouds parted and the sunlight poured through. I wanted to put my arm around her shoulders and have her rest her head on my chest. These filmy thoughts surprised me.

'When you called, I was worried but now I'm just delighted.'

'That makes two of us,' I said and meant it.

Suddenly Fatima said, 'I want to dance, I'm so happy.'

'Here? Won't people think it odd?'

'I'm dancing for you, not for people.' Then she added. 'Even if you say no I feel like dancing. I can't dance on demand. Anyway, the next time I feel like dancing you're not to say no.'

As always, we had tea and coffee and then we got up to go back.

'Thank you, Fatima. I've been feeling a bit depressed for the last few days.'

'Is this about Chitra?'

'I don't know. But I'm feeling so much better now that we met.'

Before I could start the bike, she stopped me. 'Will you listen to a poem? It's only three lines and it's mine.'

I waited.

'Surya maaka dipkaaytaa, dipkaaoon di.
Wotaat haanv korpotaam, korpum di.
Tujya udaas manaacher mojhi saawli podun di.'
'The sun shines down on me. Let it shine.
The heat scorches me. Let me burn
If I may cast cool shade over your sad mind.'

*

Over Christmas, we found a new place. Bambolim beach. It was very rocky but there were no crowds. We sat on the rocks for there were no benches either and watched the waves. Chitra called on a schedule: one week me, one week

Fatima. She knew that what she said to either of us would get to the other.

*

Fatima found an excuse to meet me. It was an assignment. She had to write an essay for Hindi class: 'The Significance of Books in Our Lives'. Her reading in Hindi stretched only as far as ghazals, shayari and poetry.

'I can't think what to write,' she said. 'That's why I called you so that you can give me some points.'

The next day again. Five minutes on the topics and fifteen minutes of conversation.

She complained that she did not find the time for studies but would suggest that we go here and there.

I had enjoyed Chitra's company. That was because of her extensive reading. Fatima was interested in poetry and dance. I was interested in neither. And yet of late I had grown to like her. Perhaps because she was Chitra's friend. She took me into another world altogether. At first, I thought of it as her world but soon its outlines became familiar.

*

Towards the end of the Christmas holidays and before the end of the year, we went to Bambolim. Suddenly Fatima seemed struck by an idea. 'Have you seen *Guide*?'

I hadn't. Fatima loved watching old films. I didn't care much for cinema.

'I want to dance like Rosie today. Shall I?'

'Feel free to break an ankle.'

Undaunted, she rose to her feet. She found *Piya tose nainaa laage re* on her phone and began to play it. Turning those rocks into a platform, she started to dance. She gave it her all, singing along as she moved. I had to admit that she danced beautifully. It was a song that allows no pauses but Fatima kept up with it, her expressions and movements, fluid and sensuous. I could not take my eyes off her. And then as she executed yet another spin, she lost her balance and fell over. Some people who had been watching from a distance applauded. I went over. Her feet were bruised. I picked her up in my arms.

'Are you hurt?'

'If you pick me up like this, I'm willing to fall over again and again.' I set her down. She rested her weight on me and we began to walk. She said, 'Do you know why I like to dance?' And without waiting for an answer, she added, 'It's like falling in love.'

'With whom?'

'With anyone, with me, with you…' she said and pinched my arm. When we arrived at Panjim I offered to drop her home but she hired an auto and left.

That night I ordered R.K. Narayan's *The Guide* on Bookganga.

The next morning Fatima called. 'I won't be able to meet for the next couple of days. Don't be looking for me.'

I wasn't going to be looking for her but I still asked, 'Why not?'

'I've hurt my soles, both of them.'

24

Fun Week

Ma's health took a turn for the better over the next few months since I imposed a strict dietary regimen and made sure she took her medication on time. Dr Costabir said, 'It's a miracle that you're well again. But you have Babu to thank for this.'

But Ma was a bad patient who resented my strictures. From the moment she woke up she would begin complaining. 'Someone's having nice sweet tea and serving me this bitter brew.'

Since I had taken over the housework, she did not help at all. This meant even less movement and so I had to insist on her getting up and walking about. Even this she saw as imposition. If she had earlier blamed Daddy for not making her happy, now she blamed me for making her unhappy.

Looking after Ma and doing the housework meant I had to miss college. But I didn't want to stop studying. It was not possible to study Konkani literature on the Net so I tried not to miss those classes. It was not because I cared about whether I passed or I got good marks; I just wanted to learn about Konkani.

Then came Fun Week. The college set up a committee.

Amrut took the lead. He tried to get me involved too. I managed to stay out of it. Since the college would not spend any money, the cultural committee had to raise sponsorships on its own. I donated a thousand rupees.

Amrut brought in sponsorship from a beer company: fifty thousand rupees. That made him a hero.

'Tomorrow there's a dance competition. I'm going to give a solo performance. But you have to come and see it,' Fatima said.

'Sorry, not interested.'

'Please. Just because I'm asking...'

'But I haven't seen even one other...'

'All the more reason.'

I refused to budge.

'If you don't come, I won't dance.'

'You must do as you choose.'

'Okay. Then I'm going announce in front of everyone that since you're not here, I'm withdrawing. And you should know I keep my word.'

Fatima was stubborn and a bit off the wall. I didn't want her to be announcing these things and she knew it. Hence this blackmail. I said nothing.

'If I don't see you in the audience, I won't dance. Be warned.'

And so I was forced to go. The last entry was Fatima's. She danced as if we were alone in the auditorium. The students gave her a standing ovation. They clapped and whistled and stamped their feet. Fatima danced as if she had been born with paizonaa tied to her ankles, as if she were a trained dancer.

Balam pichkari jo tune mujhe maari
Toh seedhi saadhi chhori sharabi ho gayi

When you sprayed me with your pichkaari
You turned an innocent girl into an alcoholic.

When she finished there was a roar of applause and the usual comments: 'Once more...Ultimate...!'

There was no doubt who was the winner. Then she was back on stage and took the mic to say: 'I dedicate this performance to the man who saved my life.' Another storm of clapping. I was not sure who had understood Fatima's reference but then one or two voices shouted, 'Phantom, Phantom!'

Fatima was standing in the spotlight. I was among the audience. For a moment I wanted total darkness, a spotlight that could darken me, black me out. Then I would become invisible. Unfortunately the lights were on and everyone could see me.

*

Generally, government programmes find few takers. But the Art and Culture Department's D.D. Kosambi Festival of Ideas generally drew crowds, or so I had heard. I had never gone myself. And it is likely that I would not have gone if Martin Sir had not told me that I should go. 'The speakers are very good. I suggest you go today. Professor Anil Kumar Gupta is going to speak on grassroots innovation. It may motivate you.'

If Martin Sir had taken the trouble to call me, I figured I should go. Perhaps he was a regular at these lectures. And then he might wonder where I was. I thought I might go with Fatima but then it occurred to me that Martin Sir might see us and ask, 'Who's this?' and then what would I say?

*

At around three o'clock, Martin Sir called again.

'Are you going for the lecture?'

'Yes, sir.'

'How are you planning to go?'

'I thought I'd take the bike.'

'If your pillion is free, can I hitch a lift?' he asked hesitantly.

'I shall be honoured, sir,' I said and meant it too.

'It's likely to be a full house. We should get there early.'

And he was right. The hall was almost full of people eager to hear the professor's ideas. Many of them were young. I found it odd to be sitting next to Martin Sir. But the excitement was contagious.

'My life has been a journey of discovery,' Professor Gupta said at the very beginning. He used no fancy flourishes but spoke simply and from the heart. His audience was spellbound. He spoke of the many small innovations he had witnessed and the responses he got from the youth, which were fascinating. He emphasized that each innovation arises at some sensitive juncture and can rarely be attributed to a single person. Instead, he talked about the idea of the hive-mind where nameless, faceless people come together to make change. Everyone has a creative mind which can give rise to new ideas but if these are not given encouragement, the mind settles into routine thinking. One has to keep one's heart open and one's mind receptive and only then will new concepts come alive. He offered the example of very young children who can often have startlingly original ideas but if they're made to feel that they will be laughed at, they do not express themselves. And in this silence, we lose any number of original ideas...

Professor Gupta spoke for forty minutes. The hall was

packed but the crowd listened in silence. He spoke now about teachers. He said there were four kinds of teachers. The first is the teacher within, the second is nature, the third is one's social environment and the fourth is one's peers, the knowledgeable people around one. 'These four teachers take us forward,' he said.

I resisted the impulse to look at Martin Sir. Professor Gupta offered the youth an open challenge: 'When you have an idea, new idea, however strange, however extraordinary, bring it to us. We will consider it seriously.' He even gave his email ID. The lecture ended with thunderous applause. Then there was a question-and-answer session. Martin Sir looked at me encouragingly as if to say, 'Go on and ask your questions.'

I thought back to the time I had been sitting in another audience when Fatima had dedicated her dance to me and I had wanted a spotlight (a spotdark?) to hide me. Could that be at all possible? Could one construct a device that would block light, erase it from a space and so create a patch of darkness? Of course, there were opaque objects but what we needed was something that would erase all light, prevent light pollution, create real darkness? But I could not get myself to say anything.

Outside it was dark already. I dropped sir home. When he got off the bike, he thanked me and asked, 'What did you think of the lecture?'

'Awesome, sir. It was because of you that I could...'

'I thought you'd have had something to ask him.'

I was silent.

'Be open. Be frank. Didn't you have an idea to share with him?'

'I've been thinking about this for a while, sir. It's a

thought that keeps coming back. When it is dark one turns on the torch and it becomes light. But what if one wants to do the opposite? What if one wants to cast darkness into a lighted area. Say for instance, I want to erase light pollution so that I can study the stars. This is all very tenuous right now. I don't even know if it's feasible.'

Martin Sir took a while to process that then he said, 'You should have asked. Who knows what might have come out of that? Did you note his email ID?'

I hadn't. Sir handed me a slip on which he had written the ID.

'Drop him a line, quick.'

25

The Three-word Equation

'We are on holiday now. When do yours start?' I asked Chitra over the phone.

'From tomorrow.'

'Tickets booked?'

'Yes, but not for Goa. I'm going to Shimla with Preetam.'

'And who's this guy Preetam?'

I was surprised to find that I wanted to know more about Preetam than anything else.

'He's not a guy, Preetam's a woman. My roomie. And a really good artist. So I said to her, "Okay, this time we'll go to Shimla but next year you have to come with me to Goa." She has agreed.'

And then I had to listen to a tale of Preetam's exploits and wonderful qualities.

'And here I was waiting to see you this time. Last time, we missed each other.'

'And who didn't show up? I remember all too well. How's your mother now?'

As expected, Fatima called immediately afterwards. 'I supposed you heard? Chitra's not coming. I told her I would miss her. She said, "Simple, when you're with Vipin, pretend I'm with you as well."'

I maintained my customary silence. She continued, 'You know, Vipin our friendship is a *teen lafzon ki kahaani*. Guess what those three words are?'

But before I could answer, she had told me: 'You. Me. No.'

'You've dropped Chitra from this equation?'

She said: 'If Chitra were here, I would have loved it. But she's off with her friend to Shimla to have a great time. So, let's you and me have a great time here. Just the two of us and our three words.'

I didn't like the subtext that Fatima was happy that Chitra was not coming.

'Look Fatima, I think I'm going to be housebound this vacation.'

'No problem, Vipin. I'll come to your house. But let's deal with that when it comes up. Let's just meet this evening.'

Fatima was right when she said that the coffee at Café Coffee Day on the Campal was good but I didn't enjoy my tea very much.

*

Perhaps it was all for the best that Chitra had not come to Goa for this vacation. The last time, Ma had had a diabetic neuropathy attack. And now that she had fallen it had worsened. This was because of her irresponsible behaviour. Every day she would sneak some money to the baker who brought us our daily bread and ask him to buy her some sweets. She had hidden these away in a glass jar among her saris.

One night I heard a thud, someone falling. When I went into her room, she was lying on the floor, the jar shattered next to her and a piece of glass stuck in her foot. I tried to get her up but it was difficult so I first pulled out the glass piece and the blood began to flow out of her in a small, gurgling stream. I tied it up firmly and went off to look for a bandage. When she was bandaged, I managed to heave her near dead-weight back on to her bed. She spent the rest of the night moaning and complaining while I sat by, helpless.

I had suspected something of what happened but Dr Costabir came and looked her over and confirmed my diagnosis. 'Her ankles are swollen. We'll have to increase her insulin. But if the swelling doesn't come down in a couple of days, we have to show her to an ortho.'

He had to put four stitches into her foot and told her, 'If you don't follow advice, you'll have to go to hospital.'

Ma was shocked. 'You'll dump me in a hospital to die? Is that your plan, Babu? To send me off after your father?'

What must Costabir be thinking? Surely he knew her and me well enough to discount this.

I took on the responsibility of monitoring her round the clock. Her medicines, the insulin injections, the glucometer, feeding her, cleaning her right up to clearing her shit and piss. In between I managed to read some books online. I had brought a collected Shenoy Goembab from the library and spent some time studying that whenever I had time. And so the days slipped by.

*

When Fatima called, I told her about it. Though I said I would prefer her not to come, she turned up. When she arrived, I was giving Ma a sponge bath. When Ma dozed off, I made tea for myself and coffee for Fatima.

'Are you managing all this single-handed? You will need help, Vipin. See if you can find a maid?'

And holding her coffee cup she said, 'May I come and help you?'

'Do you think I can't manage?' I asked her, taking a gulp of tea.

'I would never say that. I know you. If somebody told me you had given birth to a child tomorrow, I would believe that,' she said and burst out laughing. I took a moment to think about this. Who knows whether in some distant future this might not be feasible? Deliveries through Caesarean section.

'What are you thinking? Your tea will get cold.' Fatima brought me back to the present. I finished my tea and got to my feet. I wanted Fatima to stay a while longer but there was just too much to do. 'Time for her insulin.'

Fatima got up. She took the cups into the kitchen. She washed them and slung on the hooks above the sink.

'You're acting as if you're at home,' I said, the words coming to my lips before I could stop them.

'I am in the house of my friend. Surely, I have some rights?' Then she came right up to me and recited a poem.

'The road is long, the destination unclear.
But I know how to be a friend
If we are to part,
I will not stop you.
But do not stop me when
I try to enjoy our
Moments of togetherness.'

As she spoke, she drew even closer and putting her hand on my shoulder, she buried her nose in my chest and inhaled deeply.

'What would you know of the scent of friendship?'

In the next moment she had slipped her feet into her sandals and she was gone.

26

The Rules of Friendship

Krishna came over, looking for a job in a good hotel to gain some experience over the vacation. When he saw Ma's state, he offered to come back to work. I knew than gaining experience in a real hotel was more important that coming to work for us and so I refused. Ma called Krishna over and asked him make her biryani. I had warned him that all such requests had to be routed through me. So he said, 'I'll ask Babu,' leaving Ma quite annoyed with him.

*

I called Fatima which made her very happy.

'You're learning the rules of friendship at last,' she said.

'What makes you say that?'

'All it took was a single verse. I had no idea it would work so quickly.'

I changed the subject. 'Remember you told me your uncle works at Sher-e-Punjab?'

'My mother's brother, yes. Why?'

I told her about Krishna. 'If he gets to work there for a month, he'll earn something and learn something. Will you ask?'

She called the next day, 'He's in luck. An assistant cook has gone on leave for two months. Can he start tomorrow?'

I thought it best to make things clear. Krishna had worked in a small restaurant. He had some experience of cooking and loved doing it. But I wasn't sure that he would be ready to stand in for an assistant cook.

'Don't I know Krishna? I've told them all about him. Uncle says he'll bring him up to scratch. And if he's quick, he'll learn what he needs to know.'

I sent Krishna to Sher-e-Punjab that very day.

*

Ma's blood sugar responded to the insulin but the swelling did not subside. The wound in her foot had improved but she would not set the foot on the floor. Dr Costabir also advised she should keep her weight off it.

When college reopened, I could not attend. Despite my telling her not to, Fatima came on two separate occasions. Chitra would phone regularly. And Krishna would drop in whenever he had a free moment. That night, as I was browsing, I found a book called *A Grief Observed* by C. S. Lewis.

The name was not familiar but I thought, from the synopsis, that Martin Sir might like it. I read the preview and the reviews, all of which brought back memories. Sir's birthday was in July. I ordered the book.

In between I managed to squeeze in a few lectures in college. But other than Konkani, I felt no interest in the other subjects. Even English Literature, a subject which I had looked forward to, bored me in class.

But perhaps because I had hardly read anything in Konkani or because the teacher was good, I did enjoy those classes. I did not think I could get enough time to attend class regularly so I spent most of my time in the library, reading Konkani books.

As soon as Fatima saw me, she would come racing up, and we would go off for tea and coffee. Meeting in the evening was no longer possible.

'No problem. If you can't manage the evening, come in the morning. Or the afternoon. Whatever. I'll bunk,' Fatima said.

'But listen, it's your final year. You need to concentrate.'

'No problem. No one is going to notice. And if I have any difficulties, you're there. What you did for me in the first year, you can repeat in the third year.'

*

When Krishna came to see me, I asked him, 'On July 10 can you bring me a Black Forest cake?' Perhaps Ma heard this. So on the tenth, she was waiting with bated breath. As soon as Krishna arrived, she called out, 'Babu, what has Krishna brought with him?'

'Nothing much,' I said.

But she insisted, 'I know he's got cake. And I want a piece.'

'Listen Ma, it's for Martin Sir's birthday.'

'Whatever. He's not going to miss a small piece.'

'Ma, your diabetes...'

'Arre one piece of cake is not going to kill me.'

I ignored her. But I went to the chemist and got some sugar-free sweeteners. In the evening before going to Martin Sir's house, I made her a cup of tea with milk and a sugar-free pill. When she took her first sip, her face brightened and she said, 'God bless you, Babu. This is heaven.'

*

Agnes Aunty opened the door. She invited me in. 'Martin is not at home. He's gone to Panjim to see a doctor.'

'Nothing serious I hope?'

'His blood pressure keeps rising despite the pills. The doctor said he'll change his medication. He just called and said that there's a crowd at the doctor's and he'll be back late.'

'I'll come again,' I said but she would have none of it. 'I know you enjoy my tea,' she said and went in.

When she returned, she saw the book on the table.

'What's this?'

'I hope he likes it and there's this cake as well. I think this is the first time I've got him anything.'

'Cake!' she exclaimed and her eyes filled. 'In years gone by, Stella would bake a cake herself. I'd forgotten all about baking a cake for him.'

We drank our tea in silence and then Agnes Aunty said, 'Martin says he wants to take voluntary retirement now.'

'So soon?' I asked, surprised.

'Yes. He's seems to have lost all interest in life.'

'But why?'

Agnes Aunty made no reply, only shaking her head and wiping her eyes.

'What will he do then?'

'He says that there are lots of books to read.'

*

While Ma's condition had not worsened, it had not improved either. She still depended on me to get everything done. The sugar-free pills had made a difference; she was not complaining so much. I had also figured out how to telescope the chores so as to free up some time for myself if I wanted to go out.

I learned, for instance, what tasks could be postponed for a day. Fatima benefited from these moments, of course, or was I the one who made her the beneficiary of this free time?

'You could always find time to meet Chitra. But for me, you never have any free time,' she would complain and I would work out something. Did I do this for her? Or for me? I had become accustomed to getting out of the house. But once outside, I didn't have too many options. When Chitra was around, I would meet both of them and now that she wasn't, I only left home to meet Fatima.

Even when Chitra was around, I knew that Fatima enjoyed spending time with me. But slowly I began to enjoy Fatima's company too. She must have known this for she had grown bold of late.

Once she asked me, 'Why are you so detached?'

What answer could I make?

'Have you ever fallen in love?' she asked me once and when I did not reply for a while she added, 'Do you love yourself?'

'Have you?'

'Come close and look into my eyes. What you will see there is my love.'

*

'I think Fatima has begun to like you,' Chitra told me over the phone.

'Did Fatima tell you that?' I asked.

'You don't have to be *told* some things,' she replied.

'Then how come you don't know that a day doesn't go by without me thinking about you?'

'This Fatima certainly told me.'

*

'I have a wish. Will you fulfil it?'

'You're asking like it's your last wish.'

'Think of it that way then. I know you don't like watching films in a cinema hall. But today, make an exception. Come with me. Please.'

'Why ask me to do what I don't like to do?'

'Because I like it?'

'I'm not stopping you from going.'

'I've booked two tickets. Just this once. Don't hurt me by saying no.'

Was there something different, something more intense that day? Or was it just another Drama Queen stunt?

'I think it's selfish to ask someone to do something they don't...'

'So be it. Call me selfish but just come.'

She ended the call as if it were all settled.

*

A 3:15 show. There was a crowd outside the multiplex. We went in before the film started. There were about thirty people in a hall that could seat three hundred.

'What are we watching?'

'Does it matter?' she answered in a droll tone.

'I hope it's a good film?'

'The critics gave it two stars.'

'That bad? And still you booked?'

'That is precisely why I booked,' she said and took hold of my arm. Even after the film began, she kept talking to me. Perhaps she didn't want people to overhear for she brought her mouth close to my ear and whispered into it.

'If you didn't want to see this film, why are we here? We could have just gone out, as usual.'

'I wanted to break that routine so I brought you here.'

'In this darkness?'

'I thought you said you like the darkness. That's what you told Chitra, anyway. Have you forgotten?'

Perhaps she knew that any mention of Chitra would have me interested.

'Do you know what Chitra said to me on the phone yesterday?'

I made no response so she went on: 'She said, "Now Vipin is all yours."'

'So was I a shared territory earlier?' I asked, somewhat irritated.

'Nothing like that. Let me tell you what she said: "Out of sight, out of mind". Anyway, that's what she said and I accepted that for what it's worth. But truly, I don't think I miss her the way I used to.'

I felt the same way too but I didn't say it.

'Because you have made up for the loss,' she said but just then a dance sequence began in the film. Since it was a semi-classical dance, she paid rapt attention. And I watched her eyes sparkling in the darkness.

In the interval, I made to get up. 'I'll get you some coffee.'

'No, not now. Let's just talk. We can have tea and coffee later. On the way home.'

Before the film could start, she asked, 'Doesn't Ma tell you to get married?'

'Why would she do such a thing?'

'She must be alone at home. Your wife would be a support, maybe company for her?'

'Ma keeps her hand in. And if she needed help, we can always hire someone. Why marry for that?'

'But just suppose she were to say you should get married, what then? Hypothetically speaking. What would you say?'

'I'd say I have no thought to get married.'

'But if you were to fall in love you would get married, right?'

'I don't know,' I said, hoping to end the conversation.

'But then how will I get married?' Fatima asked plaintively.

I was silent.

'Don't you know, Vipin? How can you not know? I love you very much.'

'I don't.'

I didn't want to hurt her but I didn't want to fall into her trap either.

She must have been hurt. She was silent for a while and then she said, 'Okay, that's all right. Don't. But I love you and you can't stop me.'

Her voice rose, threateningly. She hit me with her fists, once, twice. A couple of the audience turned around to see what was going on. But just then the screen exploded in bullets. Fatima buried her face in her handkerchief. I had no idea whether she was sobbing or wiping her eyes.

By the time the film ended, Fatima was calm. I took her hand and we followed the audience as it straggled out of the theatre. But outside, her eyes widened with fear, she shook my hand off and bowing her head, she began to walk away so fast that I had to scamper after her. I got the bike out and said, 'Let's get some coffee into you. You might feel better.'

'No, no, Vipin. I'm scared. Just drop me at the bus-stand,' she said. Her eyes were scanning the crowds, still frightened. As we rode to the bus-stand, she told me that she had seen her brother, Aslam. 'He was with that Tablighi

Imam I told you about. He gets people all hot and bothered. Now, he's going to tell Abbu everything.'

We were at the bus stand.

'Are you afraid of him?' I asked but before she could answer, the bus had arrived and she jumped in. I couldn't say farewell properly. It was as if a flowing stream had suddenly frozen over.

*

I could not go to college the next day and Fatima did not call either. Ma's blood sugar level had not come down but was steady and so perhaps because of that, I was a little complacent. Then she began to complain of pain in her legs. When I examined them, there were bluish-black marks all over her calves right down to her ankles.

I didn't even bother with Dr Costabir; I just called 108 and got an ambulance to take her to the hospital. I suspected it was gangrene and it was vital to control it immediately. The next few days were spent in a medical maze; there were injections and tests, saline bottles and catheters, reports and conferences. I spent most of my time in the hospital and in the middle of it all, a call from Chitra.

'I'm coming to Goa on Saturday. Let's meet.'

'Sorry, Chitra, I don't think it will be possible this time.'

'Are you angry with me?'

'Where's the time to get angry?'

'But I am coming specially to see you,' she said.

I had to tell her then about Ma's condition. 'They're talking about amputation.'

Chitra paused for a moment before speaking. 'Have you any idea what state Fatima is in now?'

I had suspected that she would have been scolded by her parents or that Imam.

'They've stopped her going to college and...' Chitra stopped, perhaps waiting for a response. Then she went on: 'We can talk about that later. Take care of Ma. Anyway, I'm coming down. You won't be able to make it so I'll come to the hospital. I have to talk to you.'

She ended the call.

*

I signed the form for surgery with no real feeling. But there were still questions that plagued me. The doctor asked me whether they should amputate her leg beneath the knees or above. The question left me puzzled. Post-operative care would be easier if they cut above her knee. What would Daddy have done if he were here? Or would he have simply refused to sign and got his Baba to perform an exorcism?

After the surgery, Ma spent a day and a night in the ICU before she was brought to the ward. Chitra called. She was coming by the Mangalore Express and would get down at Canacona. She would meet her father, have lunch and then set out to meet me. 'I should be there by four thirty,' she said. 'We can talk for an hour or so and then I'll have to go to the airport to catch the nine thirty flight for Mumbai.' She seemed to be in organizational mode, more of a business traveller than a friend.

I went to see the staff nurse on duty. 'Ma seems to be out of it. Can I go home for a couple of hours and come back?'

'Someone has to be by her side at all times,' she replied.

I called Krishna in the afternoon. His last lecture ended at four, he said. 'I may be ten or fifteen minutes late,' he added. 'But I'll be there by four thirty latest.' He was as good as his word but by then Chitra was already in the ward. It had been more than a year since I had seen her last. She seemed very different.

How different? I couldn't say. Her face, her walk, her hair, her clothes? Or just her eyes? What had I seen in those eyes? What had I thought I was seeing in those eyes?

The tea and coffee in the canteen were decent but it was not the kind of place where you could linger and talk. I got the bike out.

'Where are you taking me?'

'Not too far.'

At Bambolim, we picked our way across the rocks to the usual spot.

'This is where Fatima hurt her foot, no?' she asked

And then she came right to the issue at hand: 'That day you guys went to the cinema together and Fatima ended up in trouble.'

'I didn't take her there. She insisted on going.'

'So it was all her fault? Is that what you're saying?'

'No, but she must have known that she could end up in trouble, right?'

'That was why she asked you to go for a film with her. So she could tell you of her love. To ask you for a commitment. If you had acknowledged your love for her, she was ready to face the consequences, whatever those might have been.'

'She's so frightened of her family or what?'

'You think she'd be afraid of her family? She had confided in Aslambhai. Her parents are progressive people at heart, you know. But then there are these orthodox Islamic leaders who exaggerate things. Those are the people she fears. They don't approve of a Muslim girl being friendly with a Hindu boy. She wanted to tell you about this. That was why she called off her invitation to come for Eid lunch; her father insisted. You remember when you would ask whether you could drop her home and she would refuse? That was why. How much she cried when she told me all this on the phone, poor mite. I was crying too by the end of it. Which was why I came down to explain things to you.'

'To explain things to me? What did I do wrong?'

'First listen to me,' she said. 'You have no idea, Vipin, what she has gone through. She has suffered terribly even as a child. She was a girl when she was raped. The whole thing was hushed up by her family to save her from wagging tongues. She ended up with a severe case of depression. But she got counselling and that saved her. But still she held aloof from the others at school and in college. She was like a rabbit, always tense, always poised for flight. I remember the first time I saw her, such a pretty girl, but always alone. I noticed her eyes. Vipin, have you? Such expressive eyes. I wanted to paint her and that's how we got acquainted. And you know how coffee unites us but imagine, she had never dared to go into the canteen alone. I pushed and shoved and finally got her out of her shell. And when she shared her poetry, I was struck by it too. She seemed to know a lot of poetry. And her voice, you've heard her sing, you know how beautiful it is. She's never studied dance but she's a gifted dancer. I was so proud that she was my friend and my friend alone—until we met you.'

She paused for a moment. 'That fateful day when you saved her? She was so terrified. Luckily, I was also close by. I reached her home afterwards. I was so scared that she would sink back into depression. Then she wanted to meet you to thank you but again she was worried that you'd try it on with her, act the hero, you know. She was going to thank you and run. But you turned out to be different. You refused to take credit for what you had done and barely even looked at Fatima. When she tried to get close to you, you pushed her away. That hurt her. I kept reassuring her. It was I who invited her along when we were going to meet up. You can't imagine how much she changed after meeting you. She wouldn't even sing for me and there she was, willing to dance for you in public. You have no idea how much she loves you...'

'And you?' I asked, looking into her eyes.

Chitra ignored the question.

'Fatima has no secrets from me. She's said it so often: "I feel safe when I'm with Vipin." You are the first man who treated her like a person and not a sex toy. You didn't seem to care whether she was a Hindu or a Muslim. Nor were you concerned about whether she was younger or older than you, your college senior or junior. I think she began to feel free in your company.'

Chitra was sitting with her eyes fixed on the horizon. She pointed at a boat far out to sea. 'The waves are beating against it but it is still. But even that boat isn't as stolid as you. The wind can move it. In a storm, it will dip and buckle like Fatima. But if there is an expert boatman, it will be at peace and find its way out again.'

Chitra was finding a way, I thought, to come to the point. 'All this while you've only been talking about Fatima. You haven't said a word about yourself. But you were my first friend. Fatima came after that.'

'I will always be your friend, Vipin.' And then she added as if she had finally chanced upon what she needed to say: 'How can you not know that she loves you, Vipin? You have reached the point of no return. You have to make a decision. For Fatima's sake.'

'What are you saying I should do?'

'Propose.'

Suddenly I was filled with a great sadness. The waves came roaring up to the beach and collapsed into silence.

My head felt numb. Chitra was waiting for my reply. I waited until I felt a little calmer and said, 'When we were in the theatre, Fatima said as much to me. "How can you not know that I love you?" And I said, "I'm willing to be friends. Love? I've never looked at you that way. So now don't force me to propose."'

'You are such a stubborn coot, Vipin. Why can't you accept that Fatima loves you?'

'Because I love you,' I said impulsively.

Chitra was stunned.

'Oh. Fatima would often say that. "I think he prefers you," she said. And truly, Vipin, I do like you very much. But it's a different kind of liking. On the other hand, Fatima *loves* you.'

I thought of the difference Gautam Buddha had suggested between liking and loving. When someone likes a flower, the impulse is to pluck it. When someone loves a flower, the impulse is to look after the tree on which it blooms. I wanted to tell Chitra this. But before I could open my mouth, she had silenced me with a gesture. She took a deep breath and said, 'Not everything is for saying. But since you're a friend, I'm sharing it with you. I haven't even told Fatima yet. I will though. But let's get this out of the way first. I am in a relationship. It's been a year. I'm a lesbian, Vipin. And I've found someone to love.'

'Preetam?' I said spontaneously.

'You remember? Yes. The one I went to Shimla with.'

The sun set. It took a jumble of feelings and thoughts with it.

'I have no check-in baggage so I can get to the airport an hour and a half before the flight. How about a coffee? And tea for you, of course.'

We stopped at a coffee house on the way.

Perhaps because she was stuck for something to say, Chitra said. 'I've often wanted to ask you. Why don't you write a novel?'

'Martin Sir asked me that too. But I take my cue from Isaac Bashevis Singer: "Life is God's novel; let him write it."'

'Didn't stop Mr Singer from writing.'

'I think the words pushed their way out of him. If the words push, I might even do some writing.'

While we waited for our tea and coffee, I asked Chitra: 'Reading anything new?'

She pulled a book out of her bag, 'Right now, this.'

Babyji by Abha Dawesar. I read the back. It was a work of lesbian fiction. When I handed it back quickly, Chitra laughed. Then her gaze must have fallen on the bike parked outside.

'Fatima really liked your bike.' And then for want of anything better to say: 'She wanted to go on a long ride with you.'

Our order arrived. We picked up the cups. We raised them to our lips and Chitra said, 'So symbolic, no?' And then I realized that I had picked up her coffee cup and she had raised my tea cup to her lips. 'Everything seems a bit mixed up now.'

As she got into a taxi, she said, 'When I said that you should propose, I didn't mean that you have to get married right away. Propose now and then give it two years. Fatima says she'll wait. Now the ball is in your court.'

*

When Ma's amputation was being planned, I called the uncles at her instance. The doctors had told me that they needed blood donations for her surgery. I said I was willing to donate but they said they would need more. I called Uncle Senior again. He said, 'I'll see if I can make it but if I can't, check at GMC; they have blood donor lists.' That was a useful piece of advice; eventually Krishna and I donated and I bought the other bottles that were needed.

The nurse had warned me: 'We will need a woman by her bed at all times.' I called my uncle again but he evaded taking responsibility for this too. Until the surgery, I had spent my days outside the ward. My uncles seemed to have washed their hands of us. But when Ma was brought back to the ward, I had a real question before me.

When I went to meet Chitra, Krishna had taken over for the evening. When I returned, he told me that my uncle had come in my absence. Krishna said that my uncle had clicked his tongue at my handing over responsibility to him. But once again his advice came in handy. Uncle Senior had said paid attendants were available and even left the contacts for one of them. I heaved a sigh of relief and relieved Krishna of his duty.

*

That day, for the first time, I felt that my mind was in the grips of some confusion. The Chitra who had made me aware of my own independent existence, who had awakened my sleeping creativity, who had offered me friendship, that Chitra was slowly drifting away; of course, I was going to regret the loss. I had no rights over her or her affections. How could I have been completely unaware of her homosexual predilections? Was I resenting her finding a gay partner or was I resentful of the new distance between us? Why had I returned her book so abruptly? Even as I was dealing with this rush of questions, I found myself ordering *Babyji* on my mobile on Bookganga.

I was awake into the wee hours and fell asleep where I was sitting. And I could hear Fatima singing in the distance.

Tere mere sapne ab ek rang ke
Jahaan bhi le jaaye raahein, hum sang hai.

Our dreams are now each other's;
and wherever the roads take us, we will be together.

Someone else was listening to this song on the mobile, sitting on a bench next to mine. I was now wide awake. This was one of Fatima's favourite songs. On our return from Dona Paula one day, she had clung to me on the bike. She had hummed this song from *Guide* in my ear and then she said, and I remember this clearly: 'I can't let go of your *nasheelaa badan*, Vipin.'

Embarrassed by this reference to my body, I said, 'Enough of this filmy dialogue, please.'

She warned me: 'Try to get rid of me and see.'

And in a voice that was almost intoxicated, she said, 'When I dance, when I sing, I draw you to me. So close, so close, I feel I am hugging myself.'

I remember that I had liked this sentiment then, but why had I resented what Chitra had said about Fatima? Chitra had found someone. Why should Fatima not find someone to love? A partner maybe? When Ma had been ill, Fatima had come over and behaved as if she belonged in my home. I had no idea how people behaved in her home. But with me she was a breath of fresh air. I had never drawn her to myself but when she put her arms around me, I had felt stirrings of desire. Chitra had said, 'You never saw her as a sex object.' And she had not been a sex object to me either. Even when we had stood in each other's embrace, no sexual thoughts had crossed my mind. Now she was appearing before me in a new light. She had said, 'I love you' and I had replied, 'I don't.'

Was I wrong?

In the morning, Chitra called. 'What have you decided?'

I had no reply.

'Give me some time. I'm thinking about it.'

I didn't even know what this meant.

*

'The number you dialled is currently out of service.'

After I received this message four times, I gave up calling Fatima. But every time, an unknown number showed up, I would answer immediately just in case it was Fatima calling. Each time I would be disappointed.

I had hired two ayahs to be with Ma. They worked out a shift between them. A doctor would visit to give Ma counselling. He would explain what would happen when prosthetic limbs were attached. From time to time, he would chat with me as well. Rehab proceeded with GMC but there were times I had to get medicines from outside. There were routine blood tests and sometimes samples to be delivered to a lab in Dona Paula and reports to be collected. Ma's diet had to be closely monitored. When she had been in the ward, she had lost all notion of day and night and would suddenly wake up screaming, and demand to see me. The she would claim she was hungry, could I at least get her some tea? All this even as I tried to sort out my feelings for Fatima.

Seeing me keep these long vigils outside the ward, a Malayali nurse by the name of Rebecca took me aside to say, 'Those ayahs are taking good care of your mother. Why don't you take a break now and go home and rest. You can even skip a night or two.' I was in the habit of going home to take a bath. But that day, I took my time. I even got in a half-hour at my laptop. Then I turned out the lights and had a deep sleep, a four-hour nap. After that I returned to the hospital since I did not think I should leave Ma alone for too long. But there was Krishna, sitting outside the ward with soup for Ma and chapattis and bhaji for me.

'When do you bring her home?' he asked. And truth to tell, until he asked, I had not even thought about it.

I went inside and asked. Sister Sugandha, an unsuitable name if ever there were one, for she gave off a rank odour of sweat, snapped at me: 'When do you want to take her? Today? Right now? Should I get the discharge papers ready?' And then to a nurse sitting by her side. 'They think they're doing us a favour, putting their relatives in here. We have to slog it out for them and then they can whisk them off home. And will they take care of them once they're home? Oh, dear me, no. In a few days they'll be back, saying the pains are back, this is back, that is back.' My ears were burning but I went out of the ward and sat down again. After a little while the Malayali nurse came out. She looked around, making sure no one was listening. Then she said in a gentle voice, 'Don't take what she says to heart. Just don't ask her anything. She's a bit…' Here she seemed to be at a loss for words. Then she added, 'It will take another eight or ten days before you can take your mother home. But she will require a great deal of nursing: dressings, cleaning, medicines on time, all that. There's a shortage of beds here so they really would like to send her home quickly. It would be to their advantage if you take her home but don't consider it right now, okay?' That was when I discovered why Rebecca was so popular with the patients and their relatives. She had a comforting presence about her.

Even though it was a government hospital, the bills kept mounting. I checked the balance in the bank on the computer and tried to forecast what things might cost. If we went on at this rate, we would run out of money by the end of the year. It seemed like a good idea to move the money from a fixed deposit to a mutual fund to earn some more interest.

The Net warned me that this was not without risk. But this, I believed, was a calculated risk. I made the shift.

*

One day when I got back home, a courier had left an intimation. If I didn't call, my packet would be sent back within four days. I called and he delivered *Babyji* the next day. I made an immediate start. And as I read, an idea occurred to me.

This was how I could propose.

'Hello, Chitra. I think I love Fatima. She will be a wonderful partner. I am going to propose to her. But not marriage. No rituals of any kind. We should live together as life partners—a live-in relationship,' I said in a rush, barely paying attention to whether Chitra could hear me or not. When there was no response from the other side, I began to wonder. 'Hello, hello, Chitra. Can you hear me? Hello...?'

'I'm here. I'm listening. But Vipin, I'm afraid you're a little late. Fatima's nikaah has been fixed.'

27

And Amanda

After forty days in the hospital, Ma was finally discharged, with a warning: 'Those wounds will need to be dressed for some weeks, maybe even a couple of months. Let her walk with crutches. Taking her to the toilet, sponging her, changing her, all this will be the responsibility of the women of the house. Or a female nurse. If she is allowed to lie in bed all the time, she might end up with bed sores. And if a bed sore gets infected, it could be fatal.'

Although I knew my uncles were going to wiggle out of taking any responsibility, I called them.

'Arre Babu, is your aunt a nurse or an ayah to come and stay with you? There are ayahs available around GMC. If you want a nurse then talk to the social worker or the parish priest. There are nursing bureaus too. Prepare to spend a little money. If you don't get anyone, call me. I'll keep an eye out too.'

But that wasn't necessary. When I was getting Ma discharged, Nurse Rebecca came up to me and said, 'If you want a home nurse, let me know. My sister is a trained nurse. She's a widow but a very skilful nurse. She's at home in the village. It will take a few days for her to get here. She could start on Monday.'

I jumped at the offer. We agreed on her fees as well. And Ma came home with an attendant I hired on daily wages.

It was all tougher than I thought. The attendant took care of everything during the day but the nights brought their fair share of work. The medicines were easy enough but I had to get her up to pee, sit her down on the commode, empty it, clean her up, get her back into bed...I felt truly sorry for her as I took care of her. I tried one day to walk about on only one foot, to have a bath and go to the loo on one foot. It proved quite difficult. I would have to take greater care of her. I moved the television into her room. I bought a new CD player and crutches too. And until the nurse came, I made my bed in her room. I installed a zero-volt bulb and in that half-light, I did fall asleep but I did not feel rested when I awoke the next day.

Most people put out the lights when it is time to sleep. I was a creature of the dark. Chitra had also said she enjoyed sleeping in the dark. 'Perhaps because we know the light will return again in the morning,' she said. In my case, I wished the darkness would go on when I awoke in the morning.

One of my uncles stopped by on the evening we brought Ma home from the hospital. I could not tell whether she was happy to see her brother. 'Bai, I'm sorry I came empty handed but then you have to be careful of your diet, no? Get well soon. Then you can ask for whatever you want.' Then he was gone again. No question of him bringing anything for his nephew. He had never done so before.

The next day, the younger uncle did his duty.

They had not come to reassure me. Nor could they in my current state with Chitra far away and Fatima locked away from me. Martin Sir did visit. He brought apples with him. He asked after Ma's health. 'If you need anything, I'm here,' he said. He picked up my copy of *Babyji* from the table, read the back and set it down again.

*

On Monday, I went to GMC to meet Nurse Rebecca as agreed. I looked for her among the crowds and in the ward. Then I remembered that Monday was her holiday. As I turned to go, there she was in the middle of the corridor. I had almost failed to recognize her, so different did she look in a sari. She looked like the statue of Our Lady of Fatima from the church where the statue portrayed her with dark skin. Just then someone came running up to talk to her. He seemed familiar. By the time I reached them, their conversation was ending. And just as he turned away, I recognized him.

'Aslambhai,' I said. 'Hold on.'

He looked at me for a moment but then rushed away as if in a hurry.

'Do you know him?' Nurse Rebecca asked.

I nodded.

'He's in a rush. His sister is getting married.'

Should I ask? Shouldn't I? I asked.

'Who did he come to meet?'

'He came to the psychiatric department but then he also stopped by to meet me.'

Seeing the question in my eyes, she smiled. 'You probably know his sister...'

'Fatima?' I blurted out.

'Yes.' For a moment, she was caught on the horns of a dilemma: to tell or not to tell. Nurse Rebecca said: 'She was being treated here six years ago for depression.' Nurse Rebecca was then in the psychiatric department, she said.

Fatima had recovered. But from time to time, she needed some medication.

'Such a sweet girl. Poor thing...'

'She is sweet all right but why would you say, "poor thing"?'

She closed up. 'We can't talk about our patients to other people. I only said something because you said you knew her. Her marriage has been fixed and that has made her nervous again. Her brother came to get a prescription from the doctors.'

I did not need to make any further inquiries. I changed the subject: 'Hasn't your sister come?'

But she was standing right there, behind Nurse Rebecca. The family resemblance was so clear there was no need for introductions but Rebecca introduced her sister Amanda anyway.

'Shall we?' I asked. 'I brought the bike. You guys can follow in an auto.'

I flagged down an auto for them and we set off.

*

Nurse Rebecca took stock of the house. When Ma saw her, a smile crossed her face for the first time in many days.

I thought they might look askance at the state of the house but the only comment Nurse Rebecca made when she came to my room was: 'Why is it so dark in here?' She asked this as she opened a window.

'I am used to the dark.'

She left the window open and went off to check up on Ma. Then she explained what needed to be done to Amanda. The sound of Malayalam was beautiful. But did Amanda know Konkani?

'She'll learn. Meanwhile, she knows English. And a little Hindi.'

She left Amanda with her new charge and came out.

'Parob...'

'Call me Babu, Sister.'

'Babu, I have been watching you all this while so I know you are a gentleman. But I must tell you that Amanda is very sensitive. Oh, she's not frightened of work. She will not be a burden on you in any way. But as her elder sister, I worry about her. She's borne a lot. Her husband died in an accident and his family then harassed her a great deal. I brought her here so that she could be close to me. Take care.' I could not tell whether she meant I was to take care of myself or of Amanda.

Then she summoned her sister for some parting instructions and though these were in Malayalam, I got the general drift. 'Try to fit in. Work well. Keep your mobile phone charged. And call me from time to time.'

Nurse Rebecca left and for a moment I felt that she should have been the one to look after Ma.

*

The next day I got a letter from the college. It was from the Controller of Examinations. I would have been surprised if it had not come. I had not attended classes for two months. Nor had I submitted any assignments for internal assessment. Some lecturers would not have so much as seen my face.

I went to the Controller of Examinations.

'Do you know, Parob, what your attendance is?'

What could I say?

'Thirty per cent. Which means you've been absent about seventy per cent of the time. Your intra-semester assessment is also very poor. The rule says you have to have seventy-five per cent attendance. If you had been in class sixty per cent, or even at least fifty per cent of the time, some concession could have been made if there were a genuine reason. But thirty per cent? But still the Examinations Committee has not made a final decision. Do you know why? Because they say you're a brilliant student. We can consider your case but on one condition. You will have to give us a letter stating that you guarantee full attendance from now on.'

I got up and left. I went to the canteen and ordered a cup of tea. Then I wrote, 'I quit' on two separate sheets of paper and signed them. One I delivered to the Principal's office, the other to the Controller of Examinations.

That day I went to meet Martin Sir. 'Sir, you may not approve but I thought I should tell you. I've dropped out of college.'

I thought he would get angry or be disappointed or at least look surprised.

'Well, you must have made the decision after thinking about it,' he said. Then with a slight smile: 'Even if you have given up college, don't give up on educating yourself. I don't think a formal education is the sine qua non of success. Henry Ford was no college graduate. And Thomas Alva Edison had not completed his formal schooling either. Bill Gates says proudly that he is a college dropout. They were all geniuses. Like you. The only difference is that they were ambitious; you're not.'

On the way back from house, I stopped at Vasudev's restaurant and bought chapattis. I wanted some hooman but I was told that the chicken curry was ready. I figured I could go home and cook some rice. When I got home, I found rice, daal and rotis all ready. Cooking had not been included in Amanda's duties. I could understand her making a little soup for Ma but a full meal?

'I get time, so I cook. Don't worry, sir.'

Then came the awkward moment of eating. Could I say, 'Come, let's eat?' So I said, 'You go on. Eat. I'll eat later.'

To which she replied: 'You eat first. I will wait.'

And so I put away the food I had ordered from Vasudev and served myself, adding some chicken. Then I washed up and set out a plate for Amanda. After a while, when there was no sound, I came out and found the plate untouched. So, I went into Ma's room and said, 'You should eat now,' and only then did she go and eat.

I don't know who was more embarrassed.

*

On Sunday, Krishna visited. He was happy to see the new arrangements. He went to Ma's room to ask after her and when a considerable time later, he had not emerged, I went in to find him chatting cheerfully with Amanda in Malayalam. That was the first time I saw a carefree look on her face. I discovered that day how one's language was so important in one's happiness.

'Where did you learn Malayalam?' I asked Krishna.

'I can only speak it,' he said. 'There were some families from Kerala in our neighbourhood. I learned to speak from them.'

Krishna made a list of the things we needed in the house and went off to the store to buy them.

The list now had items I had never purchased before: urad daal, idli rawa, sambar masala, pure ghee, moong daal, brown rice and of course, other household familiars such as cooking oil, flour, washing powder, agarbattis, dhoop, brooms, Vim...it was a long list.

'Babu, Ammai gave me her list as well.' Krishna showed me a two-hundred rupee note and a short list: some shampoo, Parachute coconut oil and Colgate toothpaste. I said, 'Buy these and add them to my list. Give her money back to her.'

Amanda took the list and the money back. When she saw her items among the other groceries, she mumbled to herself in Malayalam. I did not understand what she was saying but I figured out that she was not pleased.

In the evening, Nurse Rebecca called, 'I forgot to mention it that day. Monday Amanda should get a half-day holiday. Because I'm off on Mondays too. I'll come tomorrow at around nine o'clock. And I'll bring her back in the evening. Okay, Babu?'

*

When Krishna left, Chitra called. She asked after Ma.

'Who's looking after her?'

'A nurse. Twenty-four hours.'

'Who cooks the food?'

'I do that. She helps.'

'College?'

'I dropped out.'

'Any news of Fatima?'

'Only what you told me.'

'I did call, you know...'

I cut in: 'How come you get through and I don't?'

'She doesn't have a phone now. I call on Aslam's phone. And we talk only when she's alone.'

'Aslambhai lets you talk to her?'

'Fatima is his favourite. He isn't mad at you either. He's worried about society and about that Imam. That Imam would not even have approved of a friendship between you and Aslam. And Aslam doesn't dare oppose him.'

'Why this rush to get her married?'

'Vipin, you have no idea. When they forbade her meeting with you, she told them she was in love with you and was ready to run away with you. And she was.'

'You mean she would have run away with me if I had proposed?'

Chitra was silent so I pressed my point. 'Do you think she would have been ready for a live-in relationship?'

'What's the point of discussing it now? Her family is busy preparing for her marriage.' Chitra added: 'After that, she will be coming to live in Mumbai, you know. Her husband is Mumbai-based.'

Was Chitra happy that Fatima was going to live in her city? That their friendship could now resume? My mouth felt sour and I ended the call.

'Sir, chai,' Amanda put a cup of tea down in front of me and went off with soup for Ma. The first sip cleared my palate.

Now that I thought about it, I could see that if I had asked, Fatima would have readily consented to a live-in relationship. She would even, I realized, have been willing to live as my mistress. But I had not been able to see it. The thought had not crossed my mind. With my head full of Ma's ill health, I had had no time to think. When Chitra had tried to get me to act, I resisted, thinking she was putting pressure on me to get married. Perhaps if I had said then, 'I will be happy to have her come and live with me,' Fatima might have been with me today, happily spinning her poems. There would have been a Fatima mehfil each night, a solo performance. And she might have brought some energy, some soul into this house. Was it possible even now?

I called Chitra again: 'Sorry Chitra, I cut you off when you were saying something.'

'You never let me speak. But never mind that. Listen to me. I phoned Fatima and she was very depressed. But I told her what you said to me, word for word. "I think I love her," and your willingness to accept her as a life partner. Fatima said she hadn't wanted anything to do with these rituals either. She even said she would have been willing to live in with you. But by then it was too late. You delayed far too long.'

'Sorry,' I said instinctively. Perhaps it was the first time I had used that word.

'But what surprised me was the effect your words had on her. She perked up immediately. "Really? Did he really say that, 'I love her'? Finally he realized it." She was very excited, she said, "Vipin is really stubborn. He just refused to accept his feelings. But now I am happy. He said it, right, 'I love her'? Now I'm even ready to die." Wait, Babu, don't interrupt. She wasn't talking suicide. Listen to what she said after that: "I am his first love and he is mine. And no marriage can change that reality." That you accepted her love was enough; even that much made her happy.'

I found I had nothing left to say.

When I took the empty cup into the kitchen, I could smell the aroma of coffee. Amanda had made coffee for herself.

28

A Nurse Like You

Little children see doctors or nurses armed with injections as their enemies. Ma seemed to take this view of me. When Nurse Rebecca came to take her sister away for her weekly off, she went in to check up on Ma. Ma was happy to see Rebecca. She made no complaints about Amanda but hardly had the two of them left before she started on me. 'Bad enough you got one of my legs cut off but now what about my tongue? Why are you making my poor tongue suffer like this? You've spent thousands on the medicine but you're too mean to put some sugar in my tea? Okay, no sweets. I understand that but no fruits either? No bananas, no chickoos? You won't buy them and you won't let anyone else buy them either, will you? You told Vinoo not to buy me any food, no?'

Daddy would have simply ignored her. But since I had some sympathy for her state, I listened as she rattled on and on. She had agreed to the amputation because she believed it would make her well again and then she would be able to eat her fill as she had before her diagnosis of diabetes.

'And if you had to hire a nurse for me you should have got that one who came here in the morning. The one you've got carps at me; she's just like you.'

'Would that hospital nurse let you eat what you wanted?' I asked.

'At that point, I had no appetite. Now that I feel like eating, I'm sure she wouldn't deny me anything.'

I thought she might stop if I left the room. I went and got myself a book to read but I could hear her grumbling away to herself.

'I'm sure you're living it up,' I heard her say. When it was lunchtime I took my plate, served myself, and went into her room to eat. As I started, she asked: 'What's for lunch?'

'Good stuff. There's karela, roti and salad.'

'No rice?'

'No,' I said and she slapped her forehead.

When I had finished, I served her some soup and rotis but she grumbled, 'At least a banana...That doctor, the nurse and you must have been my enemies in some last life. Let me eat and let me die, I said, but you lot have made rice a luxury. If I don't get what I want to eat, what's the point of living?'

And so it went until she fell asleep.

*

At around six thirty in the evening, a rickshaw brought Amanda and Rebecca back. As was her habit, Rebecca went to meet Ma. Amanda went straight back to work. Rebecca gave me a packet of banana chips and said, 'They're from Kerala. Amanda brought them when she came. Don't give your mother any.'

'Do you know what Ma's new song is? Why didn't we hire the nurse who looked after me in the hospital?'

'Any complaints about Amanda?' Rebecca asked, worried.

'No, no complaints. It's just that she wants to send her away and hire you instead.'

'What about you?'

'Who wouldn't want a nurse like you?

'Should I take Amanda back?'

'Nothing of the kind. Ma thinks you'll let her eat what she wants and so she wants you to nurse her.'

Rebecca smiled. 'Amanda is a very good nurse. Her only problem is the language; otherwise, I'd say she's even better than me.' She checked that no one was around, 'I wanted to tell you something else.'

I thought she would ask for an advance payment. But no.

'See, you bought her some shampoo and hair oil and didn't take the money. She didn't like that. She hates feeling obligated to anyone.'

That surprised me. I had somehow managed to offend her sensibilities with my own cultural assumptions. 'If she asks again,' Rebecca said, 'And I don't think she will but if she does, please just let her pay, okay?' I nodded. She spoke freely now, 'Truth to tell, Babu, it's an odd situation. Here she is, a young woman and there's just you and your mother in the house. It isn't just she who is worried; I am too. But I pride myself on being able to judge people and I trust you.'

'And Amanda? What does she think?'

'She has no complaints.'

Then I remembered. 'There was one thing. She was hired to look after my mother. She does that very well. But she also helps with the cooking. Tell her that I'll manage that as best as I can. Or I'll hire someone. She wasn't expected to do the cooking.'

Rebecca smiled. 'She just can't sit around doing nothing. Let her do what she can when your mother has no need of her. She cooks because she enjoys cooking. Don't worry about it.'

She went off and had a long chat with her sister.

Before she left, she said, 'The boy who would come to the hospital? The one who came yesterday...'

'Krishna?'

'Yes. Amanda liked him very much. She said he was a good boy. He promised to come next Sunday.'

For some reason, I felt pleased about this.

29

Call Me Philippina

'No one gets married during the month of Mohurram,' Chitra informed me, 'So the marriage will happen in December.' The groom was a wealthy businessman. He had hired a bungalow in Dona Paula for the wedding. Around fifteen to twenty guests were expected to come from Mumbai and other places. The shukraanaa would be the night before. After joharnamaaz, the muhurat was fixed for 11:38 a.m. After the nikaah, the baalima ceremony. Chitra had been invited to all these rituals. In the middle of all this, Fatima sent Chitra a message, 'After the nikaah, I'll harass you.'

What she had to say only she knew. But the thought of her teased me through the week that followed.

*

'Babu, Akka was asking if she could have a holiday for Christmas.'

'Akka? I thought you called her Ammai.'

Krishna smiled. Ammai was the word for an aunt; Amanda wasn't that much older than Krishna. She had asked him to call her Akka or elder sister. She must be about ten or fifteen years older than Krishna, I figured. Him calling her Akka would not reduce that age difference.

'She says she wants to attend midnight mass on Christmas Eve. She will go on the twenty-fourth in the evening and return on the evening of the twenty-fifth.'

I could see no reason to refuse.

'Sister Rebecca won't be able to come for her. I'll pick her up and bring her back,' Krishna said.

A brother-sister relationship was obviously developing between them. Amanda began to call Krishna 'aniyan' or 'younger brother' and every Sunday, they would talk up a storm either in Ma's room or in the kitchen. And Krishna began to teach her some basic Konkani. In turn, she helped improve his Malayalam. Dishes out of Kerala, made specially for Krishna, appeared on my menu. One day I heard Krishna singing, '*Hanv Saaiba poltodi voyta*' to her. And she was teaching him Malayalam songs. She was trying to sing softly so that I would not hear but I did. There was no sweetness to her voice and she certainly couldn't hold a tune but something in the singing reminded me of Fatima.

The next day I went to a music shop and bought three CDs of popular Malayalam film music and handed them over to her. Better to hear some good Malayali music sung well instead of this tuneless singing.

*

The usual rhythm of Krishna coming over on Sunday and Rebecca collecting Amanda on Monday was disrupted. Amanda came to tell me: 'Rebecca will not be able to come and pick me up; she's busy with Christmas preparations. Aniyan will take me.'

On the evening of the twenty-fourth, Amanda got dressed in a new sari and sat down to wait for Krishna. Only Krishna did not come for a very long time. When he finally raced in, he was full of apologies. 'Sorry, Babu I got really late. And now we won't get a bus. Can you drop her? I'll sit with your Ma until you're back.'

This was the very pillion seat Fatima used. Amanda was holding herself away from me, taking care that our bodies should not touch; and all through that night ride, memories of Fatima rode alongside.

*

'Happy New Year, Vipin,' Chitra called early in the morning. She asked after Ma, out of habit. Who was looking after her? Did Krishna come to help? I don't know if she could possibly understand what looking after an elderly woman whose leg has been amputated, entailed. I explained that Amanda did most of the heavy lifting. Then she asked after me. What was I doing? What was I reading? What was I missing?...and only then to the crux of the matter. 'I talked to Fatima yesterday. She called me. You won't believe it but she isn't very far from where I stay. She's in Kandivali; I'm at Andheri.'

When my heart begins to beat faster, the words clog up in my throat but I did manage, 'How is she?'

'Better than I expected. Quite composed, in fact.'

I had an inkling of what state Fatima would be in at this time. How could we even expect that she might be 'quite composed'?

Chitra's voice sounded embarrassed 'By mistake, I asked her such a stupid question. I shouldn't have but I did. I asked her "How's life?" Her answer was a slap across my face. "You're asking someone who is being raped everyday how life is?" I can't imagine what she must be going through.'

Chitra took a moment to compose herself and then said. 'But she did ask after you. She remembers so much. She said even if she has got married and come to live with her husband, she still thinks of you as her life partner. She's going to call you today.'

A burst of adrenalin.

'She asked me to tell you. She wants to be able to talk to you freely so she's figured out a way. She isn't going to call you Vipin. She's even saved your number on her mobile as Philippina. That's how she will greet you and talk to you only in Konkani; that too when no one else is around. You are not to call her. For everyone else, Philippina is a friend of hers, a Catholic girl-friend from Goa. You get it, right?'

I didn't have long to wait.

'Hello Philippina! Happy New Year!'

I heard her voice and my throat closed up, my voice failed me.

'Hello? Philippina? Can you hear me? Just wish me. I've longed so much to hear your voice.'

'Thank you,' I managed but I wasn't sure I could wish her happiness, that I could use the word 'happy' for her. 'Wish you the same.'

'Look after yourself. Don't worry about me. I'll call you again tomorrow. Okay, bye.'

Could she not manage anything more without crying? Or had a family member turned up? I stood there for a long time holding on to the phone.

Then I heard a bike come to a halt outside and returned to myself. I had no idea that Sister Rebecca had a Kinetic. She generally came to fetch her sister in an auto.

'Happy New Year!' she said, offering her hand. She went straight into the kitchen and set down a bag, before going in to see Ma. Ma was on the throne so she waited and when she was done, wished her. 'Happy New Year, Aunty.'

'Have you brought me some cake or must I make do with your wishes?'

Rebecca's face fell.

'You're just like the others,' Ma said, turning her face away. 'As though I don't know. You must have brought cake for your sister. Nothing for me.'

I thought it best to intervene. I glared at her. 'Are you being starved, Ma? Even though it's a New Year, Amanda stayed here with you and didn't go to see her own sister. She makes soup for you, porridge for you, nachni aambeel...'

'And don't you pay her to do that?'

It was all to the good that the sisters had gone into the kitchen. In a little while, Amanda came back with a piece of cake. I thought this was for me but she gave it to Ma. Before I could protest, Rebecca said: 'Don't worry, Babu. I told Amanda that we could increase the insulin dose just for today. Let her celebrate the New Year too.'

'I knew you would give me some cake. It's only this Babu who wants to starve me.'

As Rebecca left, Krishna arrived. He had brought cake too and whisked into the kitchen. Though he said it was for me, I felt it was really for Amanda. Rebecca did not forget to wish Krishna before leaving.

As I flicked through the messages on my phone, I found New Year wishes from Amanda. And she was living in the same house too. Truly these phones did not conquer the distance between people. They increased it.

'Babu, Akka's calling you to eat.'

'You know I'm not in the habit of eating at this time,' I said, remaining seated.

'But it's New Year today. Come, na? She'll feel bad.'

When I followed him into the kitchen, I found that Rebecca had brought appams and mutton. She had obviously meant this for her sister. Now if Krishna and I were also to eat, what would be left for her? I took one appam but without asking, she put another on my plate. The mutton was rich with kadi patta and tasted great. When she saw that I was hesitating, she opened the cover of the vessel and showed me how much there was.

'I get it. But please, you and Krishna must join me.'

But until I was done, she would not sit down to eat.

30

Pin Money

Ma's health was improving but the dressings had to continue. One day Nurse Rebecca said, 'I think you should get her checked by a doctor. Those wounds should have healed by now.' I followed her advice. The doctor changed the antibiotic and increased the insulin dose. By March, the wounds finally healed.

And just when things seemed to be all right, Ma called me and said, 'Get married. Bring home a wife.'

I asked, 'For what joy? To put her to work?'

She said, 'To have children. To further your line.'

My line? Had I been conceived only to continue the family line?

I thought of a poem by Kaifi Azmi that I had read. Ma always said, 'You remember things you don't really need.'

> Today my children asked me
> Why did you have me?
> I had no answer
> I remember however
> That I asked my father
> That very question.

And he, in turn, asked
His father and my grandfather
Had asked my great-grandfather.
Son, do me a favour:
Before you father a child
Think about this and prepare
Your answer to this question:
Why did you have me?

I said to Ma: 'I do not want to get married. I do not want children. As for the family lineage, I don't think there's much point in extending such a glorious line as ours.'

The poor thing was silenced.

*

I was not sure whether Ma's improved health pleased me or worried me. As long as there was a nurse, there was someone to listen to her moaning and groaning. If she stuck to her regimen, the doctors were sure she would improve but as soon as she made some progress, she began to insist on having her own way. At some point I would have to dispense with Amanda's services. Twenty-five thousand a month, not counting medicines, was not sustainable. The switch to mutual funds had brought in some more, it was true. But it was not a guaranteed amount.

Sister Rebecca had said that in another two or three months I should no longer need a nurse, but Ma would need some kind of companion to look after her. And though I had no hopes of this bearing fruit, I dropped a word in my Uncle Senior's ear.

To my surprise, both uncles turned up the very next morning. They said that they felt it was their duty to make sure there was no stone left unturned to ensure that Ma got the best care possible. If they could get one signature from me and one from Ma, they would make sure she was well cared for. I remembered the time Daddy rebuffed them. But I said that I had no objection and could they please tell me where to sign? The younger one had the paper to hand. When I looked at it, I found it was a general power of attorney. I said that I was not going to sign this. I wanted to be told specifically what it was for. The two of them were immediately on their guard. But since I was adamant, they came to the point. They wanted to hand over their father's house and a property in Assagaon to a developer. They needed Ma's signature and since Daddy was no more, my signature too. They would give me ten lakhs and Ma ten lakhs too. I asked to see the plan of the property. I asked whether the deal with the builder had been fixed and at what price. These questions startled both uncles. They withdrew to the verandah for a hurried consultation. Then they returned and the younger one made their final offer: twenty-five lakhs now and fifty lakhs after the signing of the deal.

I went into Ma's room and asked her. She said she was willing to sign but she had one condition 'How much will you give me as pin money?'

'How much would you like?' I asked her.

'Ten thousand,' she said.

I agreed and her face lit up with victory. Daddy had never given her any money for herself. I came out and said we had a deal and the papers could be made accordingly.

*

Every two days, Fatima would call. If she didn't, I grew uneasy. Our calls followed the old pattern: jokes, shaayri, maybe a song or two. She behaved as if neither of us were married yet. If she felt any sorrow or pain at her marriage, she did not bring it to these calls. Each time I keenly felt the physical distance between us.

Once I said, 'I miss you' and she replied with a line from a nazm, '*Dosti ka ahsaas tabhi hota hai jab dost judaa hota hai/Na jaane yeh judaai kab khatm hogi. Kya zindagi intezaar mein hi kat jaayegi?*' (One only knows the value of friendship when one is parted from a friend/And then one wonders: will this parting end? Will our lives be spent in waiting?).

Slowly I fell in love with her poetry. It was not always her original lines. Sometimes they were her compositions, but she would often take lines from some other poet and rework them to suit her mood and her need. Sometimes they were Konkani, sometimes Urdu. Once I asked her whether some lines were Hindi or Urdu and she said, 'That's for the listener to decide. It makes no difference to me.' And it did seem also as if her marriage had made no difference to us even though she was far away. I still had the pleasure of this encounter with my Fatima.

One day I said to her, 'You haven't changed at all, Fatima.'

She replied in a poem.

'I am a book. However old I get,
My contents will remain unchanged.
When you remember, turn one of my pages.
There you'll find me, as I was, as I will be.'

When she said something like this, it was as if the fine silk of her dupatta brushed gently past my heart and the rest of the day would be spent in a Fatima mood.

*

I should have known something was afoot because Amanda kept wandering out of the house and on to the verandah as if she were expecting someone. Then Krishna arrived with a box of pedhas and I remembered that it was the day his results were being declared. He had got a first class, scoring sixty-eight per cent. When he went to touch Ma's feet to take her blessings, she was quick off the mark: 'Where are the pedhas?'

Amanda said, 'He did bring sweets. I'll get you some.'

I knew that she would not rest until she got her pedhas, now that she had been told she was getting them. In a little while, Krishna came to my room to say, 'Akka is asking for you.' When I went into the kitchen, I found she had made payasam.

Obviously, she had expected good results from her aniyan. And since she knew Ma would demand her share, she had made a cup of payasam with Sugar-Free. She sat Krishna and me down at the table while she remained standing. I could not take this. When I told her to sit down, she refused. It was only when I got up and threatened to leave that she sat down uncomfortably at the table with us. Krishna grinned and said something in Malayalam. She smiled too. We enjoyed the payasam together.

I invited Krishna over for dinner. I told him to come prepared for a sleepover. I bought chicken and ice cream. When Amanda's duties were done, she made rotis. The three of us ate dinner together.

'You have to prepare for the next stage now,' I told Krishna. I asked whether he had made some inquiries about courses and he said, 'I want to do a catering course in a private college.' I was rather surprised. We had already discussed this before his eleventh standard. Now where had this private certificate course come from, even though he had got good marks?

'A certificate course lasts a year and it only costs about forty or fifty thousand.' Now he began to talk up a storm. 'A diploma course takes two years. And each year costs about sixty thousand rupees. Babu, I know you said you would give me the money. But you already gave me sixty thousand and with these two years, it will get close to two lakhs. And I can see how much Ma must be costing you. Appa says it will take us years to pay that much back. He says I should do a one-year course, get a job and start paying off the debt.' He dipped his head and continued to speak. 'Of the sixty you gave me, we've managed to hold on to about twenty-five thousand. Appa says he'll manage the rest of the money.'

I got angry with him. 'Why not go back to Vasudev's joint? I want to see you become a chef, not just a cook. I have no ambition; you do. If you don't do as I tell you now, then the doors of this house will be closed to you forever.'

'Sorry, Babu,' Krishna said contritely, 'I'll go tomorrow and collect the admission forms for the degree course.'

I went into my room and wrote him a cheque for a lakh. I gave it to him with no thought for whether my uncles' cheques would come in or not.

That little piece of melodrama—the 'closed doors' speech—did its work. I wonder now what would have happened if Martin Sir had tried that on me when I had taken admission in science in the eleventh standard. Would I still be studying today?

*

On the way back from Broadway Book Shop, where I had bought some books, I passed a morcha accompanied by the police. I remembered that an elected representative of the ruling party had made a comment that madrasas were factories producing terrorists; this had caused a storm of protest across the country; no doubt this was one of those protest marches. I parked my bike near Samrat Theatre and joined the march. Some of those marching were familiar to me. Many of the marchers were wearing skullcaps. They were shouting slogans: 'Hindostan Zindabad', 'Delhi Sarkar Murdabad.' (Down with the government in Delhi.) Then I saw Aslam. I made my way towards him. I caught his eye and I was sure he recognized me but looked away hurriedly. I got closer, said, 'Hi'. He gave me a quick fake smile.

'That politician should be taken to court,' I said. 'When he's made to break rocks, he'll get it.' I had to speak in an artificially loud voice so that he might hear me. He agreed.

The morcha was headed to Azad Maidan. Near Gujarat Lodge I said to him, 'Let's have a cup of tea. Then we can go to Azad Maidan.' For a moment he hesitated but then agreed.

While we waited for our tea, I said, 'It takes guts to stand up to the government these days. Good for you.'

'You said it! Do they think this country is theirs by divine right? Why would we be teaching treason in the madrasas? We follow the Qu'ran and teach what's in it.'

'And you follow what's in the Qu'ran in your lives too.'

He grew cautious at that but nodded his head.

'Now let's do one thing. You raise the slogan "Dilli Sarkar Murdabad" right here and I'll follow you. I'll say it too.'

Unwittingly my voice must have risen for other people began to look at us.

'Here?' he asked, incredulous, 'Not here. What will

people say? Let's go to Azad Maidan and raise slogans there.'

At that point the tea came. Aslam blew on it repeatedly to cool it down. He was in a hurry but the tea was hot.

'You're so worried about what people would say that you couldn't protect your sister's right to freedom? And now you're off to save the entire Muslim population of the country?'

Aslam put down the cup, ignoring what remained of the tea and ran in the direction of Azad Maidan.

*

Now I did not have to make my morning cup of tea, it came to me. Krishna told me that Akka had asked him about my likes and dislikes. Krishna said I wasn't fussy. 'He'll eat what is put in front of him. But he does like a strong cup of tea.' And from then on, I got a strong cup of tea every morning. That morning she reminded me, 'Tea powder is getting over.'

I took a gulp of tea and my phone rang. I thought my phone was in my room so I went to look for it. When I came out again, Amanda brought it to me. She said I had left it in the kitchen.

I answered quickly.

Of course, I had assumed that it was either Chitra or Fatima. Who else called me? But this time it was the younger of my uncles. He needed signatures on some documents. Ma's and mine. 'I don't want to waste your time so I'm sending Kalpesh. Sign them and send them back with him. We have to submit them by tomorrow.'

And though I kept an eye out for my cousin all day, Kalpesh only turned up in the evening.

'Did you walk from Mapusa?' I asked

He grinned unrepentantly. 'I got late because of Emily.'

He obviously wanted me to ask who Emily was but I was really not interested. And though I didn't ask, he decided to enlighten me. 'She's from Argentina. She came to Goa alone. She asked me to come in the morning but she only woke up at twelve. So no breakfast, straight to brunch. And then her shopping. She kept asking me to stay the night. But Kaka said it was urgent so I came here.' His tone of voice suggested that he had done me a favour.

I made tea for him while he went in to see how Ma was doing. When he came out of her room, his eyes were glittering.

'Is that your nurse? Full item number! When I heard nurse I thought it would be some old hag...'

I felt a flicker of anger at this, 'What bike did you come on?'

'Bike? I came by bus.'

'Let's have those papers,' I said. I signed mine and got Ma to sign hers. Then I asked Kalpesh, 'How do you propose to get back? It's nearly eight.'

He looked at his watch and said, 'No point going back now. I'll just stay over and return tomorrow morning. If he gets the papers by ten, that should be okay.'

This was unprecedented; a guest who invited himself to stay over. I didn't like it but I could scarcely tell him that he must leave.

'We can catch up, you and I. I haven't seen you since Grandpa died. And yes, when your Daddy died, I had come over.' I did not want to be reminded of that time. But he changed the topic and said, 'Chal, let's go out. Take me for a spin.'

I got up but in that instant I made up my mind. The seat on which Fatima had clung to me? I wasn't going to let Kalpesh park his butt there. Others had sat there: Martin Sir, Chitra, Krishna and even Amanda. But not Kalpesh.

'No bike. We'll walk'

So that Amanda might hear, I told Ma. 'Kalpesh and I are going out for a walk. He'll spend the night here. I'll get some food when we come back.'

Amanda objected. 'No need. I'll just make some more rotis. There's vegetable. And eggs. No need to order food.'

*

'Do you know why I like your company? Because you don't talk much and enjoy listening.'

Kalpesh was now going to tell me what I liked and what I didn't.

Just before we arrived at the market, there was Babush's Bar.

'This is a bar?' he hooted. 'You should see the bars at Calangute and Candolim. What bling! At midnight it's as bright as day. This looks empty. You need a good crowd for a bar to swing. It should be so crowded, so noisy that you can't hear what anyone is saying. That's when you can really cut loose, do shots, take potshots.' I walked on, listening to all this with only half an ear. When we got to the bazaar, it did not meet with Kalpesh's high standards. 'What's all this? Let's turn back. I'm thirsty. Let's kill a beer. You have dosh, na?'

There were empty tables at Babush's but Kalpesh got a separate table set up in the corner.

'Beer, right?' he asked as if we were in the habit of doing this regularly.

'I don't like it.'

'You took the words out of my mouth. I don't like it

either. Whisky for us boys.' And without asking me, he asked for a half. I thought this meant a half peg but half a bottle was set down in front of us. Two pegs were poured. I did not like it that Kalpesh was making all these assumptions about me. Even before he could raise his glass in a toast, I sipped mine. It burned my throat.

'Neat, huh? Have some soda?' he said, seeing my reaction.

He ordered chips too. 'I don't carry cash,' he said. 'My money is all in the bank. You know how I earn? I get about two thousand rupees a day. But that isn't everyday. Some days I draw a blank. But then there are foreign women. They come from all over the world: the US, Canada, and they travel alone. These chicks are loaded. If they take a fancy to you, then you're in. One of them is a regular; she comes every year. And she asks for me as a companion. I do all her stuff for her. When she left day before yesterday, she gave me five hundred dollars. I must have at least a lakh in my account now. And then our house is going in for redevelopment. That will bring in some crores. I told Baba: I want a new car. And that will mean a whole load of fun.'

And how will that be fun? Kalpesh finished his glass and filled it again. He urged me to finish mine. He ate all the snacks and pushed me to eat more.

'Once I get a new car, the sky's the limit, I won't have to wait for clients. They'll line up. Foreign ones. And Indians too.' He touched the side of his nose, the sign for sex.

'Indians?' I asked, which was a mistake.

'Oh yes. Indians too. Single women come to Goa from all parts of India, from Bombay, Delhi, Ahmedabad. They need transport and a young driver. Do you know what they pay for twenty-four hours? Five thousand. That's fifty kilometres and some service from the driver too. Until his metre goes down!' and then he turned to me. 'So how much do you earn?'

He drained his glass and poured himself another. I was already feeling the effects of the two pegs I had drunk. But Kalpesh was in form. 'How many girlfriends do you have? Have you banged a chick yet? When I was your age, I'd already slept with a fifty year old. Get this, people spend thousands of rupees to bed a woman, but me? They pay me for it. One thousand, two thousand, five thousand for a go...you know how much that means a month? Uncle is a lawyer. What does he make? People scrounge and scrabble for a few thousand rupees. Then they get married. Why? So they'll have a woman to bang. What others have to work for, I get free.' And once again his finger went to his nose.

'Do you live for all this?' I asked. I was feeling repulsed. But he answered cheerfully enough. 'That's the fun of being a gigolo.'

My head was beginning to ring now. I couldn't tell whether this was because of the alcohol or because of his stories. I felt like throwing up.

'Come on, let's go, its past ten,' I said and paid the bill.

'Wait man, let me finish,' Kalpesh said. He was not done yet. 'To earn you need a brain. A nurse was staying near us. One day, I saw that she was alone at home so I took my chance. She beat me to the floor, man. I gave her an idea. I told her to offer massage services on the internet. First, she would go anywhere. Then she learned the knack of the business. She expanded her business: not just men, she would massage women too. They would pay double, those lesbians. I tell you women are hot to trot; they can beat a man any day.'

'All women?' I spat at him.

'*All* women!'

'Do you mean my aunts too?'

Kalpesh was left speechless. His intoxication came down with a thump.

He got up and we left the bar in silence.

When we got home, I said I did not want to eat. I did not have to tell Amanda that I had had a drink; she turned her face away with a barely concealed moue of disgust and cleared the food from the table. My head was feeling heavy. My eyes were ready to close. I splashed my face with cold water which provided temporary relief. I washed my face and hands. When I came back out, I found Kalpesh sprawled on the sofa. I went into my room and threw myself down in the dark.

A thunderous sound woke me up. I dashed out of my room to find Amanda sitting on the floor, banging the vessels about. She stopped when she saw me but her eyes were spitting fire, her chest heaving. In the hall, I found Kalpesh curled up, the bedsheet over his head, pretending sleep. I ripped the sheet off him with one hand and pulled him to his feet with the other. He was terrified but before he could say anything, I made his ears ring with a good slap around the head. I spent the rest of that night on a chair in the hall, keeping vigil. In the morning, I watched Kalpesh creep out of the house. I went into the bathroom and had a bath in cold water. Then I made two cups of tea and going into Ma's room, I gave Amanda one. I could tell she hadn't slept much either. That Ma had slept through it all was the only silver lining.

I was in a state of suspended animation, waiting for Nurse Rebecca's phone call. I decided that if Amanda said she was going to quit, I would not try to stop her but I would not hire another nurse in her place either. I would manage as best as I could.

Fatima called twice and Chitra once during that time. I was too guilty to answer their calls. Amanda went about her daily chores in the usual fashion but this did not alleviate my discomfort at all.

*

On Sunday, Krishna came and spent some time chatting with Amanda. After a little while, he came out.

'Babu,' he asked, 'who came to meet you here day before yesterday?'

My heart began to pound. I thought she was going to say what she had to say through Krishna. I tried to prepare myself for it but he changed the subject himself. 'She says you're to come and have tea with us.'

'I'll have it out here,' I said but then I realized that I had to lance the boil once and for all. I went into the kitchen. Amanda was sitting at the table, drinking tea. Now she did not have to be told to come and sit down. Looking me straight in the eye, she said, to Krishna, 'Your Babu is now keeping bad company, you know? Very bad, very bad.'

I felt truly ashamed of myself.

'If that man ever comes here again…' Here it comes, I thought, the threat to quit…'I will kill him.' Her voice was filled with disgust.

Without averting her gaze, she said to me, 'Please stay away from him.'

I nodded, dumbly, guilty.

'I had heard so much about you from aniyan but he never said that you touched alcohol. I can understand that man drinking. But why did you have to? Very bad. Please never again.'

Again I nodded. Then I said, 'Amanda,' and realized it was the first time I had used her name 'I promise. It will never happen again.'

'Thank you,' she said, making it sound as if I had done her a favour.

The tea had cooled. She took it away and made me a fresh cup. Her face had a tranquillity I had not seen before.

*

After Amanda had put me on the witness stand, I called Chitra that night and made a full confession. I didn't have the courage to tell Fatima myself so I told Chitra to tell her what had happened.

Fatima called the next morning, 'Philippina, I hear you've been hitting the bottle? I only wish I had been there. Neither of us would have needed alcohol to help us lose our senses.'

'Have done, Fatima. I almost died of shame and you're joking?'

'My dear Philippina, read between the lines. What did I say?'

These romantic lines and the use of English reached me. 'No one's around I take it?'

'You are.'

No one must have been around.

'So what was I supposed to read between the lines?'

'If you want to lose your senses, why not lose them in my embrace?'

At that moment I longed for Fatima to be close to me.

*

After a long silence, a text message from Martin Sir: 'Come and see me.' I wondered if this meant he was ill, and set out immediately.

'What are you doing these days?' he asked.

I had no real answer.

'You must be busy looking after your mother.'

'No, sir. There's a nurse who handles it all.'

'I don't think a job would suit you at all. But you cannot simply waste your time doing nothing.'

He was right. I was doing nothing. But what could I do? A job like my father had done? I didn't think I could.

'I can lead you to the water. Whether you drink or not is your decision,' he said. 'You can write. You have potential. Much has been given to you and it is only fair that much is expected. Do something. Write articles. Social commentary. Fiction. Leave it to me to get it published. If you have no ideas, translate a book you have liked. Review books. Do some research. But whatever you do, apply your mind.'

I said neither 'yes' or 'no'.

*

As if they were communicating telepathically, Chitra said over the phone: 'I can't believe you've been drinking. Some evil influence must have taken over your empty mind. Or it's the distance you've suddenly discovered between yourself and Fatima. May I say something?'

I wanted to say that she had already said a great many things without ever feeling the need to ask permission. 'You must find something to occupy yourself. Take on a project. Find something that will engage your mind. You have to find something that you can do at home.'

While Chitra enjoyed dispensing advice, Fatima was

unconcerned with my activity or lack of it. It was all the same to her whether I was busy or whether I was idle. She had the rare ability to be content with whatever time I could spare her, earlier when we met in person or now on the phone. She made no complaints. 'Do you know what a splendid night I had? May I tell you about it? You appeared in my dreams and you were tantalising me.'

'And now you're awake.'

'A-ha, why do you assume that I was asleep then? Don't you know one does not have to sleep in order to dream?'

*

From the Konkani classes I had attended in college, I had discovered how little Konkani there was on the internet. You could not find lists of synonyms or antonyms. No one had bothered to record the vivid differences in all the versions of Konkani one might encounter. There were no etymologies.

Shenoy Goembab's writings had caused me to fall in love with the language. But if the foundations he had laid were to be built upon, if the beauty and variety of the language were to be adequately recorded, a search engine would have to be created. I could see that this was something that would have to be addressed at a fundamental level. Google told me that there were no thesauri available. I could not find evidence that anyone was working on this.

Since this seemed like an academic enterprise, I decided it might be worth my while going to meet the Goa Konkani Akademi, a government enterprise. The President was unavailable but I did meet his deputy. He assured me of his complete support were I to take on this project. He said that he would have to seek the approval of the executive committee but I should begin work anyway. He told me that the committee would meet next month and asked me to get a proposal ready with a work plan and some samples. When I saw that the assistant director was seized of the importance of the project, my own excitement increased. I went to the bookshop and bought the *Collected Shenoy Goembab*, a four-volume Konkani dictionary and eight other books on Konkani. I lugged this bundle home and set out all the books and got down to the work of devising a Konkani thesaurus. First, I did some research on how thesauri had been constructed in the past. Next, I scanned all the dictionaries I had bought and chose the words from Shenoy Goembab's works and fed them in. Meanwhile, I got to know the mechanical translation project undertaken by Asmitai Pratishthan. There were 30 lakh words that had already been gathered and which had been tagged, categorised and classified which had been passed on to the university. Even a spellcheck was ready but it was not perfect. Nevertheless I got the basis of what I needed for my proposed project.

*

'Good to see you so deep in this,' Krishna said and respect was clear in his tone. 'Akka says you're so engrossed you don't even eat on time.'

I spent a huge amount of time on my laptop. I didn't even think about tea until Amanda would bring me some and I would realize that I wanted a cup.

Now Krishna was asking whether he should bring some tea in or would I come out? I thought to ask him to bring it to me but changed my mind. I had been hunched over my computer for hours. It would do me good to stretch my legs. After my first gulp of tea, I noticed that Amanda had a bright red spot on her forehead. She saw that I had noticed it and said, 'Aniyan brought it for me. Did you like it?' I was at a loss for an answer. I was not in the habit of giving compliments. But Amanda was looking expectantly at me.

'So Krishna, what did you think?' I asked him.

'I liked it. I think it looks great, no, Babu?'

'Yes, you look good,' I said. Amanda looked pleased.

By the next month, I felt the work had progressed well. I went to the Konkani Akademi well before the deadline with a CD on which I had loaded my proposal, my methodology and a sample of my work.

This time my reception was very different.

'What do you want?' the secretary asked, his frown and sneer of cold command making it clear that he saw me as an irritant devised specifically to disturb him.

It occurred to me that I had better not tell him what I was doing.

'I would like to meet the President,' I said.

'Gone,' he said triumphantly.

'His deputy then.'

'The President and his deputy have both resigned,' he said. Now he was in his element. The rest of the staff looked on, mute spectators.

'Anyone from the Executive Committee?'

'Dissolved.'

'When will a new one be constituted?'

'Now that's a question for the minister,' he said. Then to show that he was too busy for such conversations, he buried his head in a file randomly selected from his table. I was not ready to give up.

'I have a proposal here. To whom should I submit it?'

'Leave it here,' he pointed to his table.

'Can I have an acknowledgement?'

'What kind of acknowledgement? Have you brought cash?'

'An acknowledgement of this proposal.'

'Leave it here. I'll read it and then we can talk.'

I took the print-outs I had brought with me and tore them in half and then half again. I tossed them on his table and walked away.

Another roadblock.

Chitra said, 'What of that? You have so much potential. I believe you can do anything you want. Choose another project. Keep at it. Stay busy.'

Easy to say. When Martin Sir called to find out how things were going, I had to tell him. He reminded me of Professor Anil Gupta's talk and the excitement I had felt then.

Fatima's regular complaint: 'You tell Chitra everything. You tell me nothing.' When I told her what Chitra had said, she replied, 'You get worked up when someone who has no idea of your worth says something. And you ignore those who are worried about you.'

At this time my mobile and my laptop were my best friends. I spent most of my time with them as I regained some semblance of composure. Just as I was recovering, Sister Rebecca called. Some guests from the village were visiting Goa and she was wondering whether I could spare Amanda for a long weekend, Saturday to Monday. I thought this might help distract me. Thanks to Amanda's diligence, Ma's condition had showed a vast improvement. She wasn't very keen on getting about but her diet was under control and her medicines were administered on time. The insulin injections were now a daily thing. Amanda explained exactly what I had to do. And so I shook off my lethargy and set to work. When I had finished my chores, I would go to Ma's room and watch TV with her. I played a CD of the Malayalam film songs that I had bought Amanda and watched a Malayalam film too. Perhaps her sister had given it to her, I thought. But when Krishna came that evening, he told me that he had got it for Amanda when she had told him of her love of cinema. I asked him how he happened to be there on a Saturday, he said that Amanda had asked him to come on Saturday and Sunday. I did not like that she was asking him to do this. I told him to go and said that he need not come the next day either. But Krishna did come. Then he and I watched the Malayalam film. Krishna told me that he had watched the same film with Amanda and Ma three times already. I told him, 'Bring a couple of good Malayalam film CDs the next time you come.'

I did not feel good about going back to my room to sleep so I dossed down in Ma's room. Ma did nothing much all day but still managed a good night's sleep. When I made tea in the morning, she asked if I would put some sugar in it. I used some Sugar-Free which pleased her. But when I got her up and slipped her crutches under her arms and told her to try and walk for ten minutes, she got annoyed. She complied but kept up a steady mumbling and muttering. Those two nights and three days taught me what nursing really meant. I had to give Ma her commode at least ten times a day.

What with meals and tea, I had to get her up on her crutches about four to six times. There were three insulin injections that could not be skipped and antibiotics too...if she were asleep I had to wait until she woke up. Amanda could tell when Ma was really sleeping and when she was playing possum. And since she was my mother, I did not see all this as an imposition even if I did not find pleasure in doing this. But why should someone unrelated to her be willing to do all this without getting annoyed, even if that person were paid?

Then Monday evening rolled around and Amanda came back, ready to relieve me of my burden.

*

One Sunday, Krishna came home, full of excitement.

'Do you know someone called Sarvesh Namshikar? Last week, he came to our institute.'

'Does he study there?' I had no idea that Sarvesh had opted for hotel management.

'No, Babu, he's at the degree college. Brilliant. In the final year. Even before he graduated, he has an offer from the Taj Group. He says he'll get a year's experience with them and then open his own hotel. He'd come to do a little talent spotting at our college. And right there, he made me an offer.'

I was happy to hear that Sarvesh had followed his dream.

'So he managed to break out of the cage of his father's expectations.'

'He says you inspired him. He thinks a great deal of you.'

Oddly the news that Sarvesh had followed his dream, woke something up in me. I began to work again. Martin Sir's words came back to me. I researched Professor Anil Gupta's grassroots work. I looked up the mechanics of the honey bee network and how it functioned. I began to research the causes of people's failures and the reasons for their success. I made such copious notes that I began to run out of A4 paper. It was afternoon already. I got up and dressed and came out. I found Amanda who it seemed had just had a bath sitting there. Her hair was wet and loose against her neck. She had put on the fan and I could not tell whether this was because of the heat or in order to dry her hair. She saw me and got to her feet quickly. I went off to get my helmet.

'Raincoat?' she asked.

It was threatening to rain outside. The sky was dark with clouds. I didn't want to waste time looking for a raincoat but Amanda brought me one.

I went to JD in Panjim, bought a ream of paper and then saw an old woman selling fresh mogras for the hair.

I bought one and managed to beat the rain home. After eating, I settled down. I lost track of the time. The scent of mogras filled my nose and then suddenly, Amanda brought me some tea. She put down the cup and said, 'Thank you.'

'For what?' I asked.

She turned her head and showed me the mogras in her hair. She smiled and left the room.

I thought suddenly of Fatima's long hair and how these mogras would have looked in those dark locks. I wondered why I had never thought to buy her any. Maybe because her hair had always been covered by her odhni. I felt the urge to talk to her but the rule was that she would call Philippina. And then, suddenly the phone rang.

'Hi Philippina. What you up to?'

'Just thought about you and there you were.'

'See we have telepathy. So tell me, yaad kaise kiya?'

'I suddenly thought today: I never gave you flowers. I wonder why not.'

She was quick on the uptake.

'Because it was never the time of blooming.'

'Today I saw some mogras and thought of you. We met for two years and yet I never...

'Wait.

Were you to give me flowers
their fragrance would fulfil me.
Were you to give me thorns
their fragrance would fulfil me.
Were you to give me nothing
your fragrance would fulfil me.
So why let it worry you?'

'It worries me that everything amuses you.'

'It worries me that no one looks past my amused lips to see my sad heart,' she said and ended the call.

*

That ruined my mood. I could only see Fatima's melancholic face. I browsed aimlessly. It was six in the evening when I came out. Amanda was in Ma's room, watching a film on CD. Ma was watching and drowsing. For a moment I stopped at the door and asked, 'What's the name of the film?'

'*Rati Nirvedam*.'

I did not understand the title. I told her to stay where she was with a gesture and went into the kitchen to make tea. I went back to my room and began to browse available films. I came upon *Rabne Bana Di Jodi* and began to watch it. When it ended, it was way past dinnertime. In the kitchen I found dinner was on the table and Amanda was waiting for me. I ate and went back to my room looking for another film to watch.

I could not decide which one to watch. It must have been close to ten thirty. Just then Amanda burst into my room.

She was obviously ready for bed. 'I'm so sorry, Babu but we've run out of insulin. I should have told you but it slipped my mind. I don't even have a dose to give her now. Please get it immediately. Very urgent, very urgent.'

When I was ready to leave, she was at the door with my helmet 'Sorry, my mistake,' she said.

It was drizzling outside. 'Raincoat? Wait,' she said. She began to look for it.

'Where did you leave it?'

'I'll look,' I said but then I remembered. I had taken it with me but I had not brought it back. I must have left it on the counter at JD's. The rain wasn't coming down so I left anyway. But after I bought the insulin, it began to pour. I waited for it to lessen a little and fifteen minutes later, I set out again but I got home drenched.

It was eleven when I reached. Amanda was waiting for me at the door. I put the bike on the stand and took off my helmet but by the time I got up the stairs, the bike had toppled over. Perhaps the rain had turned the ground to mush. I went back to set it right and Amanda came to help.

'Go back in,' I said. 'No point you getting wet as well.'

But she was wet by the time she got back to the house. I went in and handed over the ampoules. 'It's not too late? Ma is awake?'

'No but she will take it anyway,' and she ran inside.

I needed a cup of tea but I was drenched to the skin. I stripped off and wrapped a towel around my hips. The laptop had settled into sleep mode. I wiggled the mouse and the screen lit up. I thought this might be a good time to watch *Last Tango in Paris* which for some reason I had been delaying. Just then Amanda entered my room with a towel and said, 'Sorry, Babu, you got wet because of my mistake.' She came to where I was sitting and began to towel my hair dry. I did not think this was necessary but she gave me no chance to protest.

'You will get a cold,' she said, 'Let me...'

And when she was done with my hair, she began to wipe my chest dry. Since she was standing in front of me, her breasts touched my forehead. The scent of her body filled my nose. This was not the scent of mogras; it was her scent, the scent of a woman. When she had finished with my back, she took me by the hand and urged me to my feet. She began to dry my chest. Her breath began to come quickly. Mine was beginning to heat up too. She stopped drying me and suddenly wrapped her arms around me. In order to keep my balance, I put my arms around her too. She seemed to be slumping completely against me as if her legs had lost volition and so my grip tightened. Her eyes were shut but she raised her head towards mine. Her lips drifted apart. Her breath was now coming in short pants. Her breasts were pressing against my ribs. Picking her up, I placed her on my bed and somewhere during this time, my towel slipped off. My hands began to explore her body. I reached out to stroke her breasts but her bra got in the way and I had no idea how to unhook it. She reached behind herself and freed her breasts. Now the computer went back into sleep mode and plunged the room into darkness even as we fell together into each other.

*

When I awoke the next morning, as from a dream, Amanda was no longer by my side. The night had passed in exertion and I got out of bed with the satisfaction of someone who had made a rite of passage, who had arrived at the estate of manhood. I got dressed. I felt the need for a cup of tea. I went into the kitchen and made myself a cup.

I heard the sound of footsteps and turned to see Amanda standing there, her head lowered. She was wearing a white sari with a pink border. This was what she wore when she went out. Her head was still lowered.

'A cup for you?' I asked. She did not move. I sipped my tea but she remained unmoving.

'What happened?' I asked and then realized how stupid the question was. As if I did not know what had happened.

'I am leaving,' she said, her voice low. She made no attempt to conceal her guilt, refusing to meet my eyes.

'Where are you going?' I asked, noticing then the suitcase she had packed and which was near the door.

'Home.' And without raising her head, she added, 'I am sorry.'

I did not know what to say. I could not tell how she could be responsible for what we had done the last night. Was it something wrong? Was it not natural? No one had used any force. If we had done something wrong, we were both equally to blame. The silence was extending, lengthening and she broke it again, 'My mistake.'

'Don't go,' I said. 'It was my mistake too.'

She kept shaking her head.

'Will you leave me like this?' I asked.

Finally, she raised her head.

'Please,' she said.

'Listen to me, please,' I said. 'It will not happen again.'

Then for the first time that morning, she met my eyes. 'Yes,' she said. 'Me too. Never again...Sorry.'

And even before she had finished that last apology, I added: 'Never again.' She picked up her bag and went back inside.

The tea had cooled. I poured it into the sink and made three cups. I gave Ma hers and gave Amanda a cup.

'Thank you,' she said and her eyes, I saw, were wet.

*

A host of questions swarmed into my head after that. At some point in my life I had read '*Kamaturanam bhayam na lajja*' or 'Those caught up in the sexual urge feel neither fear nor shame'. Who did this apply to? What was the source of the shame she felt? Or for that matter, what did I feel? Daddy was openly libidinous. Ma had often told me that when she had delivered, Daddy had been having it off with the woman who was attending to her. Elsie too had had problems with her sexuality. Daddy must have had some kind of relationship with her. Had his satyriasis descended to me? Ma had refused to have any household help because she felt that Daddy would have affairs with them. She had hoped he would hire some male help but he had refused to hire a male servant. Daddy had never satisfied her sexual needs. So how had I been conceived? Nor had Ma given Daddy the physical satisfaction he had sought. She had told me clearly, 'He never gave me the kind of happiness I wanted.' Are all the sexually depraved without shame? Those who had some thought for the way the world looked at them eased themselves with masturbation. Was that how Amanda dealt with her current state? After her husband's death, society had kept her from any physical satisfaction for five years. Had she ever strayed from this socially ordained straight and narrow? I thought not. She had been here for seven months. I could not remember her looking at anyone with anything resembling lust. Sex was a natural bodily need. But it seemed that society felt the need to hedge it around with all kinds of limitations. Who had set up the limits of this decency? Daddy had exercised his rights as a man or those he thought were his rights—and had denied Ma the same rights. Were these the limits of decency?

Ravindra Kelekar had said, 'Where minds meet, sex is moral.' Had ours been a meeting of minds? Not at all. Our bodies had come together. Did the absence of anything other than sexual pleasure make the encounter immoral? We had found pure physical pleasure in each other. In that unguarded moment, her resolution had faltered and her feet had slipped. But she had not stepped on anyone's toes. These desires, so long held back, had finally found release...Now she was blaming herself. But at least she had not just taken her pleasure but had given pleasure as well which made the account even on both sides. Amanda had no husband to deceive. And yet she was feeling guilty. For what it was worth it had happened and the little drama was over. The curtain had fallen and there were to be no encores. 'Never again' we had said and meant it.

As the questions began to settle, one remained: 'Putting aside the guilt, did you have an orgasm?' But I knew I would never be able to ask that question.

I felt the need for a cup of tea. I went into the kitchen to get the makings together when Amanda came out. She told me to sit down and said she would make tea. She did not look at me. Without knowing it, I was watching her back.

She set the tea down in front of me and remained standing there. It was as if she wanted to say something but did not dare, or so it seemed to me. She stood there, rubbing one foot against the other and then said, almost inaudibly: 'Thank you.'

'For what?'

She smiled, embarrassed and left the room.

Had I received the answer to the question I could not ask?

*

And then it struck me. I had deceived Fatima. I had not even thought about her. While I was absolving Amanda, why had I never thought of what I was doing to Fatima? When Amanda rode pillion with me, I had thought of it as Fatima's seat. And so, when we had begun to touch each other last night, how come I had not thought of Fatima who said things like 'Your intoxicating body never seems far from my arms'? When I had picked Amanda up and laid her on my bed, how come I had not thought of Fatima whom I claimed to love? And if a memory had come back to me, would I have pushed Amanda away?

Another thought: Perhaps it was all for the best that I had not thought of Fatima while in Amanda's embrace. Did she think of me when she lay in her husband's arms? Chitra would know. I tried calling her but the phone was busy. When she called back much later, the desire to ask her had passed. We chatted about other things. Up to yesterday, I thought that there was nothing I could not share with Chitra and Fatima. True, I had not told any lies. but concealing the truth is also a form of lying. *Satyam bruyaat, na bruyaat satyam apriyam* (Speak the truth but not such truth as might hurt.) By that token I should not be telling Fatima any of what had happened with Amanda. Hadn't Chitra too concealed her relationship with Preetam in its early stages? Perhaps it was because she thought it would hurt me.

All through that day and much of the night I tried to wrap my head around the ethics of that pleasurable mistake.

In the morning, I got up. I made up my mind that tea would not enter this room again. I went into the kitchen.

31

A Photo of Your Girlfriend

'You don't seem to have what it takes to bring a project to its logical conclusion,' said Chitra. 'Fatima is right: you can do anything you choose. But if you want to lead a meaningful life, perhaps you should take up a project that will benefit Goa or even the country at large. Think big and start working.'

She was annoyed when I told her that I had given up the idea of investigating the possibility of developing a dark light in the honey-bee network.

Chitra thought nothing of giving me advice regardless of my state of mind. Fatima was different. When I was despondent, she would joke and tease until she had rescued me from the Slough of Despond. Then I could resume my work with renewed vigour.

*

'My Philippina can do anything she sets her mind to...'

I cut in: 'I know that line by heart now. What do I do when I'm out of sorts?'

'Are you impatient then?'

'Very.'

'If I were in your arms, this impatience would evaporate like water on a hot pan.'

'Enough poetry.'

'It's not just a line. I'm telling you what I believe. You can do anything you want but you need me by your side. Then you'd see how well you would work.'

'So I have to wait until you come to Goa to get back to work?'

'Why wait? You come here.'

'Why would I come there?'

'To fulfil your dream.'

'I do not dream.'

'I do. I dream for you as well. I dream enough for both of us. I dream when I'm awake. Listen:

When I lose myself in a dream,
    What do you lose?
When I take you in my arms,
    Do you understand me?'

'Go on dreaming then.'

'I live on dreams, if not...'

'If not what?'

'Let it go. Tell me when you're coming.'

'Why would I come?'

'To torment me.'

*

I felt I was not in command of my moods. There seemed to be an immutable logic to this: I would find the energy and enthusiasm to do something and soon enough, something would happen that would derail me.

Then one morning Amanda came running into my room, crying, 'Ma, Ma, Ma.'

Ma would not be roused. I tried her pulse. I put my ear to her chest.

'Call the doctor,' Amanda shouted.

I phoned Dr Costabir and fetched him on the bike.

'I'm sorry,' he said and closed her eyes gently, but they remained half open. She must have passed on a while ago.

Amanda said that she had changed her diaper at two in the morning.

'At that point she was awake. She didn't say anything much. She seemed a little low but she didn't complain of any pain,' Amanda said forlornly

'A heart attack. Diabetic patients often don't feel the pain when one comes on. It must have happened about two hours ago.'

Dr Costabir said he would sign a death certificate. I reached him back and waited while he prepared it.

I called my uncles. I rang Krishna and asked if he could come. I called Chitra and told her the news and said we would talk the next day. Amanda must have called Rebecca for she arrived. She offered her condolences and then asked, 'Should I take Amanda with me?'

I said yes.

My aunts who had never come in many years turned up. As soon as they arrived they put sugar in Ma's mouth. And so a handful of sugar went into the mouth of a woman who had yearned for sweet things for years. And though two and a half years had passed since Daddy's death, nothing had changed. The same rituals that had been conducted then were conducted now. The two aunts stayed at home. Otherwise, it was all the same. And those traditions prevented Krishna from coming to the cremation grounds.

Now that they had some money to throw around, the

uncles had brought their wives in taxis. They supervised the purchase of the wood for the pyre, they ordered the hearse, they organized a pundit, candles, camphor, the wood. Then, vastly satisfied that their sister had had a better send-off than their brother-in-law, they went home.

The next day there was an announcement in the papers, regarding the death of their beloved sister.

Over the next few days, a series of visits. Even Sarvesh and Amrut turned up. The only exceptions were Chitra and Fatima. Martin Sir came empty-handed this time but left with some advice. 'Don't waste time. Don't let your mother's death become an excuse. Get down to work. You have a creative mind, keep it busy. Everyone who is born must die. I will die one day, so will you. But works of genius do not. They remain in the public memory.'

Fatima's response was not just in accordance with her character but also an echo of what I was feeling. 'I should have been by your side today. Not to wipe your tears but to hold an umbrella over your head in this rain storm of loneliness. To keep your dreams from getting soggy and washed out. I feel I should come to you, not to hold your hand but to give you a hand.'

I too felt that she should have been by my side. I confessed: 'I'm missing you, Fatima. I'm not sure I have much to say. I have so much to tell you. I wish you were close by.'

'If only,' she said and hung up.

*

Now that twenty-five lakhs had been deposited in my account and another fifty lakhs were on their way, my uncle was under the misapprehension that I would agree with anything he said. While Daddy was around, they had not the courage to advance their plans. Now that both were gone, they were confident, Uncle Senior had an agenda this time: how the rituals for his dear departed sister should be conducted. He had brought his younger brother along. No doubt he had told him: Just see how I smooth it all out.

They had eaten lunch and come, no doubt aware that no fish could be cooked for twelve days in the house of the bereaved. However, after their sister had married, her gotra had changed and so those rules were no longer followed. They began to tell me about the fish they had had. They went into ecstasies over the prawns tempered with drumsticks and described in detail the hooman Uncle Junior's wife had conjured up with some succulent and fresh-from-the-sea kingfish which had been purchased despite its exorbitant price. When this was done, they said that they were not hungry but would not say 'No' to a cup of tea. Then they got down to business. Naming a constellation I knew of only by name, one said, 'If she had died when that one was crossing the sky, we would have had to go for a Mahashaanta havan. But now it should be fine.'

'What should be fine?'

'Now look Babu, when your father died, you had your way. And we did not object because he was our brother-in-law. But this time we're talking about our sister.'

'And why did you not object? What had your brother-in-law done to you?'

Something in my voice warned him to walk carefully. But this time the clink of money in his pockets reinvigorated him. He did not want to lose face in front of his younger brother.

'Speak no evil of the dead,' he said sententiously, slapping himself gently on each cheek to prevent any other ill-meaning power from punishing him. 'Now whatever it is, she was our sister, no? We must do everything according to the shastras.'

'And what do these shastras say? If you know, perhaps you might enlighten me?'

Uncle Junior had been sitting through this exchange quietly. He had probably been warned to hold his tongue. But Uncle Senior was ready with an answer.

'Oh, I'm glad you asked that question. It is something you should know.' He must have returned fresh from meeting with the pundit of his choice. 'See your mother has passed on. Now she begins the great journey of her return. Even as her skull burst on the pyre, she began this journey of metempsychosis. This is an eleven-day journey. And so, on the twelfth day we will have the shraadh. And if there are some unfulfilled desires, her soul will find itself stuck here.'

'Here? I thought her soul was already making its way to pitrulok?'

'Now don't be literal. The journey of which we are speaking is a long and arduous journey. How can she reach devalok unless she achieves mukti? You might say devalok is Vaikunth. And getting there is mukti.'

'So what are you saying? That if we have this shraadh, she will achieve mukti? And your duty will be done?'

'Yes. And then if you choose not to go for the monthly rituals, we would understand. Really no one bothers with them now. But we must have the twelfth-day shraadh and the one-year shraadh.'

'And what is that for?'

'So that people left behind would not be troubled by the soul of the dead person.'

'And those left behind would be?'

'You. Me...'

'Is that all?'

Uncle Senior looked at Uncle Junior as if to say: And that is how it is done. The younger one sat there silent. He did not seem to have understood anything.

'Now, you listen to me, Uncle. What you call shastras make no sense to me. I believe these rituals have been created by the Brahmins to fill their stomachs. I do not believe in rituals of this kind. I believe that if Ma had any unfulfilled wishes or desires, it was because of me. I am willing to face the consequences. To the end, she longed to eat sweets but none of us gave them to her. And then when she died, it was my aunt who put sugar in her mouth, so let her reap the spiritual benefits of that act of mercy. You know what you did and what you did not do when my mother was alive. But if you think it would help her in some way, please feel free to have any rituals performed. I cannot take part in something in which I do not believe.'

And still he said, even as they prepared to depart. 'Tomorrow, you have to go and get her ashes from the crematorium. Or isn't that part of your beliefs?'

'I have no objection to you collecting them.'

'No, no. You set fire to her pyre so you must collect them.'

'If that is so, leave it to me.'

*

In the morning, Amanda came to ask after me. How I was doing, how I was managing, who was cooking and all that. Just when this was beginning to feel surreal, she said, 'I will make tea' and went into the kitchen. I was accustomed to her way of making tea. She came out carrying two cups. We continued sitting there. She said: 'I leave tomorrow.'

'Are you going home?'

She nodded.

'Akka says you are a good man. A gentleman.'

'And you? What do you say?'

'Very good.' And then hesitantly: 'I will miss you.'

She had her hair in a chignon. I thought of her hair loose around her shoulders. This seemed an improvement.

'What is it?' she asked, puzzled by my prolonged stare.

'You're looking nice,' I said.

She smiled gently. 'May I ask you something?'

How could I say 'No'?

She looked straight into my eyes and asked, 'Do you have a photo of your girlfriend?'

That threw me. What did she know? I was about to say 'I don't have a girlfriend' but that felt like a lie. After a moment, I asked, 'How do you know?'

'A guess. When you talked to her on the phone, I could see the glow of happiness on your face...'

I looked for a picture of Fatima on my phone. I had never taken a picture of her. I found a couple that Chitra had sent me which I had not deleted but which I had not looked at in a long time since I took no great pleasure in these images. I tapped on one, expanded it with two fingers and showed it to Amanda. She looked at her for a long time. I thought I could see a series of emotions pass across her face.

'Very pretty,' she said sincerely.

She washed up and came out of the kitchen, wiping her hands on her pallo. She came up to me and said, 'Our last meeting.'

Then she hugged me.

'Thank you, Babu, for everything.'

It was a warm hug, full of gentle affection.

Even as she was at the door, a taxi stopped outside the

gate and Chitra got out followed by Fatima. Chitra came up and gave me a hug. Right behind her Fatima came close and took me into her arms, winding them about me so tightly that I almost suffocated. Chitra turned to Amanda and introduced herself. Amanda's attention was however fixed on Fatima. Fatima's eyes were closed tightly and two tears squeezed themselves out. I freed her hands. I wasn't sure whether Fatima had even seen Amanda but when she came closer, Amanda pulled her into her arms and hugged her. She kissed Fatima on the forehead and said in her ear, 'You are lucky, very lucky.'

To which Fatima could make no coherent reply; she simply made do with a hurried 'Bye.'

Chitra watched her leave. 'That's the nurse, right? Such a sensitive person. And what expressive eyes.'

*

'Fatima just wouldn't take no for an answer. She insisted we should come and meet you for however short a time.' Chitra kept talking while Fatima remained silent, her gaze fixed on mine. She seemed to be in a trance, so steady was her gaze. Not even an eyelid fluttered. It was as if she were challenging me: will you blink first? And yet I could see the myriad emotions in her gaze: love, sympathy, compassion, concern...I could not but hold that gaze if only to keep this connection going. My ears recorded somewhere that Chitra was speaking; I heard but was not listening. At some point, she came to a halt and was looking at Fatima, worried.

'He-llo! Fatima. Earth to Fatima?'

That registered and I looked at Chitra. Fatima was still looking at me. I would have loved to stand there forever, looking and being looked at but I finally conceded:

'Okay Fatima, you won.'

Had it been a competition? Had I only imagined the challenge in Fatima's eyes?

'You have always lost,' Chitra said sombrely. 'You never saw how much Fatima loved you. And even your love for her? She recognized it before you did. You refused to acknowledge it. She was even willing to accept your live-in relationship idea. But you left it too late. By then, she had accepted the marriage proposal. And yet she loves you as much today as she ever did. Her love is like Radha's, like Meera's. Day before yesterday she told me that you said you missed her. And after that she could find no rest. She started after me. For the world, Fatima has come home to see her parents. But we came here straight from the airport. Now to settle things she will go and see her parents. I will visit my father too. We have a return flight this evening.'

I listened to all this, bemused. 'They treat her well there, right?'

'At home? Home for her is a place where you and she live together. Or so she told me.'

'Enough of this,' Fatima seemed to recover herself although her eyes were still fixed on me. 'Can we all stop talking about me? Tell me about yourself...'

'I will. Come on in. I'll make some coffee.'

*

Coffee was drunk; tea as well. But Fatima still did not say anything. Chitra told stories out of art school. And some about her father too. When she left, she asked what project I had taken up.

They sat with me for a long time. Chitra talked a lot. Fatima's eyes were fixed on me and were saying, 'Take me into your arms. Draw me close. Whisper into my ears.'

Then they left. Had no one noticed? We never spoke of Ma's death.

*

Krishna called with bad news. Agnes Aunty had had an accident while riding a hired motorcycle. She had not been hurt badly but was slightly injured.

I went immediately. 'She was alone so she got onto the back of a motorcycle for hire. The bike hit a pothole near the Kadamba Circle and skidded. She fell off the bike. Luckily there were no fractures or anything. We went to the doctor who said she should be fine in a couple of days,' Martin Sir told me.

At which we could have simply agreed that the number of potholes had increased because of the sub-standard work of the Public Works Department. But why did the roundabouts at the Kadamba and Merces Circles develop potholes every one or two years? I thought this might be something I could look into. I left Martin Sir's house and went for a spin on those roads, looking for answers. I came back from Panjim to Merces and saw that the road looked dangerous near the red signal and at the traffic island. Perhaps, it was because those were the spots where the cars had to brake hard. And because the work was substandard, the road went bad again within the year. I thought that it might make more sense to ask why this was happening than to complain about it.

I focused all my energies on this. After six days of concentrated research, I arrived at a solution. What if one were to add some kind of adhesive solution to the mix? In the next week I prepared a fifty-page report. I went to show it to Martin Sir.

'The Chief Engineer of the Public Works Department

was my student. Go see him. He will be able to guide you.' Armed with an introduction from Martin Sir, I went to meet the Chief Engineer. He was busy but when I said that Martin Sir had sent me, he made the time to hear me out. He took my report and said, 'I'll take a look.'

He called the very next day. He said he had read the report and had been impressed. He said he was going to try and get an appointment with the minister immediately. 'If he likes it, and we get the sanction, we can go ahead.'

*

The minister seemed to have time on his hands for we got an appointment quite soon. The Chief Engineer presented my proposal with enthusiasm. When he began to go into the details, the minister interrupted.

'Cut to the chase,' he said.

When the Chief Engineer finished, he asked, 'What do you expect to get out of this?'

'If you mean money, I want nothing,' I said.

'Then what's the benefit?'

'Goa benefits. Fewer potholes. Less accidents.'

'No, I mean how will I benefit? What do I get out of this?'

I had no answer.

'Look here, in this world no one does anything unless they have some reason to. If you have no expectations you can leave.'

'Sir, I expect to reduce the number of accidents and improve the condition of the roads...'

'We have our PWD engineers for that. Let me look at this,' he said and ended the meeting.

The Chief Engineer was even more disappointed than I

was. 'Sorry Mr Parob, that's how the government works. If you had asked for, say, twenty or twenty-five lakhs for this, it might have gone through.'

Then as we were parting, he asked, 'Do you mind if I keep that report? I could try to implement it at my level. But you'll get nothing, I'm afraid. Not even the credit.'

Since I had only wanted to try and improve the condition of Goa's roads, I felt nothing.

*

When I was working on the proposal, another thought was circling in my head. Now this came to the forefront. And then Fatima called: 'There has to be some limit to waiting.' I looked at my phone and realized I had put it on silent when I had gone to meet the minister. I had not noticed that Fatima had called twice during that time.

'Do not get so involved with your work that you forget about me.' After Fatima and Chitra had come to Goa, her melancholy seemed to have eased a bit. She even had an explanation, in her own poetic fashion.

I have endured enough pain.
So, I came to you once again.
When I saw the hurt in your eyes.
My pain eloped with your hurt.

From then on her teasing and her poetry began to weave into each other as of old.

I brought her up to date: 'The minister cut me down but I made some headway with the Chief Engineer. That's something. Isn't it?'

To which she replied. 'Good. Now that it's over you can come to Mumbai.'

'To do what?'

'You are alone there. I am lonely here. But together there's so much to do.'

'I may be alone but I have work to do. I'm looking for a new project.'

'Wow. All the best.'

'I haven't even started.'

'Then start. but remember:

Take me with you
And you'll succeed.
Take me with you
To clear every obstacle.

Will you remember that?'

32

Deep Dive

I started out with great enthusiasm the next day. And like a bad omen, the electricity went off. I kept telling myself the current would come back any time now. Then I saw that the day was done, evening had come. Darkness outside and within. I was outraged at all this. Here I was thinking up lamps that might create areas of darkness but what would happen to them if the electricity were to fail?

If I had thought to install solar panels in the house, this would not have happened. This was no original idea that I could claim but it was one to which I had always been drawn. Solar power. What if I were to study that? I knew that one ought not to leap into deep waters without knowing how to swim. But failing was better than idling. One of the great obstacles to the country's progress was the lack of a reliable electric supply. But this was held to be an engineering problem. To address that it was held to be necessary to have a sound technical background.

Necessary? I thought of Thomas Alva Edison. He had been a school drop-out. Like me. And yet he had conducted ground-breaking research that had resulted in inventions like the light bulb and the film camera. I thought of Dharmananda

Kosambi, universally respected as a great scholar for his research into Buddhist literature, for his revival of the Pali language—and how much had he had by way of formal education? These were autodidacts. They were powered by their determination I had that. I could also start learning on my own.

Time to take a deep dive.

I would learn to swim as I went along. At some point I would get to the other side.

Just as this decision was made, the current came back. I shovelled some food into my mouth and set to work.

The problem of a dependable energy supply had been with us since independence. When the Nehru government had started with the Bhakra-Nangal project, it had been under the assumption that all of North India's power needs would be met by this one dam.

And today, after so many dams and projects, we were still labouring with a power deficit. We should have had a surplus by now. Why was this happening even when we were rich in resources? There were miles of concrete and tarred roads. Could solar energy be generated by those roads? A Google search told me that this had been tried successfully in some western countries. After a little research I came to the conclusion that even if only the Thar Desert were to be exploited for solar energy, there would be enough power generated for the whole country. The problem was how could it be transported from there?

The demand was there. It was necessary to think of ways and means of storage and distribution. In other countries, vehicular transport generated energy and this was used to light street lamps. This could be one solution but surely there were many others. Only it would mean thinking of ways to store up millions of megawatts of energy. This was the problem on which I zeroed in.

I began to collect information and store it on my pen drive. I had one that could store 4 GB. I bought another one that would hold 32 GB. At the shop I learned of a new generation of flash drives whose storage capacity would approach 1 TB. In the next decade capacities would go much further than 2 TB.

If a finger-sized device could store so much information why could devices not store a similar amount of energy?

To accumulate and understand the information that was available was easy enough. The difficult part was in thinking up the change that would revolutionise the storage of energy. I began to see the extent of the problem and also the nearly infinite amount of research that would be needed. Difficult I concluded, challenging, but not impossible.

In my room again I saw the magnitude of the task. It was not something I could accomplish single-handed. I would need help. Like-minded fellow researchers. There would be project costs and material costs too. A laboratory, instruments, human resources...I would need a sponsor, someone who would give me a free hand and allow me to work. I needed institutional support of some kind to proceed.

Chitra suggested that I go and meet some expert in an engineering college and see if I could get it involved. I chose an engineering college and simply turned up. I didn't even know who I should meet. I made inquiries in the electrical and electronic engineering departments. Finally, I was sent to an assistant professor. 'Why are you here? What do you want? Who do you want to meet?' he asked suspiciously.

When he had heard me out, he said, 'All the teachers are in class right now. You will have to wait until the evening.'

I waited.

Finally, I did meet a professor who brushed me off. He said I should meet the Head of the Department. I did. I showed him the notes I had made and explained the broad outlines of my proposal.

'Have you applied for a PhD?'

'I don't want a PhD or a degree. I have a concept, an idea. I need direction of some kind,' I said.

He gestured to a chair. I sat down as he glanced through my paper. Then he looked at me and said, 'How many hours has a year?'

'8765, sir.'

'Do you know how much power we generate in this country, right now?'

'330 gigawatts, sir.'

'Do you think the country could generate more power than it needs?'

'Assuredly. But we need to increase our harnessing capacity.'

'You mean increase the grids? But there are other ways, right?'

'There are grids, there are batteries. Lithium and ion batteries have 100 MW capacities. In the near future these will probably increase.'

'What do you hope to achieve with this project?'

'An energy surplus is even an export opportunity, sir. But we need portable eco-friendly devices to be able to do that.'

'As in?'

'I'm thinking of the equivalent of a USB, sir, and the way you can store information on it.'

He began to glance through my paper again. 'I don't see how I can help you. But you're at the right place at the right time. You may see Professor Ramamurthy of the Institute of Science and Technology, Bangalore. He is coming to inaugurate a seminar here. Come back tomorrow morning. Attend the seminar. I'll find a way to introduce you.'

I went home and checked on Google. The Institute of Science and Technology in Bangalore was a reputable institution. I was reassured that I would get the right kind of guidance and set off to Goa Engineering College the next day.

I had no interest in the topic of the seminar. Professor Ramamurthy inaugurated the seminar and spoke well. Then came a break for tea. I made my way to the Head of Department. He immediately took me to Ramamurthy who was surrounded by a group of the staff. How could I talk to him there? But when I was introduced to him, I said, 'Sir, I need some time with you. I'll come wherever you say. Wherever we can talk.' But Professor Ramamurthy was in a hurry. He had a return flight in the afternoon. The HOD told me to give him a brief synopsis. I handed him my paper and summed up my proposal.

'Why are you doing this?' he asked, frowning.

'The research will benefit the nation.'

He smiled. 'With no formal education in the subject, you think you can pull this off?'

'Yes, sir.'

'And what do you base this on?'

'My faith in myself.'

'You are overconfident, my boy. Do you think no one else in the world is working on this?'

'They are. But no breakthroughs so far, right?'

'And if one happens tomorrow?'

'No one will be happier than me, sir.'

'Then better stop toiling over this and be happy now.'

Everyone laughed. He looked at the HOD and said, 'So childish.'

That day I went home and hid myself away in the darkness of my room. Professor Ramamurthy, the PWD minister, the Secretary of the Akademi, Professor Namshikar, Gaonkar Sir...I had always been dismissed as childish by all of them.

Fatima called, 'Hey Philippina, how's it going?

Hiding from the world of the wise, I had grown up learning my lessons at Daddy's knee. And so I had learned to hold my cards close to my chest and yet that day I told Fatima everything. 'I think my faith in my intelligence took a beating today.'

'How's your faith in your stupidity?'

I was in no mood for raillery but she continued 'There isn't much difference between intelligence and idiocy, Vipin. Don't take it to heart.'

Since I still said nothing, she went on. 'Have you seen *Makdi*, the film I mean?'

I had not.

'You have heard of Vishal Bhardwaj?'

I had not.

She said that he had written the script of *Makdi* and sent it off to the Children's Film Society of India with great enthusiasm. They rejected it. Perhaps they thought it childish too. But he didn't give up. He made the film himself. And he got the Best Film Award for it. And some international awards too. She told it as if she were telling a story. And that held me.

'So tell me, what do you think was the reason he got those awards?' she asked. Then she answered her own question: 'Rejection. He took that rejection as a challenge. And he made his own film. And he won.'

She paused a few seconds and then asked, 'Moral of the story?'

'In the land of the blind the one-eyed man is king,' I said, my mood beginning to change.

'Is he really? Or would the land be built around blindness?'

I felt cheered.

'Thank you, Fatima. I was feeling defeated. Not anymore.'

'As long as I'm around, I won't allow such feelings.'

When had I started talking of victory and defeat? And why was I seeking solace from Fatima? But it was true that she had cheered me up.

'Do you know why I called today?' Fatima asked, throwing me into a quandary. 'This is an anniversary. What kind of memory do you have?'

By now she knew me well enough not to expect a reply. 'There was a day, Vipin, when you rejected my love with the darkness of a theatre as witness. You can have no idea, Vipin, how that destroyed me. I do not want to remember that day. But today was the day that one year ago, you said to Chitra: "I love her." Those words came like a breath of life, reviving my soul.'

'I left it too late,' I admitted.

'What had to happen, happened. The prodigal must be welcomed back.'

'But I put you through such agony...'

'True but you brought me relief too. You made space for me in your life. As a life partner.'

I did not know what to day. But Fatima was in the mood for words. 'I have found love. Now there is one thing left on my bucket list.'

I did not think I could keep up with her in this mood but I asked, 'What is it?'

'I am a chapter, a short chapter, in the book of your life. It is an incomplete chapter but I would like resolution. Tell me when you're coming to Mumbai.'

'I can come tomorrow,' I said without thinking.

'Tomorrow is no good.' I thought she was going to say that the next day was a problem but she added, 'Come today.'

'I know you're asking me to come but I need to know if it will cause you any problems.'

'If you don't come, it will be a problem.'

'Let me see.'

'What is there to see? My impatience is growing.'

'Ever since you've gone to Mumbai, this shaayri business has been increasing.'

'Don't you like it?'

'I love it.'

'So come quickly. My poetry and I and even Mumbai are all waiting for you.'

'Why is Mumbai waiting for me?'

'This is where the resolution of our love is set to happen,' Fatima said.

'Fatima, in Goa, I was always trying to push you away. Now I don't want to end this call.'

'Same with me. When I talk to you, spring bursts out in my heart. And when I hang up, it's cold and sad again.'

*

In the morning, Martin Sir called. 'Come, see me,' he said. I went. The Chief Engineer of the PWD had called him up and had sung the praises of my proposal. He said he was going to personally supervise the pilot project. He had told Martin Sir that he regretted his inability to pay me anything. I felt some satisfaction that at least one of the projects I worked on had come to fruition.

I told him of my experience with Professor Ramamurthy. Martin Sir was even more distressed than I was. But I reassured him, 'I have not given up on the project sir. I will keep looking for someone to provide direction and funds. Until then, I'll continue to work towards it. If necessary, I will put in my own money and prepare a draft document.'

Martin Sir listened to all this and said encouragingly, 'Do not give up. You will succeed.' Then something occurred to him, 'You have read Thoreau? Many publishers rejected his writing as useless. Finally, he put his own money into the publishing, and only then was its value understood. Gandhiji and Tolstoy both understood the importance of this work. And you know about Franz Kafka? Publishers thought *Metamorphosis* was rubbish and look at how well respected it is. So don't give up.'

His words stiffened my spine. After I had drunk the tea Agnes Aunty offered me, I left and Chitra called. 'When are coming to Mumbai?'

Once again, I told her the tale of Professor Ramamurthy.

I also told her of the apprehensions I had.

'Fatima keeps inviting me to Mumbai but I don't know how that will go down with her family. I don't want my visit to cause her any more suffering than she is already going through.'

'Don't let that bother you. She is looking forward to your visit with so much excitement that I am afraid she will sink into a depression if you don't come.'

'But where do I stay? And where do I meet her?'

'Oh didn't she tell you? I thought she would have. You're staying with me and she'll meet you here.'

*

I did not think I was the kind of person to get excited at the prospect of travel. But this was different. I could not think why. Finally, I concluded that it must be the prospect of Fatima's company. I did not want to waste any time getting there.

Fatima was impatient too. 'I hope you have booked your tickets? Come by air, okay? And send me your ETA soonest.'

'As soon as I book my tickets. When should I book my return?'

'Don't book your return. Just get here. Tomorrow. I yearn, Vipin, I yearn.'

'Yes, but...'

'Tomorrow evening belongs to you. I have no time day after tomorrow.'

'Then I'll book my return for the day after tomorrow.'

'As you wish. And should the Fates wish it, we will meet again.'

Why should I stay on in Mumbai if Fatima had no time? I booked my tickets online.

*

A 2:30 p.m. flight reaching Mumbai at 3:30 p.m. Chitra had told me to download the Ola app. Since I had booked it in advance the car came to the airport in ten minutes and by 4:30 p.m., I was on the street outside Chitra's Andheri flat.

'Come in, come in, sit down. I'll make coffee in a moment. Oh yes, tea for you. I haven't forgotten. Meanwhile you can look at my paintings.'

All her paintings were stacked in the hall of her 1BHK. I looked over them. After getting to know Chitra, my viewing of art had changed a little. But today all I could think about was meeting Fatima. They say you can tell much about a painter from the paintings. There were many landscapes, beautiful ones that sought to capture Goa's natural beauty. Some were nostalgic depictions of Canacona. Then one caught my eye and just then Chitra emerged from the kitchen. 'Oh, that's a self-portrait. Nude. How do you like it?'

This was not a 'Do you think I look good naked?' kind of question. But I really did not have the vocabulary to talk about painting.

'It's an experiment. There's an Anne Brigman portrait that has become very famous. But she used a photograph; I haven't. There are Frida Kahlo works like that. This is just me trying something.'

'I think it's good. But as a layman let me say you look better dressed.'

'Am I a different person nude and dressed? Both are facets of the same me,' Chitra said and led me into the kitchen. She continued, 'Frida once said "I am the person I know best." Which was what made me try a self-portrait.'

Chitra took up her coffee and gave me a mug of tea. 'When we met the last time, our cups got interchanged and I wondered if that was to be our last meeting. But here we are again, thanks to Fatima.'

'I did not think Fatima would forgive me.'

Chitra looked at me, unflinchingly. 'Have you noticed something, Vipin? How you've changed? How isolated you were and now...'

'Yes. I felt lonely then. Now I don't feel it. Thanks again to Fatima.'

Fatima had said she would get there by 5 p.m. I was on tenterhooks.

'She will come,' Chitra reassured me. 'Five minutes early, mark my words.'

'But what if she has problems when she goes home again?'

She took a gulp of coffee and said, 'You have expressed your concerns. Now I want to ask you something. Has Fatima ever spoken to you about her home, her new family, her problems?'

I didn't think so.

'It's been nearly a year now that she's been married. She's visited me at least four times but I've never been asked to go there and I've never set foot inside her new home. If she talks, she only talks about you. I've never heard a word about her husband, her home, not a word. If I ask about it, she immediately changes the subject. Once she said to me, "If you want to know how I relate to Vipin, it's simple. In everything, I think of him first." I found this a bit much but she meant it.'

After a while she added, 'I have no idea whether she will accept it or not but I thought I should ask: are you still game for a live-in relationship?'

'Even more than I was before. But what about her?'

'Can't say. But she seemed willing to do anything for you. You remember how she came to Goa saying she was missing her parents? I think it's time you ask her for yourself.'

'What do you think she'll have told them to come here?'

'This morning she told me that a girl who used to study with her at the madrasa had come from Goa. I don't think she meant to lie to me; she was telling me the story she was going to tell her folks so if anyone asked me, I would have the same story to tell.'

At 4:58, the doorbell rang. Fatima came in and wrapped herself around me. Then she spotted Chitra who was standing there watching us and clicked her tongue in a pretence of disapproval. 'Voyeur! Go away.'

Chitra picked up a sling bag full of clothes.

'Where are you off to?' I asked, surprised.

'To Preetam's hostel.'

'When do we expect you back?'

'Ask Fatima,' and she winked at Fatima and left.

'See you in the morning.'

*

Now we were alone together, the distance between us ended. I wanted to take Fatima in my arms immediately but as I took a step towards her, she took a step back. 'Wait. I want to cleanse myself.' And she went off to take a bath, a long bath. She came out clad in a nightgown. She brought to mind a hibiscus after a monsoon shower. Again, I took a step towards her and again she stopped me. 'Wait. I'll make us tea and coffee. In the meantime, you have a bath. You'll feel fresh.' When I was in the bathroom, she said from the kitchen, 'If you haven't brought a change of clothes, don't put on any. But don't put on the used clothes.'

I had already drunk tea but for fear that she would not drink her coffee, I said nothing. I had my bath and came out wearing shorts and waited for the tea.

That was the first time in my life that I had a silent conversation. Perhaps I had never noticed it before. Fatima's hair was damp, loose around her shoulders; another first.

Even without lipstick her full lips looked pink. Her

cheekbones were prominent. Strands of hair fell over her damp forehead. Her large eyes gazed into mine with a distinct challenge. I had never been interested in the grammar of beauty. But if beauty did indeed lie in the eye of the beholder, Fatima looked extremely beautiful today. I wondered how I appeared to her.

'What are you looking at?' I asked.

'I can see the light of my love for you in your eyes. I don't think I have ever loved myself so much...but how much you made me suffer.'

'But I'm here now, right?'

'You're here. And the fetters have fallen from my feet.' She stood up and came and sat down in my lap. 'Now I'm free. I am a free bird and I've chosen you as my branch.' And she laid her head on my shoulder.

When some teardrops fell on my shoulder, I raised her head. Her eyes were filled with bliss. 'Are you happy?' I asked.

'Fool. I'm swimming in the ocean and you ask if I'm wet?'

'Fatima, I'm worried about you. When you go home tomorrow...'

'Have you heard of a bird making friends with a catapult? Well, I have. In full awareness of the consequences.'

'So, you say you will never let me fail and you talk of ignoring the consequences?'

And taking advantage of the moment, I said, 'After this, shall we live together?'

'Aren't we together now?' she asked.

'I mean for good. A live-in relationship? I would like that. What about you?'

'I made a promise: I shall love you until death do us part.'

Even as I thought I saw pain flash in her eyes, she said, 'You know how much I love you, shall I count the ways? How could I say no to you?'

Joy flooded me. 'I will never let anything hurt you ever again. We will be happy together.' And I raised her chin and brought my lips down to hers. After a while, she said, 'In your arms I have no fear of pain and no interest in joy. My life begins and ends in your arms.' And she snuggled even closer to me.

Her poetry was now having a strange effect. In Goa, it had not meant much to me. Today even her prose seemed to be poetry.

'When do we leave for Goa? Tomorrow?'

'Why are you in such a hurry? When your hand is in mine, what have I to fear? Life is not a race, at least, not for me. As long as we are together, I will have no truck with speed.'

'I am in a hurry. When do we leave?'

'Not tomorrow. I have tickets booked for a trip.'

'Where are you going?'

'I am going to a festival.'

'Alone?'

'Does that worry you? Are you worried someone will abduct me?' And she started to laugh.

'Don't lie.'

'Me lying?'

'Didn't you say you were going to meet a madrasa friend when you came here?'

'That Chitra can't keep her lip zipped.'

'And didn't you say that you were going to spend the night with her?'

'Yes, I am to spend the night with a friend.'

'And in the morning?'

'Why these doubts? I told you: I'm off in the morning.'

'Alone?'

Fatima got up, picked up her purse and showed me a railway ticket.

Swaraj Express. To Ratlam. I returned it. Something fell out of her purse. I picked it up. It was a sim card.

'Oops. I must have left this behind. Give me a moment.'

She went into the bathroom and I heard the sound of the flush.

Before I could ask, she said, 'Hey Vipin, enough of this interrogation. I am ravenous now. You go make me an omelette. After that, I'll give you ice cream.'

She cut the onions and the tomatoes. I cracked the eggs and beat them; that seemed to be my job. The pao was ready. The ice cream was in the fridge. We ate and we talked.

'Fatima, would you dance for me?'

'Are you full?'

'What have we eaten that would fill us up?'

'True. I am ready. But you have to dance with me.'

'No. I can't dance.'

'The heart that loves makes the legs move.' She hummed. '*Har dil jo pyaar karega, woh gaana gaayega*.'

I laughed at that. Surely more hearts could love than people could sing?

'Please, "*Balam pichkaari*" for me?'

Fatima found the popular Holi song on my phone and then she danced. She danced for me alone. She danced as one lost in music and yet when the music ended, she would not stop moving. Eventually I got up and went to stop her and she slumped into my arms. She was tired, her chest heaving. I cradled her in my arms. I brought my mouth down to hers. We stood for a long time like that, enjoying the sweetness of the moment. And with our lips still locked, Fatima began to sway. Without volition, I began to sway too. Moving my head back, she began to laugh. '*Har dil jo pyaar karega...*' Seeing my embrace had loosened, Fatima drew me to herself again.

'Pick me up.'

She got on to her tiptoes. I braced my arms around her back and raised her up. My nose was buried in her breasts: She drew my head closer and pushed my nose into her chest. My breath began to fail. She laughed and let her grip weaken.

'Were you suffocating? I suffocate every night when I grip a pillow and squeeze it, thinking about you.'

I set her down and went to put off the light.

'Hello, Prince of Darkness, can you abandon the shadows for a single night and bathe in the light with me?'

And drawing close to me she said, 'For this one night will be a moveable feast that will last for the rest of my life.'

She was obviously in the grips of a madness; an infectious madness then, for it was affecting me as well. My breath began to heat up. Words abandoned me. I folded her into my arms again and she bit my chest delicately and asked in my ear: 'Must I do it all?' And so saying she pulled my hand to her chest. 'Let there be no barriers between us.'

It took me a moment to understand what she was saying. I slipped the nightgown off her shoulders but when I reached for my shorts, she stopped me.

'Let me,' she said.

All night she spun a magic web of words around us. And all night she had her way with my body. She spoke endlessly, she nibbled me, she hit me with her fists, she pulled at my hair, she drummed on me with her heels and tickled me with her toes.

We dissolved into each other.

It was only when the dawn broke that she stopped with a line of poetry: 'We spent the night as if we had not drunk deep enough of life.'

She had not allowed me to sleep nor had she slept. At six thirty she made coffee and tea. Before she drank her coffee, she poured some into a saucer and added some of my tea. 'Do you remember I asked you what you thought this would taste like?' She proffered the saucer. I drank some. Then she got ready quickly.

'You will come to the station with me, won't you? The train leaves at 7:45 a.m. from Bandra.'

'Won't you have a bath?'

'Are you mad? And wash off the scent of you?'

We took a rickshaw and all the way she gripped my arm, sitting close to me and humming her favourite song, '*Aaj phir jeene ki tamanna hai, aaj phir marne ka iraada hai*' (Today I want to live, today I long to die).

We got down at the station. I was about to pay the driver when she said, 'No, take him and go back. You can bid me farewell here. Why come any further? Bye-e-e,' she said and vanished into the mass of rushing people. I took the same rickshaw and returned. And then it came to me that she had taken some part of me with her.

33

Decision

'Are you up? So how was it? Did she let you even get a wink of sleep?' Chitra asked on the phone later 'Is she still there?'

'Gone long ago.' My return flight was at 1:45 p.m. 'I thought I'd leave around 10:30 a.m. What do I do with the key?'

'Leave it on the table. I have a duplicate. When you leave, just pull the door closed. Hold on. Preetam's here with me. Come and meet her? She'd like that. But you'll have to come to Bandra.'

I didn't feel like schlepping to Bandra to meet Preetam.

'Not today,' I said.

*

I tried Fatima's number four times after that.

'This number does not exist,' came the message.

When my flight landed, I tried again. The same answer. By the time I reached home it was 3 p.m. I had eaten a sandwich on the plane and didn't need any lunch. Our meeting in Mumbai had filled me with happiness which now was shading into a deep unease. Fatima had made love to me madly; she had left me completely satisfied but I could not shake off a feeling of dread. I had no real rational reason for the unease. I realized I would have to deal with this before I could get on with my work. In the evening, I called Chitra. She too had been calling Fatima and getting no answer. 'She must be at home. Probably processing last night.'

'At home?' I said. 'She left for Ratlam this morning.'

I could sense that Chitra was startled. I replayed our morning conversation. Chitra had asked whether Fatima was still around. I had said she had left a long time ago. I assumed she would have told Chitra where she was going.

'Why didn't she tell me?' Chitra asked.

Then I remembered, 'By the way, she said she was ready for a live-in relationship. She said she'd tell me when she was ready to begin.'

I could not tell whether Chitra was happy to hear this or lost in thought.

*

I had grown used to living alone after my parents passed. Or so I thought. And yet now I felt like a ghost wandering through that house. Perhaps it would be this way until Fatima came to live with me.

Every day I tried to call Fatima and every day I met with the same response. Each evening I would call Chitra and share my worries with her. I would not feel easy, I knew, until I had heard Fatima's voice. Was this some kind of joke? I thought back to that moment when the sim card had fallen out of her bag. She had gone to the toilet and I had heard the flush? Had she flushed the sim card down the toilet and with it, the last connection between all of us?

And then one afternoon, Chitra called to say with tears in her voice: 'Fatima cheated us, my friend. She's gone.'

Fatima? Gone? I suddenly knew the reason for my unease.

Hearing Chitra's words I felt a deep anger at Fatima but also envy. She had gone off to a consummation that can happen only once in a lifetime. I could have gone with her and what a celebration we could have made of it. This was a once-in-a-lifetime event, Fatima, and we should have been together on that last train ride together. There would have been pinches and punches, hugs and kisses, poetry and riddles...and a lot besides. And when the chaiwallah came through, I would have had my tipple. I would have made my way to the pantry car and got some special coffee made for you. I envy you now. You had fun on your own. If I had been with you, we could have stood together in the open doorway of the train and enjoyed the breeze. You would have liked that. The train would thunder over a bridge and we would have thrown our mobiles out into the river below. We would have had a little competition to see who could throw further. Or perhaps one might have got stuck in the bridge? And then your hand in mine and...one, two, three! You missed that joy of jumping together. You jumped alone, grimacing at me.

Your last words to Chitra keep coming back. And what you said to me too: 'This one night will be a moveable feast that will last the rest of my life.' As you said in your poetic fashion: 'I am a short chapter in the book of your life. I would like to complete the chapter.' How could you not see that it would hurt me to know that you had completed this chapter without me? You lured me to Mumbai with your promises. 'Come to Mumbai; I will fulfil your desires,' and 'Our love must find its resolution in the city of Mumbai.' I did not understand what you were saying but you knew all too well what you meant. 'I have only one desire left to fulfil.' I thought our desires were the same and so I came to the city. And when we had spent that night together, you said, 'We spent the night as if we had not drunk deep enough of life.' Yes, there were hints. The song you hummed in the auto: '*Aaj phir jeene ki tamanna hai, aaj phir marne ka iraada hai.*' I had paid attention to your wanting; I had ignored your longing. Why had I not taken it seriously when you said: 'We shall meet again if we are still alive'?

I wanted to scream at Fatima: 'We are all passengers on a death train, all waiting for our destination.'

Krishna was standing in the doorway.

I only regret that you went alone. Where did you go? where were you headed? Towards peace?

'Babu,' someone called from a distance but in front of my eyes, Fatima…

Asatomaa sadgamaya,
Tamasoma jyotirgamaya,
Mrityorma amrutam gamaya,
Om, shanti, shanti, shanti.

From untruth lead me to truth
From darkness to light
From death to immortality
Om, shanti, shanti, shanti

As I sat in the hall reciting this shloka from the *Upanishad*, I could see Krishna vaguely. What did he want? Before I could ask, he vanished.

Death is the ultimate truth, they say. So would the prayer to lead one from death to immortality be a paradoxical one? But what did truth mean? 'Aham', I, was that the truth? Who was that I? Was it my name? Was it my body? My mind? My family? This way led to pride. Or was that merely the reality? To be led from darkness to light could be construed in any number of ways. But why the assumption that darkness was a bad thing? I had once dreamt of building a lamp of darkness to cast darkness into light. So was I a worshipper of darkness? I had been born in darkness. What was the real relationship between light and dark? And what was birth? Emerging from one's mother's womb? Or was birth an event that occurred at the time of conception? At that time, I would have been a cell or two, a negligible amount of matter. When I was born, I had weighed eight pounds. Now I weighed 75 kilos. How could I be freed from this except through death? The plea to be led from death to immortality was another paradox. Was the plea for immortality not a rejection of death? And of peace? After all, there was peace in death. If that were true, then Fatima had found peace. Leaving me behind?

That was not fair, Fatima. In the *Gita*, Krishna says: 'Death is merely leaving one form to inhabit another'. Would Fatima's soul wait for mine before changing bodies?

I had only read about what a gift life was. I had not experienced it as a gift. Death did not seem to matter much to me. Ma had often said that she had seen only bad days after I had been born. Daddy had dismissed me as useless. Then he had conceived the idea that I should become a doctor and being a doctor, I would have some value as a human being. Even there I had failed. Chitra had said I lacked tenacity of purpose.

What did I have left that was worth living for? One needs a reason to live. Chitra lives for her art. Martin Sir lives for the love of reading. When Ma was diagnosed with diabetes, she would often complain: 'What's the point of living without something sweet to eat?' Kalpesh, my cousin, the gigolo would say, 'It's dirty work but someone has to do it.' Whatever its form, whatever its moral colouration, one needed a reason to live.

*

I remembered the last film I had seen on my laptop. The world is infected with a terrible disease that turns everyone bloodthirsty. It is uninhabitable. The apocalypse has arrived and the world awaits its inevitable end...and yes, that day will come. So what was the point of sitting around waiting for it to end? I remembered reading Pundalik Naik's *Moronkotto* or Suicide Point where a man collects a small fee from every person who wants to commit suicide. Was this Suicide Point still open for business? If death would not come for one, should one slog through the broiling heat, struggling for life? Should one drag oneself, a starving snake, wriggling on and on until something fell on one's head and ended one's life? Or should one court death? I thought I might achieve some clarity with a cup of tea but when I went into the kitchen, the powder was over. I thought I might get a cup at Vasudev's and set out. On the way, a frond of a coconut palm fell right next to me.

'You got lucky there,' a passerby said. 'If it had fallen on your head, you would have had it.'

I had been spared.

Why had I been spared?

When I got to Vasudev's he was there but the restaurant was closed.

He was sitting outside, the picture of defeat.

'No tea?' I asked him. 'What happened?'

'I tell you, Babu, I've been in this business for forty years and my marriage lasted forty years too. And in all these years, I have finally learned the meaning of life.'

Vasudev waited for me to ask the obvious question. I did not ask what had happened. Whatever had happened had happened and had brought him to this state.

He said, 'Life has no meaning.'

In Vasudev's sad eyes I could see death. Whose? His? Or mine? Vasudev had taken forty years to realize how hollow and meaningless life was. I did not want to waste time like that. What does it mean: life having no meaning? Is there meaning to meaninglessness? If I could not find an answer, I must stop living.

I had to prepare. Ridiculous. What preparations would possibly be necessary? I didn't even need a ticket on this journey. I walked to the railway station. The canteen by the side of the station entrance beckoned. But it was also time for the train to arrive. The passengers were all getting ready to board. I joined the crowd.

And then came the announcement: 'The train will be delayed by twenty minutes.'

My quandary then: Kill myself or drink tea?